David Torrance was born and brought up in Edinburgh and educated at Leith Academy, the University of Aberdeen and Cardiff School of Journalism. He was formerly political reporter for STV and is now a freelance writer, journalist and broadcaster. He currently lives in Edinburgh.

'Offers a timely and valuable perspective'
Mure Dickie, *Financial Times*

'David Torrance's short, meticulous book functions as a piece of public service journalism'
Josh Lowe, *Prospect Magazine*

'Torrance's biography succeeds because it mirrors its subject. The biographer has worked hard to capture the politician who now leads Scotland at this crucial time in its history'
Tom Peterkin, *Scotland on Sunday*

By the same author

The Scottish Secretaries (Birlinn, 2006)

George Younger: A Life Well Lived (Birlinn, 2008)

'We in Scotland': Thatcherism in a Cold Climate
(Birlinn, 2009)

Noel Skelton and the Property-Owning Democracy
(Biteback, 2010)

Inside Edinburgh: Discovering the Classic Interiors of Edinburgh
(Birlinn, 2010) (with Steve Richmond)

Salmond: Against the Odds (Birlinn, 2010, 2011 & 2015)

Great Scottish Speeches I (ed.) (Luath Press, 2011)

David Steel: Rising Hope to Elder Statesman
(Biteback, 2012)

Whatever Happened to Tory Scotland? (ed.) (Edinburgh
University Press, 2012)

*The Battle for Britain: Scotland and the Independence
Referendum* (Biteback, 2013)

Great Scottish Speeches II (ed.) (Luath Press, 2013)

Britain Rebooted: Scotland in a Federal Union
(Luath Press, 2014 & 2015)

Scotland's Referendum: A Guide for Voters
(Luath Press, 2014) (with Jamie Maxwell)

*100 Days of Hope and Fear: How Scotland's Referendum Was
Lost and Won* (Luath Press, 2014)

General Election 2015: A Guide for Voters in Scotland
(Luath Press, 2015)

EU Referendum 2016: A Guide for Voters (Luath Press, 2016)

Nicola Sturgeon

A Political Life

David Torrance

BIRLINN

This edition published in 2016 by
Birlinn Limited
West Newington House
10 Newington Road
Edinburgh
EH9 1QS

www.birlinn.co.uk

First published in 2015

ISBN: 978 1 78027 345 7

British Library Cataloguing-in-Publication Data
A catalogue record for this book is available from the British Library

Typeset by Iolaire Typesetting, Newtonmore
Printed and bound by Bell & Bain Ltd, Glasgow

Contents

List of Illustrations   vii

Preface to the second edition   ix

Preface   xi

 1 'A material change in circumstances'   1

 2 'A working-class girl from Ayrshire'   12

 3 'The best of her generation'   29

 4 The battle for Govan   60

 5 'Nippy Sweetie'   85

 6 'Project Nicola'   120

 7 Health Secretary   137

 8 'Yes Minister'   168

 9 'No greater privilege'   196

10 'Nicola-mania'   216

Endnotes   257

Bibliography   279

Index   283

List of Illustrations

Nicola Sturgeon as a toddler

An early portrait

As a pupil at Greenwood Academy

Sporting an SNP rosette as a young activist

Young Scottish Nationalists at the 1989 SNP conference in Dunoon

Pat Kane's leaflet urging Glasgow University students to vote for Sturgeon as SRC president

Sturgeon's first television appearance in 1989

On an edition of BBC Scotland's *Left, Right and Centre* in early 1992

As the SNP's candidate for Glasgow Shettleston at the 1992 general election

Sturgeon and her grandmother following her graduation in law

On the march with SNP leader Alex Salmond

As the SNP's candidate for Glasgow Govan at the 1997 general election

Sturgeon following the Glasgow count in 1999

A flyer issued as part of Sturgeon's short-lived leadership campaign in 2004

Photographic evidence that Sturgeon was prepared to transform her image

Celebrating with Alex Salmond following the SNP's election win in 2007

Nicola Sturgeon's marriage to SNP chief executive Peter Murrell in July 2010

Sturgeon participates in the 2015 general election debates

Sturgeon with the Scottish cabinet following the 2016 Holyrood election

Preface to the second edition

The first edition of this biography appeared shortly before the 2015 general election campaign got under way and what some described as 'Nicola-mania' ensued. This was both a blessing and a curse, the former because it sold well and attracted a lot of attention (some positive, some negative), the latter because parts of it dated very quickly – an inescapable hazard for any political biography published while its subject is very much still alive.

A short-run reprint in July 2015 gave me a chance to correct mistakes and include a short account of the election campaign and result, but by the spring of 2016 it was clear a fuller update was necessary. Thus the original introductory chapter ('First Minister for all of Scotland') and conclusion ('The Apprentice') have been removed and replaced with new sections that cover events in 2015–16 and the repercussions of the June 2016 European referendum. Obviously, even this edition might have been overtaken by events by the time it appears in print.

I am grateful to the Society of Authors' K. Blundell Trust Award, for financial support towards the preparation of this new edition.

David Torrance
Edinburgh
August 2016

Preface

It is notoriously difficult to produce a biography of a serving politician. My previous study of the last First Minister (*Salmond: Against the Odds*) was not perfect when it first appeared in the autumn of 2010, and an updated paperback edition in 2011 also suffered from having been written amid ever-changing events. But such biographies are arguably necessary; more ought to be known of governing men and women beyond an occasional newspaper profile or their 'official' CVs.

Nicola Sturgeon is new to the office of First Minister but is also, despite only being in her mid 40s, a political veteran. She first joined the party she now leads almost 30 years ago, has been a Member of the Scottish Parliament for around 16 years and a senior minister for half that time. That, by any measurement, is a long career, yet one that remains underexamined. At the same time, this is what might be classified as an 'interim' biography – an initial distillation of the available (but frustratingly limited) sources.

I make no grand claims about what follows for, as close readers will note, it mainly comprises contemporary newspaper coverage augmented by interviews and also some useful academic and journalistic secondary sources. I did approach the First Minister for a 'background' interview, although for understandable reasons she declined, and thus this is a fully unauthorised biography. Sturgeon, however, did not seek to prevent people from speaking to me – indeed those who sought her permission were usually told to go ahead. For that I am grateful for they often provided otherwise unavailable details and insights.

Nor do I claim to really 'know' my subject; rather I have done what biographers do: reached conclusions based on having observed Sturgeon as a politician for around 15 years, numerous conversations with acquaintances (some closer than others) and what I hope is a judicious interpretation of her public utterances covering an even longer period. Indeed, my biographical style has always been to let my subjects speak through extensive quotation so the reader can get a feel for the politician through their own words.

In an undoubtedly mischievous letter to the *Herald* on 23 September 2014, Alex Salmond sought to redefine standard conceptions of what constitutes biography. First, he said, in response to a critical column I had written the day before, 'I hardly know David Torrance', while second, 'and much more problematically for a biographer – he doesn't know me at all'.[1] Intimacy between writer and subject, however, is rare. James Boswell, one of the earliest modern biographers, certainly 'knew' Dr Johnson, but he was an exception; the Salmond criteria would render the vast majority of extant biographies – not least historical works – redundant.

More to the point, 'authorised' works written by friends tend, with honourable exceptions, to be unreliable, inevitably glossing over difficult areas and shirking from criticism. Many even veer into hagiography, which might suit the subject while arguably neglecting the genre's broader aims. I first interviewed Nicola Sturgeon at length in 2003 and, most recently, towards the end of 2013, with only sporadic professional contact in between. But that to me is a strength rather than a weakness, having allowed me to take a step back and therefore deliver a more detached assessment of her as a politician. To reduce biography, as Salmond attempted to do, to an arbitrary judge- ment as to how well the writer 'knows' their subject is to miss the point entirely.

As ever, this biography would not have been possible without the contributions of others, most notably friends and colleagues of the subject. In alphabetical order Alex Bell, Fergus Bell, Ian Blackford, Dr John Boyle, Niall Bradley, Sir Harry Burns, Craig Cathcart, Malcolm Chisholm MSP, Ewan Crawford, Mike Dailly, Ian Duncan MEP, Jim Gray, Stephen Harte, Patrick Harvie MSP, Gerry Hassan, Fiona Hyslop MSP, John McAllion, Campbell Martin, Iain Martin, Claire Mitchell, Michael Moore MP, David Mundell MP, Calum Smith, Susan Stewart, Caroline Summers, Kay Ullrich, Cliff Williamson and Andrew Wilson all gave willingly of their time and memories, as well as several others who wished to remain anonymous. Staff at the Glasgow University Archives, meanwhile, helped me locate sources relating to Sturgeon's undergraduate career.

My own friends and colleagues also provided assistance, both directly and indirectly. Ian Swanson helpfully facilitated access to contemporary news sources, Ian Smart and Alf Young put me in touch with contacts who knew and worked with Sturgeon in her pre-political career, while Murdo Fraser MSP and D. J. MacDonald, Michael Watt, John McVie and Claire Stewart of STV provided access to archive television material. Kerry Black at *The Scotsman* Publications also helped me track down appropriate photographs for the plates sections, while Tom Gordon of the *Sunday Herald* kindly let me consult his notes from several long interviews with Sturgeon. Others also read and offered comments on various draft chapters: Helen Puttick, Dr Peter Lynch, Kenny Farquharson, Stephen Boyd, Michael Torrance, Lucy Hunter Blackburn, Douglas Pattullo and particularly Euan McColm all provided additional insights into Sturgeon's career while saving me from several silly errors. Inevitably some will remain, for which the responsibility is of course mine.

Sandra Underwood of 'Ances-Tree' proved invaluable in fleshing out the English branches of Sturgeon's family tree while, for the first time in my biographical career, I had the luxury of a researcher. I took a punt on Aidan Kerr, an undergraduate at Glasgow University and I did not regret it. Bright, proactive and politically insightful beyond his 20 years, he saved me much-needed time in marshalling the contemporary newspaper sources without which this book would have been impossible to write. Finally, Nicola Sturgeon is well known to be a voracious reader, therefore I sincerely hope she finds this an accurate and balanced account of her life and career so far.

David Torrance
January 2015

Chapter 1

'A material change in circumstances'

Man, observed the German statesman Otto von Bismarck, 'cannot control the current of events, he can only float with them and steer'. Change the gender and he could have been talking about Nicola Sturgeon in the days and weeks that followed the UK's decision – following a divisive referendum campaign – to withdraw from the European Union. More colloquially, a social media meme also circulated shortly after the result – an image of the First Minister, her arms outspread, and the simple message: 'F***in' calm doon. Am oan it.'[1]

The EU referendum had not been the SNP leader's fight but arising from its surprise dénouement was a clear political opportunity and one she seized with both hands. While England and Wales voted to Leave, Scotland (like Northern Ireland and London) opted decisively to Remain. Flanked by Scottish and European flags at Bute House, Sturgeon addressed EU citizens resident in Scotland ('you remain welcome here') while talking up the 'divergence' between Scotland and 'large parts' of the UK 'in how we see our place in the world'.

'As things stand,' the First Minister continued, 'Scotland faces the prospect of being taken out of the EU against our will. I regard that as democratically unacceptable.' And, referring to her party's recent Holyrood election manifesto, Sturgeon said she was in no doubt the result represented 'a significant and a material change' to the circumstances in which Scotland had

1

rejected independence in September 2014. She would, therefore, 'take all possible steps' to secure Scotland's 'continuing place in the EU and in the single market in particular'.

It was, therefore, 'a statement of the obvious' that the option of a second independence referendum 'must be on the table', to be held, should the Scottish Parliament agree, within the Brexit 'timescale' – i.e. the two-year negotiation period following the triggering of Article 50 under the Lisbon Treaty. Legislation would be prepared to that end while, as First Minister, she would do everything she could 'to bring people together in common cause and to seek to lead our country forward as one'.[2]

That most cautious of politicians appeared to have thrown caution to the wind but, by responding as she did, Sturgeon had not only carved out a place for herself and her party in the post-Brexit landscape she had also created a sense of momentum behind the idea of another independence referendum. 'EU GO GIRL' was the *Daily Record*'s bold headline the following day[3] and, indeed, she seemed to have captured the zeitgeist. Even J. K. Rowling, an ardent No voter in 2014, tweeted that many Unionists would now 'think again' should the question be put a second time.[4] On Sunday, meanwhile, a poll for the *Sunday Post* showed support for independence at just short of what was understood to be the SNP's threshold of 60 per cent.

The impact of Sturgeon's words, meanwhile, was palpable, not just in the rest of the UK but on the Continent. As David Cameron fell on his sword and the Labour leader Jeremy Corbyn came under renewed assault from his own MPs, only the First Minister emerged looking, as the *Financial Times* put it, 'composed and in control', her response 'not just measured but statesmanlike'.[5] And as the Scottish journalist and campaigner Lesley Riddoch observed, Sturgeon therefore became 'the calm, determined voice of reason – not just for Scots but for the Remain-voting millions across the UK and worried European citizens beyond'.[6] The *Toronto Star* newspaper even touted her as the next British premier, thus putting 'her in charge of righting the British ship and steering a path through the Euro mess'.[7]

The First Minister was, as Sky's political editor Faisal Islam observed, 'the only one who seems to have a plan'.[8] With leading Brexiters revealed as having little idea of how to respond to the majority Leave vote, Sturgeon's response appeared assured. Even City firms, anxious about losing the benefits of the single market, hung on 'her every word',[9] alert to the possibility that an independent Scotland in the EU might offer prospects London could not. Nationalists were suddenly alive to the opportunities, financial and otherwise, that Brexit might offer Scotland and the economic case for independence.

A week, to deploy another hackneyed political cliché, is a long time in politics. Just days before the EU referendum stumbled towards its wretched conclusion, Nicola Sturgeon had appeared adrift, responding to events rather than controlling them. There was grumbling at all levels of the SNP about the recent Holyrood election campaign, in which the party had lost its overall majority, while its leader faced challenges both domestic and strategic. But now all that had changed, changed utterly.

One of the first things Sturgeon had done on succeeding Alex Salmond as First Minister in late 2014 was to frame the prospect of a referendum on the UK's membership of the EU in constitutional terms. She called for a 'double majority' whereby Brexit could only occur should every part of the UK vote the same way. Constitutionally this made little sense, for it was a UK-wide referendum and the EU Member State in question was unitary rather than federal but the SNP leader was, of course, making a political point.

During a subsequent visit to Brussels, Sturgeon's pro-European tone had impressed although beneath the positive meta-narrative lurked caveats. She had already spoken of making the EU 'more democratic' and 'transparent'[10] and, in a speech at the European Policy Centre, the First Minister went further in suggesting that Member States be freer 'to take the decisions they deem necessary to protect life and promote health' (i.e. the Scottish Government's plan for minimum alcohol pricing, which the European Court of Justice later ruled breached EU free-trade laws), stressing the need for 'collective reform of rules to guard against abuse of free movement' and also 'safeguards' for non-Euro Member States, a stance not far removed from that of David Cameron

The First Minster's central message, however, remained that, if the UK backed a Leave vote while Scotland opted to Remain, then she believed 'the groundswell of anger among ordinary people in Scotland in these circumstances could produce a clamour for another independence referendum which may well be unstoppable'.[11] In mid 2015, with the status quo enjoying a comfortable lead in the polls, this rhetoric was largely academic but, as that lead diminished over the following year, there was a discernable shift in Sturgeon's position. She was conscious that, even were such 'material change' to transpire, it would need to be bolstered by a significant increase in support for independence which, hypothetical polling suggested, was unlikely.

Apart from a cogent speech to the Resolution Foundation in February 2016, however, Sturgeon understandably kept out of the European debate ahead of the Holyrood election that was due to take place a few months later. She had expressed opposition to the referendum following the devolved elections so closely (and, indeed, opposed a ballot taking place at all), and only in late May did the SNP leader return to the fray, battling to preserve what her party had, since 1988, regarded as the acceptable face of Unionism – so-called 'independence in Europe'.

'Of course I want Scotland to be independent,' the First Minister took to pointing out, 'but I don't want Scotland to become independent because the UK chooses to leave the European Union.'[12] This was a sincere position but one she often found difficult to explain to SNP members and supporters, around a third of whom intended to back Brexit. Perhaps some believed doing so would provoke another independence referendum, as Sturgeon and her predecessor, Alex Salmond, had implied, while others saw an inconsistency between arguing *against* one Union (the UK) and *for* another (the EU), a frequently articulated point the First Minister simply dismissed as 'nonsense'.[13]

The two unions were, of course, very different but it did not help that many of the arguments Sturgeon deployed in defence of the EU strongly echoed those of Better Together two years earlier, not least the line that Remain would be 'better for trade and the economy and the cultural and social links that have been forged between countries'. Pressed as to whether she was a 'Unionist' for the purposes of 23 June 2016, the First Minister replied: 'I wouldn't use that term. I would call myself a Europhile, an enthusiastic European.'[14]

Elsewhere Sturgeon indulged in 'friendly fire' towards the umbrella Remain campaign 'Britain Stronger in Europe', repeatedly accusing it of not being positive enough and, in response to a Treasury analysis of the economic consequences of Brexit, warning that 'fear-based campaigning, when it starts to insult people's intelligence' could have 'a negative effect'.[15] Not only did the Scottish Government fail to provide any alternative figures but such lines were also then quoted back at the First Minister when she took part in an ITV debate along-side Labour's Angela Eagle and the Conservative MP Amber Rudd (despite having said she would not share a platform with Tories).

'I agree with Nicola!' was therefore one of Boris Johnson's better lines in that debate, in which the First Minister performed well but without recapturing the magic of the 2015 general election campaign. And, as the polls narrowed even further, Sturgeon even resorted to her own Project Fear, warning that a vote to Leave the EU could see Scots at the mercy of the 'most right-wing Tory government in modern history', while also leading to 'profound consequences for the future of the health service right across the UK'.[16]

Ahead of polling day and with the outcome on a knife edge, Sturgeon told MSPs that 'all options to protect our relationship with Europe and the European Union' (including another independence referendum) would be 'considered',[17] while she made a point of pleading with Yes supporters in more unequivocal terms: 'If you are basing your decision on what it means for independence, let me be very clear – the only sensible and logical vote is one for Scotland to remain in Europe.'[18]

On polling day Sturgeon arrived at the SNP's Edinburgh headquarters to watch the results with aides and colleagues. There followed a dramatic few hours in which the presumption of a narrow Remain vote gave way to the realisation that Leave had pulled ahead. The First Minister arrived at her official residence at 6 a.m. on Friday morning to prepare her response while staffers put in calls to Green co-leader Patrick Harvie and the Prime Minister, to whom Sturgeon offered her sympathies while making it clear her government would bypass Westminster and negotiate directly with Brussels.

Initially, a press conference was scheduled for 10 a.m. but then pushed back to 11 a.m. It was delayed again when it emerged that three Leave-supporting MPs, Boris Johnson, Michael Gove and Gisela Stuart, would be responding to the result at the same time. Sturgeon watched this oddly sombre trio before addressing journalists at Bute House. Significantly, at the end of her statement and in response to a question from BBC Scotland's Glenn Campbell about how 'likely' she considered a second referendum, the First Minister responded that it was 'highly likely', a pregnant phrase that dominated subsequent press coverage, although she had used a similar form of words a few months previously.[19]

By the following morning, however, Sturgeon's mood was more cautious. Following an emergency meeting of the Scottish Cabinet she said a second independence referendum was 'clearly an option' while making it clear her goal was to 'protect' Scotland's relationship with the EU *and* its 'place in the single market', a subtle shift from her original position which implied the latter to be a priority. An advisory panel, meanwhile, would be appointed to advise her and the Scottish Government on matters 'legal, financial and diplomatic' and, as part of continuing efforts to reassure EU citizens resident in Scotland, Sturgeon would be inviting consul generals of all Member States to a 'summit' at Bute House.

Finally, Sturgeon pledged not to take her 'eye off the ball of the day-to-day business of government'. 'As Westminster is engulfed in political turmoil and as a vacuum of leadership develops,' she added, 'I want to make clear that Scotland is led by a stable and effective government.'[20] With that the First Minister walked back into Bute House, ignoring shouted questions from journalists. 'If you can keep your head when all around are losing theirs,' the poet Rudyard Kipling had written in another gender-specific aphorism, 'you will be a man, my son.'

Nicola Sturgeon had a knack for finding the right words in any given situation, for striking the right tone. But that was the easy bit. The following day the *Mail on Sunday* splashed on what it claimed was the likely Brussels response to the First Minister's overtures, chiefly that, while EU chiefs were sympathetic, their position was essentially unchanged from that in 2014 – if Scotland wanted to remain part of the Union, then it would need to seek its independence from the UK first and then apply in the usual way.

Elsewhere in the Sunday papers Jim Sillars, architect of the SNP's 'independence in Europe' policy and, like Sturgeon, a former deputy leader of the party, said the 'perception' now taking hold was that the First Minister was 'committed to an early referendum', something he judged 'she cannot deliver'. 'The vote was on the UK in or out of the EU,' he continued. 'The ballot paper did not say Scotland in or out. By campaigning in England, Nicola gave legitimacy to it being a UK vote on the UK's future.'[21] The constitutional lawyer-turned-Scottish Conservative MSP Adam Tomkins later made the same point – that 62 per cent of Scots had voted for the UK (rather than Scotland) to Remain part of the EU. And while Sturgeon did not ignore the 38 per cent of Scots who had voted Leave, she preferred to emphasise that every local authority area in the country had backed Remain by a majority.

In a round of television interviews, meanwhile, Sturgeon shifted tone once again,[22] repeating several times that in attempting to 'protect' Scotland's position in the EU her 'starting point' was not independence or even another referendum although, if it became 'obvious that the only way we can protect Scotland's interests is by looking again at independence then that's an option that Scotland has to have'.[23] Now that temperatures had cooled a little, attention shifted to the case the SNP might make should another referendum occur. There were obvious challenges for many of the difficulties associated with the independence proposition two years earlier – chiefly concerning economics, currency and borders – had not gone away.

Without addressing these points in any detail Sturgeon promised 'an honest conversation at every step of the way' although, if, as she said in one interview, the UK leaving the EU would be 'deeply damaging, economically, socially, culturally',[24] it prompted the obvious rejoinder that Scotland leaving an even more integrated Union (with greater fiscal transfers) would be even more so. Currency was an issue, she conceded, 'we have to work our way through',[25] but did not 'want to see in any circumstances a border between Scotland and England', which of course was a desire rather than a coherent position.

'I'm not saying there are not questions and challenges that Scotland would have to face up to,' the First Minister told the BBC's Andrew Marr. 'I'm not suggesting for a second that the path ahead is without complexity.'[26] Answers to all these questions, she admitted, could not be 'conjured up instantaneously' but, if there was another referendum, it would 'not just be a re-run' of that in 2014 because the United Kingdom that Scots had voted to remain part of did not 'exist any more'.[27] Later, SNP sources briefed that, this time, 'senior figures would admit that independence carries economic risks, costs and short-term pain'.[28]

So, despite Sturgeon's assured response to the Brexit vote and despite plans (albeit delayed) to proceed with a summer independence 'initiative' intended to win over sceptical Unionists, victory in another referendum was not a given. The First Minister, however, remained on impressive form in the week that followed. On Tuesday, she addressed the Scottish Parliament, arguing that turbulent times called for 'principles, purpose and clarity', announcing membership of her 'Standing Council' of European experts and telling MSPs it was 'vital' to 'seize the chance' to ensure Scotland's voice was 'heard as widely as possible: in London, in Brussels, and by Member States across Europe'.[29]

On Wednesday, Sturgeon flew to Brussels and met Martin Schulz, President of the European Parliament, leaders of political groups and, most importantly, Jean-Claude Juncker, the President of the European Commission, who later declared that Scotland had 'won the right to be heard in Brussels'. But there was the expected caveat. Neither he nor Donald Tusk, President of the European Council, intended to 'interfere in the British process'. Spain and France similarly made it clear that any negotiations would take place between the EU and UK, not parts of the UK, although Germany and Ireland were more positive. Speaking to international journalists, Sturgeon seemed content, saying she had 'found a willingness to listen: open doors, open ears and open minds' and she, therefore, left Brussels 'in good heart'.[30]

The First Minister's trip to the EU capital had, of course, served another purpose, demonstrating to voters back home that she was 'standing up for Scotland' both internationally and domestically. Facing the Scottish Parliament for the second time that week, Sturgeon again reiterated her intention to 'give effect to what Scotland voted for', rejecting the idea that it could be 'ripped' or 'dragged' out of the EU 'against our will'.[31]

On 2 July, Her Majesty the Queen formerly opened the fifth session of the Scottish Parliament with a studiously anodyne speech which acknowledged the difficulty of 'staying calm and collected' in 'such a fast-moving world'.[32] Sturgeon, who as ever was both calm and collected, responded with more ostentatiously political remarks about the nature of modern Scotland:

> We are the grandchildren and great-grandchildren of the thousands who came from Ireland to work in our shipyards and our factories. We are the 80,000 Polish people, the 8,000 Lithuanians, the 7,000 each from France, Spain, Germany, Italy and Latvia, who are among the many from countries beyond our shores that we are so privileged to have living here amongst us. We are the more than half a million people born in England, Wales and Northern Ireland, who have chosen to live in Scotland.

So, as MSPs celebrated 'this new beginning', concluded the First Minister, 'let us look forward with hope and a shared determination to work tirelessly for the good of all of Scotland's people – and in doing so, to play our part in a stronger Europe and a better world.'[33]

As Holyrood entered its summer recess, Westminster geared up for two leadership elections – one to select a new Conservative leader (and therefore Prime Minister), another an attempt at resolving Labour's internal squabbles. They were heady days and, after Home Secretary Theresa May emerged as David Cameron's successor, her first official engagement was an Edinburgh meeting with the First Minister.

Given the new Prime Minister had declared 'Brexit means Brexit', it seemed unlikely she and Nicola Sturgeon (who retorted 'Remain means Remain') would have much of a rapport. Both, however, were business-like women who cared little for small talk and, following their encounter at Bute House (flanked by two Saltires, the Union flag conspicuous by its absence) the SNP leader acknowledged the wider symbolism of the occasion with a Tweet of the two leaders shaking hands: 'Politics aside – I hope girls everywhere look at this photograph and believe nothing should be off limits for them.'[34]

But, while May had done her best to appear constructive, making it clear she would only trigger Article 50 once a

UK-wide negotiating stance had been agreed with the devolved administrations, a few days later she also said certain scenarios, such as Scotland doing a 'reverse Greenland' *were* off limits or, as she put it in the House of Commons, 'impracticable'.[35] Sturgeon responded with a speech setting out the 'vital interests' ('democracy, economic prosperity, social protection, solidarity and influence') she was seeking to 'safeguard',[36] although political opponents claimed the First Minister did so content in the knowledge they would likely fail.

By late summer 2016 there were also signs Sturgeon might have over-reached when it came to promising a second referendum. A YouGov poll found no real post-Brexit boost for independence support, while former Scottish Cabinet minister Alex Neil cautioned against the SNP being 'stampeded' into holding a 'premature and unnecessarily risky' second ballot.[37] A trip to Berlin, meanwhile, might have kept Scotland on the EU's radar, but yielded little for Sturgeon beyond another photo-call and praise (from a junior German minister) as a 'dedicated pro-European'.[38]

Back in Scotland a proxy war between the 'impatient' and 'cautious' wings of the party was also evident in the SNP depute leadership campaign, but nevertheless those who witnessed Sturgeon during those weeks and months saw a politician with an undeniable spring in her step, a sense of purpose that would provide form and momentum to her first full term as First Minister. At the same time, she must have been conscious of the challenges ahead: initiate another independence referendum too soon and she might lose, compelling her to resign, as had Alex Salmond and David Cameron in similar circumstances; proceed with typical caution and put the question again in 2018, on the other hand, and she could well win, securing her place in early 21st-century history but then finding herself faced with undeniable challenges at the birth of a new nation. There were, as Sturgeon said herself, no easy options, but it was clear she intended to steer the current of events towards an independent Scotland.

Chapter 2

'A working-class girl from Ayrshire'

Nicola Sturgeon was born on 19 July 1970 at Ayrshire Central Hospital in Irvine. Her parents were Robert (known as Robin), an electrician, and Joan, a dental nurse (Joan's maiden name of Ferguson would become their new daughter's middle name). At that time the couple lived at 17 Newdykes Road in the coastal town of Prestwick.

Robin and Joan had only married on Boxing Day the previous year, aged 21 and 17 respectively. In those days, unmarried parents were still a relative rarity, although the relationship must have had a solid – and loving – basis, for the couple remained happily married more than four decades later when their daughter became First Minister of Scotland. 'They were really young when I was born,' reflected Sturgeon in 2015. 'I guess their own life experiences at that time must have been fairly limited.'[1]

A sister, Gillian, followed in 1975, by which point the Sturgeons had moved to a terraced council house in Dreghorn, where they remain to this day (they moved when Nicola was one). Joan hailed from Prestwick, the daughter of a 'process foreman', while, at the time of his marriage, Robin lived at a 'tied' cottage called 'The Croft' in Dunure. This was actually quite modern, having recently replaced the previous derelict gardener's cottage.

Robin's father, also christened Robert, was a gardener for the local estate house, and his mother was Margaret, the daughter of a shipwright called Joseph Mill. She died in 2001 aged 80, although more than a decade later her grand-daughter frequently referred to her during the long independence debate, citing her 'English granny' (also an SNP voter) as proof that Scottish Nationalism was not Anglophobic. 'My granny was English,' said Sturgeon in late 2014, 'and if she had been alive during the referendum she would have voted Yes.'[2]

That 'English granny', Margaret Mill, was actually partly Scottish, and her family tree illustrated internal migration between Scotland and England common then as now. Her mother's parents, William and Mary Jane Wilcock (or Willcock – the spelling was not consistent), were a shoemaker and confectioner originally from Leeds in Yorkshire who spent at least a few years in Galashiels in the early 1880s, while her father Joseph Mill was from an Anglo-Scottish family – his father Robert, a hairdresser's assistant, had been born in Arbroath but moved with his first wife Christian Mill and two children to Durham in the late 1860s or early 1870s. Robert's second wife Alma was Margaret's grandmother, and she was from Sunderland.[3]

Margaret had been born in Ryhope's Arthur Street (which was not far from Scotland Street) in 1920. Once home to ship-yard workers and miners, the area shared an industrial heritage similar to parts of Scotland. In 1943, she married Robert Sturgeon, Nicola's paternal grandfather, at St Paul's Parish Church, not far from where she grew up. Eventually, they moved back to the south-west of Scotland.[4] (Sturgeon later recalled spending 'many childhood summers' in Ryhope, and even felt 'a little part' of her belonged to the English village.)[5]

Writing in *The Sunday Times* shortly after the 2007 Scottish Parliament election, Sturgeon had clear memories of frequent visits to see Margaret and her husband in Dunure, which was about 30 miles away from her childhood home. She remem-bered, 'For me, the whole place was just one big adventure playground. The place had hens, cats and dogs, as well as a burn running through it, so you can imagine what it was like being a child in such an environment. It was such a great place to play. Out the back of the new cottage, through a gate and across a field, was a beach and the sea. It was fantastic. The property may have been small, but as a kid it felt huge.'

For a while, Sturgeon's great-grandmother lived with her grandparents, which necessitated some juggling of rooms. Of all the pieces of furniture, what stuck in her mind was a rocking chair, on which she would sit with her granny. Occasionally Sturgeon would help her granddad with his work which, as she recalled, 'meant being able to stuff my face with strawberries'. Both grandparents, she admitted, 'spoiled' her 'rotten', although Robert died when she was seven, meaning Margaret had to move to another house in the village.

Even more than three decades later the place retained a 'mystique' for Sturgeon, and she speculated that it was probably at that cottage when she first began to develop a sense of who she was and how she could express herself. 'It was definitely a place to experiment and have adventures,' she recalled. 'Having that space and freedom probably did shape me into becoming an independent person.'[6]

The name Sturgeon belonged mainly in the shires of Dumfries and Kirkcudbright, although it may not have been native to Ayrshire. Ferguson, Nicola's middle name and her mother's maiden name, was also common in the county, derived from Robert I's gift of land to Fergus, son of Fergus, although it was widely scattered and, like Sturgeon, may not have originated in Ayrshire.

Robin Sturgeon, Nicola's father, had been born at 'The Croft', as had his father before him. Robert Sturgeon, Nicola's grandfather, and James, her great-grandfather, had been gardeners in Dunure, the latter the son of a farmer also called James. Before that the Sturgeons were ploughmen, while the Fergusons – a Prestwick-based family – worked mainly on the railways, as engineers, porters and lorrymen, although further back one described himself as a 'waterman'.

So Sturgeon's family background, paternal and maternal, was, in her own words, 'a fairly standard, normal, working-class family',[7] as were the village and town that formed the backdrop to her childhood. Dreghorn was a small, quiet village two miles east of Irvine, a much larger North Ayrshire settlement. Both were historic. During the development of new housing, a large prehistoric site was discovered to the north of Dreghorn's Main Street, making it perhaps the oldest continuously inhabited village in the UK.

Dreghorn's most famous son (until the appearance of a notable daughter) was John Boyd Dunlop, inventor of the pneumatic tyre, while Irvine could boast the American writer Edgar Allan Poe, who had briefly attended its old grammar school, as well as Jack McConnell, Sturgeon's predecessor but one as First Minister. Although Irvine had been one of Scotland's earliest capitals, later it was best known as a New Town, a relic of the post-war consensus dedicated to full employment and good public housing. Although much maligned aesthetically, New Towns such as Irvine actually achieved many of their employment targets (they were intended to attract light manufacturing) while providing thousands of West Coast Scots with comfortable housing for the first time in their lives.

A quango, the Irvine Development Corporation (IDC), would have been a fixture of Sturgeon's childhood, established, along with four others, to oversee the town's modernisation. The orthodoxy of the period dictated that this involve the demolition of swathes of the old Irvine, although the Irvine Beach Park and Magnum Leisure Centre (later demolished), proved more enduring and popular – as a teenager Sturgeon would go to Frosty's ice disco at the Magnum every Saturday night.

The early 1970s was an optimistic time in this part of North Ayrshire. The local press was full of articles about Irvine's 'dynamic future' under the IDC. George Younger, the Ayr MP and newly-appointed undersecretary for development in Edward Heath's Conservative government, visited shortly after Sturgeon was born, witnessing the first phase of the town centre regeneration to the north of the old Bridgegate. The Queen's Baton had also just passed through en route to Edinburgh for the 1970 Commonwealth Games.

Politically the area was solid Labour territory. David Lambie was the MP for Central Ayrshire (as he would be until 1983, before serving as the Member for Cunninghame South until 1992), the constituency that included both Dreghorn and Irvine, although there was modest SNP activity. In August 1970, Winnie Ewing had opened the party's 'Alba Club' in Kilwinning, its first social club in the West of Scotland. Jim Sillars had recently become the MP for South Ayrshire following a by-election, although it was to be another decade before he joined the SNP, and even longer before a poster of him would adorn Sturgeon's teenage bedroom wall. Only much later did she learn that one of her uncles 'had been a member of the SNP back in the 1960s',[8] although in other accounts it was a grandfather, 'though', as she recalled in 2007, she 'only discovered that after his death'. 'You think you're a trail-blazer,' added Sturgeon, 'and it turns out it's been in your genes all along.'[9]

Despite a bold vision of urban regeneration – Irvine's new multimillion-pound shopping centre opened in 1975 – by the time Sturgeon began primary school that year the New Town had been hit by a slump in British industry. Long before the era associated with Margaret Thatcher began, old economic certainties were beginning to break down, taking with them jobs in parts of the UK like North Ayrshire.

Shelley Jofre, who was a year older than Sturgeon and later became a BBC journalist, remembers Dreghorn Primary as a 'nice wee local school', although in retrospect she could 'understand the poverty there was – you don't appreciate that as a kid'. Several years later, as Deputy First Minister, Sturgeon tweeted about her old primary school being converted into Scotland's first sake brewery. In the 1980s, however, 'it was a nice place to grow up,' recalled Jofre. 'There was a decent sense of community, even though during the marching season we would get [Orange Order] bands coming right through Dreghorn.'[10] Making a surprise visit to her old school shortly after becoming First Minister, Sturgeon said her experiences there 'had a huge role in shaping' her life.[11] She had her first crush, a boy called Colin, in primary seven.

At this point, politics did not impinge on Sturgeon's life (one early memory was getting her 'first proper bike' as a Christmas present when she was about five[12]), although she later told profilers of a political memory, 'very vague', 'no more than a sliver', of coming downstairs on the morning of 2 March 1979 to hear her parents – SNP voters but not activists – discussing the result of the first, controversial, devolution referendum. Political talk, however, did not dominate the kitchen table, and later Sturgeon could not remember either of her parents 'trying to persuade [her] politically one way or the other'.[13]

'THE GREAT DEVO DEBATE GOES ON' read a headline in the following week's *Irvine Times*, a reference to the feeling that plans for a devolved Scottish Assembly, defeated by the '40 per cent rule' represented unsettled business, and indeed a debate that would dominate Sturgeon's formative years and beyond. The subsequent general election reinforced Central Ayrshire's position as a safe Labour seat, the SNP peak of 1974–77 having become a trough the previous year.

But nor was Ayrshire, and nor would it ever really become, what in 1980s parlance could be described as a Tory-free zone. George Younger, about to become Secretary of State for Scotland, held on to his seat, as did the Conservative John Corrie in Bute and North Ayrshire, while in the first elections to the European Parliament a month later the Conservatives won the largest share of the Scottish vote and returned Alasdair Hutton, a BBC Scotland announcer, for the South of Scotland constituency.

But, if the tectonic plates of post-war economic consensus had begun to shift in the era of Harold Wilson and Jim Callaghan, they began to produce tremors just as Sturgeon was about to transfer to her local secondary school, Greenwood Academy, situated not far from her home in Dreghorn. One of the village's main industries was coal mining, and by the early 1980s most mines in the area had already closed (i.e. under previous Labour and Tory governments).

According to Sturgeon, it was at this point, with Mrs Thatcher's monetarist experiment at its destructive height, that politics 'became an issue' for her personally. 'I began to take an interest in what was going on around me.'[14] As she told an interviewer in the summer of 2014, 'When I was at Greenwood Academy, unemployment was very high and I was acutely aware of a sense of hopelessness among a lot of people I was at school with. They would leave school and, through no fault of their own, not go on to do well.'

Her memory extended beyond school. 'There was also very strong fear, particularly among my dad's generation,' recalled Sturgeon, 'that if you lost your job, you might be unemployed for the rest of your life.' Although Robin Sturgeon was in work throughout the 1980s, this was a legitimate fear – according to one survey, by 1987, 12,000 people in Irvine were out of work. (Sturgeon's first job was selling 'tattie scones round the doors' when she was 14. 'I hated it so much,' she later recalled, 'my poor dad always ended up doing it for me.')[15]

A decision taken by Sturgeon's parents also highlights the contradictions of the era: although fiercely anti-Thatcher, they were nevertheless prepared to take advantage of Thatcherite policies, buying (for £8,400) their terraced council house in May 1984 on what was known as 'the Annick estate' having previously rented it from the Scottish Special Housing Association. 'What played on me then,' recalled Sturgeon, 'is that we had a right-wing, uncaring Tory Government that we didn't vote for doing significant damage to the fabric of our society. That just seemed wrong to me.'[16] Ironically, as a minister 20 years later, Sturgeon would oversee the dismantling of the 'Right to Buy' policy from which her parents had benefitted.

Certain teachers at Greenwood Academy clearly helped shape Sturgeon's thinking as she took a closer interest in politics between the ages of 14 and 16. She attended a large non-denominational school and there were two members of staff in particular who had an effect on her – 'one positively and the other negatively'. She recalled, 'My modern studies teacher wasn't an SNP supporter but I think he was the one who awakened a real political interest in me. On the other had, my English teacher at the time was a Labour councillor who

I think assumed I would automatically join the Labour Party. Looking back, perhaps my decision to join the SNP when I did was as much to prove a point to him that there was a real alternative to Labour in Scotland.'[17]

In a 1999 interview, Sturgeon was clear her English teacher's assumption 'was the spur' that made her join the SNP[18] while, in a more recent interview, she was more explicit about the contrarian nature of her decision: 'What made me join was a conversation with my English teacher, who was a Labour councillor. He knew I was interested in politics and assumed without even asking me that I would join the Labour Party. He actually brought me a membership application form. That was the catalyst. I thought: "Stuff you, I'm going to join the SNP." '[19]

'I would have got to the SNP anyway,' Sturgeon told this author in late 2013, making the story sound less contrarian, 'but the fact that I joined at that particular moment in time was probably an act of rebellion against him as much as anything else.'[20] (Other interviewers, meanwhile, were told the impetus had been a debating competition at Greenwood Academy, a party broadcast and a school trip to the Houses of Parliament at Westminster.)

Sturgeon was attracted, as she later explained, by the SNP's 'vision and ideals', believing them to be something she 'could get behind and genuinely campaign for'. Even aged 16, she remembered, Labour seemed 'to have something quite sterile about it, being more about people making their own careers than about the ideals of politics'.[21] Whatever the case, joining the SNP – or indeed any political party – aged only 16 was an unusual thing to do. In a 2012 speech, Sturgeon sought to put her decision in context: 'Down the years, many people have asked me why I ended up in the SNP and not the Labour Party. Why did a young girl, growing up in a working class family in the west of Scotland – a part of the country where in those days, they would joke that the Labour vote was weighed rather than counted; someone who was, just like Labour was in those days, anti-Trident and pro-social justice . . . why does that person end up in the SNP instead of Labour. The reason is simple. I joined the SNP because it was obvious to me then – as it still is today – that you cannot guarantee social justice unless you are in control of the delivery.'[22] If true, it was a strikingly mature analysis for a 16-year-old to have reached. In any case, the modern studies teacher in question was Roy Kelso, who also had a 'big influence' on Shelley Jofre, who was in the year above Sturgeon at Greenwood Academy. 'Mr Kelso stood apart from the other teachers as he was very liberal, laid back and good fun,' recalled Jofre, 'and if you had an interest in politics then his classes were the highlight of the week because you got to argue about politics all day.'[23] Kelso himself later remembered Sturgeon as 'a very nice young lady', polite and hard working but also 'quite serious'. Later, as he watched her career develop, he would think to himself, 'Nicola, smile please.'[24]

Gillian, Sturgeon's younger sister, also recalled a certain seriousness. 'Nicola and I played together but we were like chalk and cheese,' she recalled. 'I was into dolls and everything girly; Nicola was into sitting reading. She did once cut the hair off my Sindy doll, just for fun. I was a lot quieter. She was a very strong-minded wee girl. I would just do what I was told. I didn't like getting a row. But Nicola would challenge.' Sturgeon, however, denied the doll torture but later admitted ditching the 'Ayrshire tongue' and affecting both the accent and 'patter' associated with Glasgow, long before she became an adopted Glaswegian. 'It drove', she recalled in 2002, 'my mother mad.'[25]

'She was a quiet and studious child,' remembered Joan Sturgeon in an interview shortly before her daughter became First Minister. 'She loved books from a very early age. She read before she went to school. Nicola was desperate to learn. She got quite frustrated, so we sat with her and she was easy to teach. Nicola would lift a newspaper at the age of four and try to read it.'[26] At her fifth birthday party, Sturgeon recalled hiding under a table reading a book while the other children played. 'I wasn't particularly outgoing,' she reflected, 'but then – I'm always slightly worried this sounds a wee bit overly grand – there was always just a sense I had something inside me.'[27]

However, as Joan Sturgeon recalled, her daughter 'was very driven'[28] but also, paradoxically, quite shy. When the comedian Rory Bremner later asked Sturgeon what the First Minister 'of today' would say to her 16-year-old self, she replied, 'Lighten up . . . and then the girl of sixteen would say eff off.'[29]

Later, Sturgeon observed that she was 'pretty focused', a trait she reckoned came from her mother, while her father was more 'laid-back . . . quite jovial'.[30] But the 'most important value' instilled in her as a child ('almost before I can remember') was 'that you do your best, you work hard and the sky is the limit. There is nothing in your background that inherently holds you back or means you can't achieve what others can achieve. You are the master of your own fate, and if you work hard you can do what you want.'[31]

Given the modest nature of Sturgeon's background, not to mention the growing inequality that would become a feature of the 1980s, her belief that there was nothing 'inherently' holding working-class children back was one at odds with other aspects of her developing worldview.

In a perceptive profile published in November 2014, the journalist Peter Ross posited that, for the teenage Sturgeon, books were 'an escape, an adventure', with her voracious reading habits providing a glimpse of her character, then as now: 'interior; introverted; interested in the lives of others yet not entirely at ease in the living crowd; in regular need of quiet contemplation and consolation.'[32]

As a teenager, for example, Sturgeon read Lewis Grassic Gibbon's *Sunset Song*, a novel that chimed with her nascent belief in Scottish independence. 'It seemed to speak to me,' she recalled, 'at a time when other things were taking shape in my head.'[33] This suggested a romantic or 'existential' element to Sturgeon's Nationalism, although much later she would prefer to place herself as a 'utilitarian'. But, at 16, she was also reading the historic novels of Nigel Tranter, thus her thinking 'might have been more of a heart rather than a head thing', at least initially.[34]

Music was also in the air and, in 1987, Sturgeon recalled the 'perverse pride' of her hometown being mentioned in a successful pop song. 'Bathgate no more, Linwood no more, Methil no more, Irvine no more' rang a dirge-like line in The Proclaimers' hit single 'Letter From America', even though, as Sturgeon herself noted, there had been no 'single cataclysmic event' in Irvine that merited its inclusion. 'But it also solidified the feeling I had – which took me into politics – that things weren't as they should be and places like Irvine should be doing much better,' she recalled. 'There was a sense of the damage being done and the song reflected that. For someone like me, who was young and becoming active in politics, it became a political anthem. I drove my mum and dad mad playing it constantly.'[35] Sturgeon also idolised the television presenter Cilla Black and the English new wave band Duran Duran, skating to '80s songs like theirs at an ice disco in Irvine. 'I'm just an Eighties girl at heart,' she said in 2015.'[36]

Sturgeon's sister remembered CND badges being more prominent in Nicola's bedroom than posters of pop stars, and indeed she recalled the issue that angered her most as a teenager being that of nuclear weapons. 'It was one of the first issues,' she reflected in 1999, 'I remember being particularly passionate about.'[37] It is not clear whether Sturgeon formally joined the Campaign for Nuclear Disarmament (whose logo had inspired the SNP's in the late 1960s) but she said several times during the referendum campaign that she 'was in the CND before [she] was in the SNP'[38] although, given that only the Nationalists 'took an unequivocal stance against nuclear weapons',[39] the path to party membership was clear. In a 1988 Certificate of Sixth Year Studies essay, Sturgeon urged the UK government 'on moral, economic and political grounds . . . not [to] go ahead with the purchase and installation of the US Trident missile system'. Britain, she added, ought to 'have the courage to stand up and put a halt to the increasing nuclear madness which prevails in the world today',[40] a point she would make consistently for the next three decades.

Although the UK's nuclear 'deterrents' were based several

miles away on the Clyde, they must have appeared a peripheral concern to those suffering from the impact of de-industrialisation, the effects of which lingered in Scotland longer than in other parts of the country. The miners' strike of 1984–85 had also hit Ayrshire hard, while rolling teachers' strikes at around the same time had done much to harden previously sympathetic Scottish voters against Mrs Thatcher's second government. Sturgeon noticed the impact, not just in terms of housing conditions and unemployment, but its broader effects on inequality, which had been increasing since the late 1970s.

By 1987, the woman most closely associated, for good or ill, with these changes was about to submit her government to the country for a third time so, one evening in May 1987, Nicola Sturgeon, just two months shy of her 17th birthday, stood at the entrance to 'Tulsa', a bungalow at the end of a quiet cul-de-sac in Dreghorn, and rang the doorbell of 43-year-old Kay Ullrich ('a friend of the family' according to Joan Sturgeon[41]) who, as in 1983, was contesting the Labour-held Cunninghame South constituency on behalf of the SNP. 'We were just about to go out leafleting and there she was on the doorstep,' recalled Ullrich, a former Butlin's redcoat as exuberant as Nicola was shy. "Hello, Mrs Ullrich, can I help you with your campaign?" So she came in, then out she went leafleting.'

But before Sturgeon started banging on doors Ullrich, a social worker at Crosshouse Hospital, signed her up for party membership, or rather that of the Young Scottish Nationalists (YSN), a youth organisation affiliated to the SNP. 'She was', added Ullrich fondly, 'very intense.'[42] And also reserved. 'I was a shy teenager so it was a big thing for me,' recalled Sturgeon of pushing that doorbell. 'I'd been trying to pluck up the courage for a long time . . . I didn't know what reception I would get. Did they want a 16-year-old hanging about? I wasn't a naturally extrovert teenager. My instinct would be to sit in my room and watch the election on telly. You know, I could easily not have decided to take that step. But I did, and the rest is history.'[43]

Later, Joan Sturgeon said her daughter's decision 'came as no surprise',[44] particularly as she, her husband and mother-in-law were all SNP voters. What Sturgeon probably did not realise, however, is that Ullrich's chances of victory were slim, not least because the incumbent MP David Lambie was defending the second-largest Labour majority in Scotland. Ullrich's campaign majored on unemployment. The Tories, she argued, had 'ruthlessly closed' Gartcosh, and Ravenscraig, she predicted, was 'next on the hit list'. She also had a message for 'young Scots', which of course included Sturgeon. 'Their teachers have had to go on strike to get a decent wage,' said Ullrich. 'Their schools are run down. Their chances of getting an apprenticeship or into university have declined. Many of them face a future on the dole or on temporary, cheap labour schemes.'

The Labour Party, naturally, did not escape the SNP candidate's attention. 'Over the last eight years Labour have proved unable to protect Scotland,' argued Ullrich. 'The Labour Party cannot win in the United Kingdom and whether or not they win in Scotland makes no difference.' Therefore the only choice for the 'people of Scotland' at the election was 'another Thatcher government or a Scottish Government' and the SNP, she believed, would 'win Scotland a better deal'.[45]

This framing of the election reflected Nationalist strategy at that time and, although clever, it proved relatively ineffective, not just in Cunninghame South but also more generally. Sturgeon, recalled Ullrich, had 'just absolutely blossomed' during the campaign although, in her naivety, she believed Kay would become an MP because she was the best candidate, the best performer at local hustings and therefore *deserved* to win.

On election day, Sturgeon helped out at Fencedyke polling station, where Ullrich remembers her being 'incensed' at the sight of Labour agents wearing party badges on one lapel and a CND logo on the other.[46] The count that evening was at the Magnum Leisure Centre and the weather was dismal. Ullrich secured just 4,115 votes while Lambie increased his majority by around 5,000. 'We came fourth and I was devastated,' remembered Sturgeon. 'It was my first lesson in electoral defeat – though not my last.'[47]

The SNP increased its share of the vote by 2.2 per cent and won only three MPs overall, including a young Alex Salmond in Banff and Buchan, and in Ullrich's speech at the count she channelled another Nationalist campaigning theme by declaring that 'Doomsday is here now', although it was not quite true. The so-called 'doomsday scenario' had predicted that Scotland would end up with a Conservative government but no Conservative MPs, but although the party's share of the vote had dipped to 25 per cent and it had lost 11 MPs, there still remained ten Tory MPs including George Younger (just) in Ayr. 'Labour are going to have to answer the question: "What are they going to do for Scotland?" now that England has voted Tory,' continued Ullrich. 'We might have lost the battle but the war for Scotland is just beginning.'[48]

This experience of helping fight – and also helping lose – a local election campaign cannot be underestimated in terms of Sturgeon's political development. Not only had she volunteered at an age when most teenagers would have had other, less lofty, concerns, Sturgeon had then chapped on doors in a part of Scotland where the reception must often have been less than convivial. At the same time, it must have boosted her confidence, not only the initial experience of conquering her shyness, but then to find herself surrounded by other young activists committed to the same cause.

Her decision to join the SNP rather than Labour, meanwhile, was proof that Sturgeon was not thinking purely in terms of a future political career. As she recalled of attending her first constituency party meeting, there was 'great jubilation' because the SNP 'had gone into double figures in the opinion polls'.[49] The party was in fact enjoying a period of relative stability and unity having come close to falling apart in the early 1980s. Party leader Gordon Wilson had sought to move the party on to more moderate territory in terms of its stance on the then European Community (against), NATO (also against) and devolution (against with caveats). Recent campaigns on the steel industry, coal and education, meanwhile, had given the party a sense of purpose if not electoral success. Jim Sillars' book *Scotland:*

The Case for Optimism, published the year Sturgeon joined the SNP, would have been required reading.

Idealism necessarily fuelled activity, something hardly in short supply among politically motivated teenagers, particularly those on the left, and it is worth pausing to consider Sturgeon's political worldview as she entered her final year at secondary school. Unsurprisingly, this was a bit black and white. 'Thatcher', reflected Sturgeon much later, 'was the motivation for my entire political career. I hated everything she stood for. This was the genesis of my nationalism. I hated the fact that she was able to do what she was doing and yet nobody I knew in my entire life had voted for her.' That may have been true, although at that time Cunninghame South was sandwiched between one recently Tory-held seat (Cunninghame North) and Ayr (narrowly retained by George Younger at the 1987 election), while however much the Prime Minister was hated personally 713,081 Scots had still voted for her party in the election, nearly 300,000 more than had backed the SNP. Sturgeon may not personally have encountered any Tory voters, but that was hardly a scientific guide.

Sturgeon's view of the Labour Party was also unyieldingly critical. Given her age, there was little appreciation of Neil Kinnock's need to balance principle with presentation in his quest to oust Thatcher. Michael Foot's focus on the former at the 1983 general election – unilateral disarmament, withdrawal from the EEC and so on – had hardly proved a vote winner. Sturgeon was convinced Labour had ditched its principles whereas the SNP had not, but then of course her chosen party, with little chance of winning a majority of seats in Scotland, arguably had that luxury.

Nevertheless, at this point, Sturgeon's path was more or less set. She had caught the political bug and therefore, no matter what she did after school, Nationalist activism would play a part. It helped that she continued to excel at school. Roy Kelso remembers writing in her sixth-year report that 'Nicola was like a good quality red wine that matured with age',[50] although being smart at Greenwood Academy would not necessarily have been seen as a good thing. 'It was a pretty rough and tumble place,' recalled fellow pupil Shelley Jofre, 'the kind of school where it wasn't easy to be clever and it didn't make you popular.'[51]

But, despite the seriousness of politics, photographs from this period show Sturgeon smiling as well as sporting very 1980s haircuts. Gillian, her sister, remembers Nicola adopting a hairdo like Limahl (the lead singer of Kajagoogoo), while, after her 18th birthday in July 1988, the Ship Inn in Irvine became a favourite haunt as Sturgeon prepared to begin a law degree at the University of Glasgow. Much later she confessed to trying cannabis at around this time ('it made me sick, I really didn't like it'[52]), which at least hinted at a rebellious streak, although hardly an untypical one for teenagers on the cusp of leaving home.

Politically, Sturgeon remained active in the Young Scottish Nationalists – indeed, she held a position on its national executive even before turning 18. The SNP used to hold youth weekends in Portsoy in Aberdeenshire, and at one such gathering ('I know,' she quipped in 2007, 'it's not really what most 18-year-olds do on their holidays'[53]) Sturgeon first set eyes on her future husband Peter Murrell or, as she later remembered thinking of him, 'Mr Gadget Man' by virtue of a belt he wore on which were clipped lots of electronic 'gizmos'.[54] Others who attended the gatherings insist they were fun. 'We played hard and we worked hard,' said one. 'We'd learn about campaigning and also general political education.'[55]

Dreghorn, meanwhile, would remain an important part of Sturgeon's personal and political identity long after she had left home; there was to be no Thatcher-like abandonment of her modest roots. Ullrich recalls Sturgeon returning from university for branch meetings and, decades later, never missing her birthday parties or fundraisers. Even after she became a minister in 2007, she continued to telephone her mother Joan every evening.

Sturgeon later remembered being driven by a 'very Scottish fear of failure', which of course was bundled up with her background. 'I grew up in a working-class family in a working-class area,' she reflected, in a way few Scottish or UK politicians of her generation could, 'and was the first member of my family to go to university.' But as the journalist Peter Ross judged in his perceptive 2014 profile of Sturgeon, hers was also a recognisable type – 'the clever girl from the small town; the lass o' pairts; sensible, dutiful, a grafter',[56] all qualities that would find an outlet at the University of Glasgow.

Chapter 3

'The best of her generation'

'I think I was always ambitious as a younger person,' reflected Nicola Sturgeon on becoming First Minister in 2014. 'I wanted to be a lawyer,'[1] while she had 'always wanted' to study at the University of Glasgow.[2] Thus, in the autumn of 1988, the newly politicised teenager from Dreghorn arrived at what was then called the Faculty of Law and Financial Studies. If 'Oxbridge' and a degree in PPE were the pre-requisites for the English political classes, Glasgow was the Scottish equivalent.[3] Stephen Harte, a slightly older law student, remembers encountering Sturgeon during an 'orientation' course run by the law school. 'Nicola was in my group,' he recalled. 'I remember she said she was interested in politics and was a nationalist. She seemed shy.'[4] Sturgeon arrived at Glasgow with a rather romanticised notion of what the law was all about. 'In my head', she later recalled, 'it was about fighting for justice and the underdog.'[5]

Law, however, would have to compete with politics during a particularly eventful period in Scottish history. Shortly after Sturgeon began her studies, Jim Sillars returned to the House of Commons, this time as an SNP MP following a high-profile by-election in which she helped campaign. The following year, there was another by-election in Glasgow Central while, halfway through Sturgeon's degree, the independence-supporting pop star Pat Kane would be elected the university's Rector and, in late 1990, the Thatcher era finally came to an end at around the same time by-elections were held in Paisley North and South.

It was an era of protests, pickets and politics. 'Probably the first couple of years at university reinforced, reconfirmed the beliefs that had taken me into the SNP,' Sturgeon remembered in 2003. 'Probably the strongest influences on me then were international.'[6] She meant the anti-Apartheid campaign, which was particularly strong in Scotland's largest city. Indeed, a few weeks before starting her studies, Sturgeon attended her first political rally, one marking Nelson Mandela's 70th birthday. 'To me,' she recalled in 1999, 'he was just the personification of everything I thought was ideal in politics.'[7]

This was hardly an unusual inspiration for a student in the late 1980s, but it enabled Sturgeon to place her Nationalism in an international context, thus her claim in one interview that events in South Africa 'made [her] a Nationalist'. At around this time, Pat Kane (also a prolific commentator) defined the SNP's ethos as 'a modern, intellectual, progressive nationalism, which simultaneously maintained our sense of nationhood and connected it with other European cultures'.[8] Indeed, Sturgeon's undergraduate career coincided with a significant shift in the SNP's thinking, away from 'independence, nothing less' and towards a goal of 'independence in Europe'.

Thus Sturgeon's Nationalism was distinct from that of the immediate post-war era in Scotland. As David McCrone put it in his 1992 book *Understanding Scotland*, modern Scottish Nationalism had developed 'without the encumbrance of a heavy cultural baggage . . . No icons need to be genuflected at, no correct representation needs to be observed in this journey into the future'.[9] Nationalist politics (which was by no means confined to the SNP) was therefore primarily concerned with the practicalities of decision-making and 'power' rather than Scottish identity.

That is not to say Sturgeon explicitly rejected the importance of cultural capital in championing the SNP and promoting independence; indeed she realised how salient that could be relatively early in her political development, including an association with Pat Kane (of which more below). It is likely she was at the STUC-organised 'Day for Scotland' in Stirling during the summer of 1990 at which bands like Deacon Blue, Hue and Cry and Runrig performed to a crowd of 35,000. 'Many alliances between politicians and pop stars were forged that day,' recalled Kane, who also wrote of a 'sophisticated sense of Scottishness' having developed in the 1980s, 'a voice both historical and contemporary, politically forthright and culturally stylish, able to define its current needs and express them powerfully'. The Nationalism of the nineties, he added, had to 'continue the development of a plural and principled national identity', embracing Scots Asians and other 'ethnic cultures', all of which would have chimed with Sturgeon's instincts.

But utilitarian concerns were to the fore, something characterised by Alex Salmond's later plea that Nationalists should not just be 'for Scotland, for its own sake: we should be for Scotland *for* social and economic justice'.[10] Such concerns dominated Sturgeon's time at Glasgow University, not least campaigns against the Conservative government's plan to introduce student loans. Sturgeon caught the tail end of a very different climate for Scottish and UK students, enjoying full grants and even benefit payments during the summer holidays. Given her modest family background, without that financial support it is possible she would not have been able to study at all.

Another motivation for studying at Glasgow may have been its long tradition of Nationalist politics. Indeed, the Glasgow University Scottish Nationalist Association (GUSNA) even predated the SNP, having been formed in 1927, and first coming to national prominence in the early 1950s when not only did a group of its members take the Stone of Destiny from Westminster Abbey but its nominee as Rector, 'King' John MacCormick, was successfully elected. Affiliated, like the Young Scottish Nationalists, to the SNP by the time Sturgeon joined in 1988, there had been a split caused by the decision of Robert ('Bob') Pollock to run for president of the Students' Representative Council (SRC) despite having lost the GUSNA nomination, which had gone instead to Calum Smith by just one vote. Pollock stood anyway as an independent in May 1988 and won, echoing a similar split the year before. Even so, next to the Labour Club (which had around 700 members) GUSNA was the busiest political society on campus, with about 250 members, of which perhaps 35 were active.

At the 1988 SRC elections, GUSNA joined forces with the Dialectic Society and Conservative Club on a 'New Deal' slate that campaigned solely on the rather narrow issue of grant allocations to campus clubs and societies, winning 36 of the 68 available seats. Although Sturgeon was not involved in the SRC during 1988–89, she was actively involved in GUSNA's campaign against the Poll Tax, which was due to be introduced in Scotland (a year earlier than in England and Wales) on 1 April 1989.

Although mythology has now distorted the sorry history of what Mrs Thatcher preferred to call the 'Community Charge', it was undeniably unpopular in Scotland. Various non-payment campaigns gathered pace as Poll Tax demands landed on the doorsteps of Scots, many of whom had never contributed to domestic rates until that point. Scottish refuseniks faced warrant sales, the humiliation of bailiffs forcing their way into people's homes and confiscating belongings to cover the value of unpaid taxes, fines and bailiffs' expenses.

More to the point, the Poll Tax was to be a flat-rate charge payable by all adults over the age of 18, regardless of income. Yearly estimates varied from £114 in Shetland to £392 in Edinburgh and, although the government eventually conceded various exemptions, most 18-year-olds were to pay at least a proportion of their Community Charge bill, while even the unemployed were expected to pay a fifth.

Sturgeon was one of those 18-year-olds, and she surfaces – already poised and articulate – in a *Guardian* report that ran just days before the Poll Tax came into force. 'I don't think I can afford it on my grant,' she told a reporter (the student rate was about £60 per annum in Glasgow), 'And it will become even more difficult if the Government goes ahead with student loans.' She also believed the anti-Poll Tax campaign had strengthened

Nationalist feeling in Scotland, particularly following the recent Govan by-election, in which the SNP's 'non-payment' stance had apparently trumped Labour's controversial 'stay within the law' position. 'The poll tax crystallises the national argument,' Sturgeon told the *Guardian*. 'It's a tax that the Scottish people have rejected, yet it's still being imposed upon them. It all shows how the Scottish people have been disenfranchised.'[11]

The SNP was committed to organising an 'army' of 100,000 non-payers, something that it hoped would highlight the supposed impotence of the 'feeble 50', Scottish Labour MPs who, despite much internal debate, chose not to advocate non-payment. Although such a stance had Sturgeon's full support, it was not without problems: leader Gordon Wilson was not keen, having spent much of the decade restoring the party's credibility and moderate stance, but he had little choice, pressured by more radical voices in his party and electoral success in Govan. It at least demonstrated the SNP could challenge Labour from a centre-left position, although it lost a degree of initiative on withdrawing from the Scottish Constitutional Convention (the cross-party body tasked with drafting a devolution blueprint) early that year. After that, Labour was able to depict the SNP as obstructive, putting Nationalists on the back foot ahead of a by-election in Glasgow Central and elections to the European Parliament that June.

By 1989, meanwhile, Sturgeon already had a modest public profile. An early *Scotsman* photograph exists from the 1989 Dunoon gathering showing a group of young SNP activists including Shona Robison, Fiona Hyslop, Angus Robertson, Ricky Bell and Sturgeon, peering at the camera as if wanting to strangle the photographer. There, 'delegates deflated and disillusioned with one MEP elected and the Glasgow Central by-election lost', the former journalist Derek Bateman recalled talking with Sturgeon and Roseanna Cunningham, 'as they wondered if it was all worth it'.[12] The fact they had managed to overturn the party's standing orders in order to debate a European issue was scant comfort, even if it had impressed Alex Salmond.

For Sturgeon, it was worth it. That same year she made her debut on television, an increasingly important medium for budding politicians, on a special 'youth' edition of Grampian TV's *Crossfire* programme that also included a young Labour activist called Gordon Archer, who later defected to the SNP. Watching was Peter Murrell, then based in Peterhead at Alex Salmond's constituency office. 'She must have been about 18,' he recalled. 'I remember being impressed by her political skills even at that early stage.'[13] Later, he told interviewers it was even possible he had suggested her for the programme. Indeed, he later shed any doubt and said he had been responsible – it made a better story.

That autumn, meanwhile, Sturgeon also stood for election to the SRC for the first time. As she recalled in 1999, although there were already 'the first signs of the deactivation of politics', Glasgow was 'certainly more active than many universities are now' with 'a vibrant political community where elections to the student bodies were hotly contested'.[14] Turnout in the campus-wide poll was just 6.8 per cent, with only 800 out of 13,000 students bothering to vote. Sturgeon stood in what was known as the 'general poll' and, to the surprise of many, actually came first. John Boyle, described by the Glasgow University *Guardian* as the 'leading Labour candidate', remembers confidently expecting to come first only to turn up at the count and find a GUSNA candidate he had never heard of topping the ballot. 'The General Poll, unlike the others,' Sturgeon told the student newspaper, 'reflects the political make up of campus and therefore this vote is obviously indicative of the widespread support among students for the SNP.'[15] Even aged 19, Sturgeon was already adept at putting a 'spin' on an election result.

Boyle also recalls someone introducing him to Sturgeon after the declaration. 'She was wearing a blue jumper and looked very plain,' he remembered. 'She said, "Well done, John", nodded abruptly and then walked off!' Bob Pollock, the outgoing SRC president, also told Boyle Sturgeon was going to be GUSNA's candidate for his sabbatical role the following year so, as Boyle surmised, 'she'd clearly been earmarked as the bright young hope'.[16]

The SRC president for 1989–90 was a Labour student called Michael Kellet who much later would wind up his term as First Secretary of Scottish Affairs at the British Embassy in Washington just as Sturgeon was being appointed Health Secretary in May 2007. When the SRC convened for its first statutory meeting on 9 November 1989, Sturgeon would also have engaged with several others who would continue to be contemporaries. Proposing her for the SRC's constitution and procedure, welfare and women's committees, for example, was Eilidh Whiteford, later the SNP MP for Banff and Buchan and also Sturgeon's flatmate for much of her time at university (they stayed near Ibrox), while Angela Constance and Alasdair Allan, future ministerial colleagues, and Aamer Anwar, then aligned with the Socialist Workers Party, were all also SRC members. Lari Don (a future SNP press officer) and Shona Robison (whose future husband, Stewart Hosie, Sturgeon had first encountered during the Govan by-election) would also move from Labour to the SNP while at Glasgow University. Such defections were not unimportant. A Labour club that had once produced political talents like John Smith and Donald Dewar now struggled, a bad omen for the future, while GUSNA gave rise to a whole generation of leading Nationalists.

Sturgeon was not elected to any SRC committees although, as a first-time member, that was not unusual. Otherwise, she does not seem to have been hugely active in this area of student politics, rarely (if ever) proposing or seconding motions for discussion, missing a few meetings and rarely, in fact, even featuring in SRC minutes from that period. As Stephen Harte, a contemporary, recalled, 'Other Nationalists had louder voices and bigger personalities.'[17] At the same time, this relatively low profile was most likely a conscious decision on Sturgeon's part. As Niall Bradley, a fellow GUSNA activist, recalled, she was not 'someone interested in playing at student politics or the petty point scoring that often involves: she was more interested in real politics than in what was happening on campus'.[18]

GUSNA was based at the Glasgow University Union (GUU), an august debating society and students' union (Glasgow had two, the other being the Queen Margaret Union) that had only recently admitted female members; contemporaries remember Sturgeon taking part in debates, although accounts vary as to her effectiveness. John Boyle remembers her contributions as 'standard stuff' involving a lot of 'pointing and shouting, which at that time was regarded as a good oratory', but otherwise 'confident and competent'.[19] Another recalled her signature being determination rather than talent. 'She'd turn up every week, and every week she was utterly rubbish, leaving completely humiliated,' said the fellow student. 'But she'd come back, again and again, trying to get it right, determined to figure out how she could get better.'[20]

This was another illustration of Sturgeon's already strongly developed work ethic, not to mention a determination to improve her political skills which, for her after all, university was for, especially one like Glasgow. Contemporaries describe her politics as 'orthodox centre-left', not quite Bennite but certainly well to the left of the UK Labour leadership, as was GUSNA in general. Her views were, not unusually for the period, pro-Mandela, anti-Thatcher, but with no glimmer of anything iconoclastic or counterintuitive.

'Even at that stage it was obvious that Nicola would go far if she aspired to a political career,' remembered Niall Bradley. 'And unlike many of the aspiring politicians I met in those years, it was never about her and her ego. It was about making a difference. She listened to people rather than just gave her opinion.'[21] Observing her from more of a distance was the student journalist Iain Martin, then editor of the Glasgow University *Guardian*. He considered Sturgeon 'unremarkable' and 'a bit humourless' but also 'driven' and in possession of an obvious 'gift for machine politics'.[22]

But Sturgeon was also ambitious and, as discussed, the previous summer had already begun to prepare for the 1990 sabbatical elections. Prior to that, there were two significant events on campus – a referendum in late February regarding

Glasgow University's affiliation to the National Union of Students (there was a majority of 822 against) and, in March, a Rectorial election. In the latter, Sturgeon was heavily involved, campaigning to elect the Hue and Cry singer Pat Kane as the students' representative – and theoretical champion – on the University Court.

Nominally the campaign was run by Niall Bradley and another member of the GUSNA executive but, without Sturgeon's 'insight or tactics', recalled Bradley, 'we'd have been nowhere'.[23] Kane himself remembered the 'best part' of the campaign being 'a bunch of steely and determined Scottish nationalist students (. . . Nicola Sturgeon among their number)' guiding 'an over-idealistic, over-lettered pop star to victory against the nicest radical in the world, Tony Benn'.[24] That nice radical's campaign was a shambles. Riven with Militant-inspired factionalism, Labour was simply incapable of mounting an effective campaign. Legend had it that, en route to a delayed hustings meeting, Benn lit his pipe, turned to the driver and said, 'Now then. Who ish it that I'm shtanding againsht?'[25]

It helped that the person Benn was standing against was a celebrity, which in itself guaranteed a fair number of votes. At that time, the SNP also appeared to be on a wave post-Govan (the SNP reached a dizzying 32 per cent in one opinion poll) and at the height of the Poll Tax controversy. So Pat Kane, unsurprisingly, won the Rectorial contest (Benn was a reasonably good second) and swiftly illustrated his hyperbolic tendencies by comparing his election to the recent triumph by Vaclav Havel in Czechoslovakia. Sturgeon, recalled Niall Bradley, 'was instrumental in that victory'.[26] She had helped fight – and more importantly win – her first election campaign.

Kane's installation as Rector took place at the university's Bute Hall on 20 April 1990, at which he delivered a speech called 'A New Generalism, A New Scotland: Scottish Education and its Future'. He called on students to 'join the vanguard fighting for the future of Scotland as a culture, economy and polity', pledged to oppose any new decision-making processes that treated students like 'mute objects' and concluded by restating his 'nationalist optimism about Scottish self-determination'. 'I believe', said Kane, 'we are about to enter a flowering of this country's culture and society that will dazzle us all.'[27]

Just four days later, polls opened for annual executive elections to the SRC with Sturgeon up against Craig Cathcart (independent) and Stephen Harte (Liberal Democrats) for the sabbatical post of president. Cathcart had a high profile on campus and enjoyed support from figures like the outgoing president Michael Kellet and Marion MacCormick, who was a grand-daughter of John, the former Rector of Glasgow University, and daughter of Iain, an SNP MP in the 1970s. At the same time, there was no Labour candidate in the running and Sturgeon's candidacy as part of a slate (unlike Cathcart) was probably to her advantage. Cathcart and Sandy MacKinnon, his running mate, campaigned on the usual fare of loans, library cuts, the Poll Tax, Wednesday afternoon sports and discrimination on campus, which at that time was a live issue. Sturgeon, recalls Cathcart, was an 'effective' opponent. 'She was as she is now, very committed, very serious minded,' he recalled. 'My style was to use humour but she was always a tough nut to crack. She was what she was: very sincere.'[28]

Some involved in the election also believe the issue of NUS affiliation played against Sturgeon. John Boyle reckons GUSNA had been instructed by SNP HQ to support affiliation in the February referendum, and thus it was damaged by the resulting vote to remain autonomous. Polling closed late on 24 April. 'The day's events', as the Glasgow University *Guardian* later put it, 'nearly didn't progress so far.'[29] Questions had been raised about GUSNA leaflets bearing a message from the newly installed rector Pat Kane and thus the returning officer offered candidates the chance to re-run the elections. They refused for, in the event, Cathcart won by a convincing 596 votes to Sturgeon's 392 and Harte's 170. A re-run would not have achieved very much.

But the controversy rumbled on, not least because many argued that the Rector was supposed to be above campus politics. Although GUSNA denied anything untoward, the leaflet in question was quite clear. Headed 'A message from Pat Kane Rector' and footed 'Strength to Strength', it read: 'You supported me to be a Working Rector committed to fighting for student's (*sic*) interests. Today you have the chance to elect a strong Student Executive who will work with me in fighting against the Poll Tax, Student Loans and Campus Racism and for the provision of services such as a Student Creche. Use your Vote and make it count.'[30] And just in case students did not get the message, the leaflet even listed Sturgeon, Alasdair Allan, Angela Constance and Sheila Oliver as Kane's preferred candidates for the posts of, respectively, President, Vice President (VP) University Affairs, VP Services and VP Welfare (Allan and Constance, incidentally, were both elected).

When the new SRC met two days later in the Williams Room of the John McIntyre Building, Kane's involvement in the recent executive elections was discussed at length, with Sturgeon offering a robust defence of the new Rector. She did not, according to the minutes, 'accept the rules had been broken and questioned the position of [the] SRC President', accusing him (Cathcart) of 'sour grapes' given that Kane had only backed GUSNA candidates. Under questioning, Sturgeon also maintained that Kane was not bound by the SRC constitution and, when Sandy MacKinnon pointed out that the election guidelines stated that 'non-matriculated persons cannot solicit votes for candidates', Sturgeon retorted that GUSNA had solicited help from Kane rather than the other way round, which of course did not really address the point. Finally, MacKinnon asked for confirmation the Rector knew of the content of the controversial leaflet, to which Sturgeon simply replied 'yes'.[31] Despite Sturgeon's best efforts, the SRC endorsed a motion critical of Kane's actions. Not long afterwards, Cathcart was surprised to receive an apologetic phone call from Kane at his mother's council house in Linwood.

Thereafter Kane, who most recall as a hardworking and diligent Rector, at least initially, became a thorn in the side of the university Establishment. Kane's walking out of a ceremony granting the former Conservative Scottish Secretary George

Younger an honorary degree ruffled feathers further (the then principal, Sir William Kerr Fraser, had served as Younger's senior civil servant at the Scottish Office). The Court, in short, saw the pop star as bringing the ancient university into disrepute and there were even murmurings about a vote of no confidence. 'He wasn't political but thought he was,' recalled one student politician of Kane. 'He tended to be very binary and very heavy handed.'[32] Nearly a quarter of a century later, Kane and Sturgeon would again work together as part of Yes Scotland.

Sturgeon's defeat for the SRC presidency, meanwhile, must have been acutely disappointing, although she was in good company – more than a decade earlier, Alex Salmond had narrowly lost election to the same position at St Andrews University. Judging by SRC minutes, her involvement in campus politics noticeably wanes in the latter half of 1990, less than halfway through her four-year law degree. It is possible she contested the presidency a year too early and, indeed, the following year Angela Constance and Alasdair Allan were elected president and vice president on a joint ticket (Eilidh Whiteford had lost to Michael Kellet in 1989 by a single vote). GUSNA was also clearly sore about the result. In May, Niall Bradley wrote to the student newspaper to complain about 'Watchtower', its political correspondent's 'blatant and self-serving political bias' during the elections. He signed off 'Yours for a Scottish Socialist Republic', which had been the old rallying cry of the long-defunct 79 Group.[33]

Although Sturgeon stood again for the SRC's General Poll in 1990/91 (this time she came last), there is little evidence of much activity, although in November that year she won election to committees on Sexual Harassment and Women's issues, nominated in both cases by Angela Constance, who was now Vice President for Services. But then Nicola, as GUSNA contemporaries recall, was heavily involved with the Young Scottish Nationalists (YSN), so although active, for a period, on campus, it was with YSN rather than the Federation of Student Nationalists (to which GUSNA was affiliated and of which Bob Salmond, Alex's brother, was president in 1988) that Sturgeon was most closely associated at the national level.

Formed in the 1970s, YSN quickly became a political salon for budding Nationalist politicians, not only Sturgeon but John Swinney, Fiona Hyslop and, later, Derek Mackay and Humza Yousaf all emerging from its ranks (in 1996, it was renamed 'Young Scots for Independence'). Affiliated to the SNP but autonomous from it, the YSN was able to formulate its own policies, devise its own campaigns and also send delegates to the annual SNP conference. This meant it could table motions, which, in the late 1980s and early 1990s, were usually left wing, therefore controversial, and therefore not exactly welcomed by the party leadership. 'We made a point as the youth movement of getting involved in everything,' recalled Fiona Hyslop. 'Nicola was one of our key communicators – a good speaker we always made sure contributed to debates.'[34]

Similarly Cliff Williamson, a former art student and YSN convener, recalls Sturgeon and the 'Cunninghame South contingent' being a fixture at the YSN conference, which was usually held in Edinburgh or Glasgow (*after* the national conference), since she had joined the party in 1986. 'YSN at that time was full of very big personalities and you had to work hard to get known and to stand out,' recalled Williamson. 'She was always a presence and well-known as a hard worker.' Until 1990, Sturgeon – like Williamson – was associated with Jim Sillars and what was known as the 'West of Scotland Activists', although many of them had begun to drift away from the victor of Govan and towards Alex Salmond, deputy leader of the SNP since the 1987 general election.

When Gordon Wilson (who had lost his Dundee seat at that election) resigned as SNP leader in 1990, Williamson, who was also the YSN's representative on the SNP's National Executive Committee, announced his (and the YSN's) backing for Salmond to succeed him. 'We feel his campaign is striking the right chords with young people not just in the party,' he said in a press release, 'but in the population generally.'[35] There had been a brief movement behind Jim Sillars as Wilson's successor, but it quickly petered out.

Sturgeon, meanwhile, had first become aware of Salmond when she had heard Kay Ullrich gush about this 'wonderful young up-and-coming future leader of the SNP who had the loveliest brown eyes',[36] and she first encountered him personally when she was just 18 years old. So, in the summer of 1990, she threw herself into the 'Youth for Salmond' campaign. 'Even then, she was a formidable operator,' recalled Kathleen Caskie, who then worked at SNP HQ. 'She was in her late teens and a leading light in the SNP's youth movement . . . She came into her own delivering the youth vote for Alex Salmond. Suddenly there were all these young people wearing Salmond T-shirts – the party was still at 15 per cent [in the polls] and nobody had ever seen that level of organisation for an internal campaign before. That was the stage that her relationship with him cemented.'[37]

Indeed, Cliff Williamson remembered being taken aback by Sturgeon's whole-hearted backing for Salmond. 'I was surprised Nicola embraced it as she was still very much associated with the Sillars wing,' he said. 'To me it showed a dexterous political sophistication and also that she had her own mind.'[38] There were other good reasons for Sturgeon's switch, not least the perception of Margaret Ewing, the only other candidate, as being from a much older generation and more conservative wing of the party. (Sturgeon made it clear she and the YSN would 'work with her and have a good working relationship'.[39]) Nevertheless, there remained what Williamson called 'a degree of distance' between Sturgeon and the Salmondites, although Alex went out of his way to cultivate the party's youth wing, not only to secure the leadership but in order to advance a new cadre of NEC members, office holders and, ultimately, elected representatives.

At that point, Sturgeon was YSN's vice-convener and the previous autumn had spoken about the 'massive problem' of homelessness among young people at a press conference, reflecting the social justice issues that had preoccupied her from the moment she had joined the SNP two years previously. 'The government is engaged', said Sturgeon, 'in a deliberate and concerted attack on the basic human rights of Scotland's young people.' The YSN argued that government regulations relating to benefits and the Poll Tax were making the problem much worse. '25 per cent of the young homeless were previously in Local Authority care. But demand for beds in crisis hostels now outstrips demand by 100 per cent. Once young people are 18 they are then forced to find the Poll Tax while often unable to get onto housing waiting lists or to draw benefit to provide money for accommodation.'[40]

Sturgeon and the YSN were short on proposed solutions but long on (no doubt sincere) outrage. Nevertheless she was making an impact within the party, and contemporaries began to sit up and take notice, indeed an 'impressive, well researched' policy paper she had produced on the withdrawal of benefits from 16- and 17-year-olds had earned her a place on the YSN's national executive in the first place.[41]

Fiona Hyslop, later a Cabinet colleague, remembered Sturgeon always being 'quite guarded', possibly 'to make sure that she didn't do or say anything that perhaps would cause difficulty later', an indication that she was considering a political career even at that stage. But, as Hyslop also recalled, campaigning often finished up at a party or club 'and Nicola was as involved in the social side as anybody else'. She had a 'very good strong sense of humour' and although 'quite sensible' was also 'good fun'.[42] Similarly another political contemporary recalled that, despite coming across as 'earnest', there was also another side of Sturgeon that was 'caring, warm, appealing'.[43]

Linda Fabiani, of an older generation within the party, recalled Sturgeon being 'pretty scary'. 'She was fierce,' she added, but 'always very articulate'. The pair first met through mutual friends but, when Fabiani later saw her in action at SNP conference (Sturgeon spoke in a debate on 'fascism' at the 1991 Inverness gathering), she remembered thinking that Nicola – then still an undergraduate – was clearly 'going places'. 'What really struck me . . . was that, for such a young activist,' said Fabiani, 'she had a very deep political sense and sense of social responsibility.'[44] Cliff Williamson put Sturgeon's reputation 'for being a bit sharp' down to 'shyness', although he said she was 'never one of those kid politicians and had none of the accoutrements of a young politician – she wasn't a freak'.[45]

Ricky Bell, a fellow YSN activist from Ayrshire, also recalled Sturgeon's drive. 'Nicola was always arguing that, if we just chapped another few more doors, we might reach another few voters,' said Bell. 'She was often the one who would say, "Let's just do another half hour" when the rest of us were ready to give up and go to the pub. She has a very strong work ethic. She never stops.'[46] Bell had played a part in bringing Sturgeon to the party's attention, initially via the YSN. At that time, he was one of only three SNP members of Cunninghame District Council, as were Margaret Burgess and Campbell Martin, who later became SNP MSPs. At one stage, they forced a debate on the impact of the Maastricht Treaty on local government in Scotland and approached Sturgeon to prepare a briefing paper. 'What she produced was excellent,' recalled Martin. 'Ricky Bell and I thoroughly enjoying wiping the floor with our Labour opponents that day.'[47]

With Bell and Sturgeon, however, it went beyond canvassing camaraderie and the pair dated each other for several years, getting together before she started university and splitting up before she graduated, two young activists with similar left-of-centre views working towards the same seemingly quixotic goal. En route to the 1992 SNP conference, the pair were 'shaken but uninjured' after a collision with a car in Pollokshaws.[48] And although the relationship did not endure, the platonic friendship did, with Sturgeon opening Bell & Felix, a café in her constituency co-owned by Bell, in the summer of 2014, which also served as the venue for one of Scotland's first same-sex marriages a few months later.

At that time, there was what one contemporary called an 'unofficial experience programme' for young SNP activists centred around Alex Salmond's constituency office on Maiden Street in Peterhead although, as she was based in Glasgow, this was not an option for people like Sturgeon. Instead, her training ground was the hard graft of campaigning. 'It was a time of constant motion and activism,' recalled the contemporary. 'We felt the more you worked, the more it was likely to happen. All of the people in the West of Scotland were grafters at a very difficult coalface; in Glasgow it was very barren.'[49]

As Cliff Williamson recalled, 'At every local authority by-election, at every action day, at everything that happened, Nicola would be there. She was a real stalwart activist. That was the way in which you earned your spurs, not only in terms of personal development but when it came to respect within the party. Even if there were suspicions from the Old Guard that you were a bit too left wing, if you were willing to go that extra mile then that meant you gained tremendous kudos and tremendous acceptance.'[50]

And, importantly, at that time the SNP lacked what Disraeli famously called a 'greasy pole', a well-established career ladder; all a hard-working activist could aim for was to become an office bearer and perhaps win election to the party's National Executive Committee, which was hardly glamorous. As Sturgeon later told the playwright David Greig, in contrast to a later generation that got involved expecting the 'prospect of getting elected and being in government', her generation had 'come into this purely out of conviction'.[51]

That was partially the case, although it was truer to say the prospects of elected office were at best remote, certainly without the added layer of a devolved parliament. By the beginning of 1992, meanwhile, Sturgeon was clearly being actively promoted by SNP HQ, something made easier by her position as YSN convener, to which she had been elected the previous year. She appeared on the current affairs programme *Left, Right and Centre* in January, holding her own alongside other budding politicians like Murdo Fraser, later a Conservative MSP, and Craig Harrow, later convener of the Scottish Liberal Democrats.

Indeed, the programme represents a snapshot of what would become the Sturgeon generation: in the audience were Angela Constance and Shona Robison, both future ministerial colleagues, and also Douglas Alexander (later a Labour Cabinet minister) and Jim Murphy, who would face Sturgeon as leader of the Scottish Labour Party from late 2014. 'It's my burning desire to see the Tories extinguished as a political force in Scotland at the next general election,' she says at one point, predicting the party would be 'looking to save deposits rather than seats'. That proved premature, while other talking points included the closure of Ravenscraig ('we would nationalise it') and the mooted Scottish Assembly that, said Sturgeon, 'wouldn't be able to do very much'.[52] She also supported positive discrimination in terms of gender balance, putting herself at odds with the SNP's policy of not supporting a 50/50 gender split.

'It's astonishing the amount of preparation she did for that appearance,' recalls Craig Harrow, who remembers turning up (as did other guests) basically on his own to see Sturgeon huddled with a few other people. 'They were firing questions at her to limber her up for the broadcast.'[53] It worked but, although poised, confident and well briefed, Sturgeon also displays flashes of irritation at questions from the audience. Nevertheless, it was a remarkable performance for one so youthful (the following month she featured in a *Scotland Today* report on 'young Scottish Nationalists'), and valuable publicity in the run-up to the general election of April 1992, for which Sturgeon had been selected to fight the safe Labour seat of Glasgow Shettleston, making her, at the age of 21, the youngest parliamentary candidate in the UK.

Speaking at her selection meeting in late 1991, Kay Ullrich, who was standing in Motherwell, declared, 'This lady here will be the first female leader of the SNP one day,' a prediction that embarrassed Sturgeon but delighted her mother Joan, who was seated among the few dozen party members in attendance. 'She [Joan] then told her mother, Nicola's [maternal] granny, who was ill in hospital at the time and she was thrilled to hear I'd said that,' recalled Ullrich. 'I genuinely thought that at the time; she had a confidence in her – an intensity – and it just came out of my mouth.'[54] Alex Salmond had 'encouraged' Sturgeon to stand. 'In other words,' she reflected later, 'he believed in me long before I believed in myself.'[55]

Although Sturgeon had the challenging task of overturning a

19,000 Labour majority in Shettleston, the SNP went into the 1992 general election with high hopes, buoyed by support from the *Scottish Sun* ('Rise now and be a nation again' screamed a front page) and even an opinion poll showing majority support for independence. At the recent party conference, Alex Neil had predicted Scotland would be 'free by 93' which, as Labour's Donald Dewar wryly observed, had the benefit as a slogan of being recyclable every ten years. Given the expectation of a Labour government and a large band of SNP MPs, it is likely Sturgeon also had half an eye on the devolved Scottish Parliament that might follow within a few years.

'I stood in Glasgow Shettleston . . . and was never going to come close to winning,' recalled Sturgeon in 2014, 'although in my youthful optimism, I thought there was a chance.'[56] 'Labour support is soft,' she confidently told the *Independent* towards the end of March 1992. 'The SNP overturned a 19,000 Labour majority in the Govan by-election. Once Labour support begins to go it will collapse completely. We could win every seat in Glasgow.' This was hubris, although Sturgeon also articulated arguments that would become more familiar, and more credible, two decades later. 'Scots tend to blame the English for everything that goes wrong,' she added. 'I think that attitude will change with independence and England and Scotland will actually become closer when we are able to represent ourselves internationally and be on an equal footing with England.'[57]

This time there were also solid policy pledges to shore up Sturgeon's youthful idealism, with the SNP targeting support from young Scots by promising to bring back full student grants (steadily eroded under successive Conservative governments) and benefits for the under-25s. 'A lot of young people feel detached from older, stereotype politicians – the men in grey suits figures,' Sturgeon told the Press Association, adding that the voting age ought to be lowered to 16 while allowing candidates to stand at 18. 'I think it's indefensible somebody can get married, pay taxes and even be sent to war,' she explained, 'and not have the right to vote or stand for election.' On that, as on other areas such as Trident, Sturgeon would remain impressively consistent throughout her career.

Sturgeon admitted that many voters in Shettleston were 'surprised' to find such a young face on their doorstep asking for support, and thus even in 1992 she found herself rebutting the implication that she was old before her time, an impression some also had of Alex Salmond as a young man. 'I don't talk about politics all the time,' Sturgeon told one reporter, somewhat defensively, during the campaign.[58] With the passage of time, however, she would become more reflective, acknowledging that a drawback to 'coming into politics so young' was being 'at the stage in your life when everything is very serious and tense . . . I did come across as taking myself too seriously'.[59]

The 1992 general election, however, turned out to be a damp squib, not only for Sturgeon but also for the party nationally. Although its share of the vote increased by an impressive 7.5 per cent, it won just three seats following a campaign plagued by tension between the gradualist and fundamentalist wings of the party. In Glasgow Shettleston, the result was:

Labour	David Marshall	21,665
SNP	Nicola Sturgeon	6,831
Conservative	Norman Mortimer	5,396
Liberal Democrat	Joan Orskov	1,881
Majority		14,834

The disappointment was palpable, with a petulant Jim Sillars, who had failed to hold Govan, dismissing millions of Scots as '90-minute patriots', although his departure from the political scene thereafter made life easier for Alex Salmond's gradualist modernisation project. 'One of the reasons young Scots have turned to the SNP in such large numbers is our internationalism,' said Sturgeon, again putting a positive spin on the result. 'We will turn Scotland from the invisible nation of Europe into a nation which plays a full part in Europe and contributes to the great international issues. While the London party leaders have engaged in a sterile negative dog fight – to cover up the lack of differences between Kinnock and the Tories – the SNP is offering a positive vision of Scotland's future.'[60]

For Sturgeon, her baptism of electoral fire had been immeasurably useful. No one had seriously expected her to win Glasgow Shettleston; rather her role had been to increase the SNP vote, heighten her party's profile in the area and make the Labour candidate work as hard as possible. That she had undoubtedly achieved, doubling the Nationalist vote in a Labour heartland while moving the party from fourth to second place. The election of a fourth Conservative government with minimal support in Scotland (although it had done better than expected) also put the constitutional question firmly on the agenda, where it would remain throughout the rest of the decade.

The experience of contesting a nationwide election also boosted the naturally shy Sturgeon's self-confidence. Within days of the election result thousands of political activists – not only Nationalists – gathered in Glasgow's George Square at a rally called, ironically as it turned out, 'Scotland United', a sort of proto-Yes Scotland seeking to create, as Pat Kane put it, 'a truly "activist" movement for Scottish self-government',[61] committed to the idea of a multi-option constitutional referendum (status quo/devolution/independence). Indeed, this provoked a split among Scottish Labour MPs, some of whom favoured the referendum initiative and the majority who did not want to challenge the outcome of a Westminster election.

Kane actually called Fiona Hyslop asking if she would speak on behalf of YSN (Salmond had said he did not think it was 'appropriate to be dragged into strikes or street demonstrations at this stage'[62]) but she recommended Sturgeon as a good young communicator who would appeal more to the left. Several of those present in George Square recall watching Sturgeon making an impromptu speech on an open-top bus during which she got stuck into Labour and its failure to win another general election (the party had also just belatedly embraced the SNP's referendum policy). She backed uniting 'the people of Scotland' in an organisation 'not only against the Tories' but all those opposed to greater self-government.[63]

Naturally, heckling from bruised Labour activists competed with the cheers from Nationalists, but Sturgeon's speech (which made it to that evening's television news bulletins) had taken considerable courage for a 21-year-old law student. As John McAllion, the Labour MP for Dundee East who spoke after Sturgeon, reflected, 'You cannot fault her chutzpah given that she had Labour MPs behind her and hundreds if not thousands of Labour voters in front of her.' McAllion's speech made a point of calling for an end to 'party sectarianism' in order to combat yet another Conservative government.[64]

A month after the general election, meanwhile, Sturgeon contested Irvine North in district council elections fought on the basis of holding a multi-option referendum, losing by 344 votes to 508 in a straight fight with Labour. Remarkably, her undergraduate studies, then reaching a conclusion, had apparently not suffered as a result of contesting two elections. As she herself admitted, 'I spent more time involved in politics than I did studying law.'[65] She had been studying for her law finals while also beating the streets of Shettleston every evening and weekend, but she graduated on 14 July 1992 with an upper second-class degree (she narrowly missed a first) having already applied to remain at Glasgow University to complete her Diploma in Legal Practice, a necessary pre-requisite for a career as a solicitor.

Sturgeon studied Public International Law, which included human rights, the United Nations declaration and issues before the US Supreme Court such as affirmative action and the right to life, so it was much more political than other types of law. In freshers' week, Sturgeon became friendly with two other students, Caroline Summers (from Paisley) and Claire Mitchell (from Glasgow), and the trio became life-long friends, all having arrived at Glasgow University from similar working-class backgrounds.

Neither Summers nor Mitchell were particularly political; Summers recalling that Sturgeon was not that opinionated, at least not in a social context, 'which made her easy company'. 'We would have lively debates,' said Summers, 'but always in the context of our legal studies. She would do political stuff but kept it separate; she wouldn't badger us or evangelise.'[66] Catriona Drew, a relatively young lecturer at the Law School, encouraged Sturgeon and Summers to 'moot' (debate a hypothetical case) on behalf of the university, for which the former prepared thoroughly, displaying an already typical attention to detail.

Sturgeon was, recalled Claire Mitchell (who later became an advocate), 'quite serious and focused when it came to work. She was fiercely bright, but more than that she was incredibly well organised, a combination that can't be defeated. I was out every weekend clubbing and then panicking at the last minute while Nicola had everything done, never missed a lecture and despite all her campaigning would turn up to exams with everything underlined and highlighted.'[67] The Law School had a good reputation, with figures such as the eminent but conservative David Walker, regius professor of private law, and Jim Murdoch, who covered public law, while Sturgeon would later reflect that one consequence of her legal training had been to equip her with 'a very analytical mind',[68] a useful transferable skill, particularly in the political domain. Another lecturer, however, later regretted his part in the future First Minister's education. Recalling having taught Sturgeon 'when she was in law classes at Glasgow University', Alistair Bonnington felt he had 'failed to instill in her the most basic rules of how the institutions of government work in the free world'.[69]

A fellow student recalled that Sturgeon was 'popular with her contemporaries studying law', who saw her 'as intensely ambitious but good company'.[70] Sturgeon studied most closely with Professor John Grant, a specialist in public international law, a wry figure who also charged his diploma student with teaching a couple of honours classes during the 1992–93 session. After completing her diploma in the summer of 1993, Sturgeon joined McClure Naismith as a trainee solicitor, a large, old and largely male-dominated firm based in Glasgow (previous employees had included the Liberal Democrat MP Menzies Campbell and the Scottish Conservative politician

Annabel Goldie). 'We'd just come out of a recession,' recalled Caroline Summers, 'so the priority for diploma students was getting a job, and Nicola didn't have a wealthy family to fall back on.'[71] 'You took', she later reflected, 'your traineeship where you could get one.'[72]

Sturgeon had done well to end up at McClure Naismith. Competition was fierce and it only recruited around eight graduates each year but, as one partner recalled, she was 'not an unusually energetic or conscientious trainee. It was quite clear even then that her interests didn't lie in becoming a solicitor or a lawyer.' During her two years with the firm, Sturgeon would have worked on litigation, property law and general commercial work but, by the end, as the partner remembered, 'There was no question of Nicola staying on, and I don't think she was surprised by that decision . . . She just wasn't a star; she didn't show any great ambition to do what we did.'[73]

Sturgeon probably would not have disagreed with that analysis for, between 1993 and 1995, she had become even more intensely involved in Nationalist politics at the local and national level. At this stage in her activism, however, she was not yet a fully-fledged Salmondite, disagreeing with, among other issues, his ostentatious support of the monarchy. When, for example, a huge row engulfed the leadership following the SNP group of MPs' decision to support John Major's government in a Commons division over Maastricht in exchange for greater Scottish representation on the Committee of the Regions (then, in the absence of devolution, considered an important forum), Sturgeon was one of six NEC members who voted against the motion expressing confidence in the MPs' decision (Stewart Hosie only voted for after having been leaned on by Salmond), no doubt the result of pressure from angry members and a blizzard of negative press coverage, not to mention her instinctive hostility to the idea of co-operation with Conservatives. At that time, Sturgeon was prepared, as one fellow member of the NEC recalled, 'to stand up against the establishment of the party'.[74]

The meeting was unpleasant and bitter; Salmond launched

such a strong attack on certain opponents that it resulted in resignations from, among others, Alex Neil and Kenny MacAskill. When the row rumbled on beyond the NEC itself, including further calls for the leader's resignation, several members (including Sturgeon, Tom Chalmers, Fiona Hyslop and Roseanna Cunningham) attempted to move on by making it clear in a letter to *The Scotsman* they did not support 'the pursuit of this issue in public argument' and would 'be committing [their] efforts to campaign for the recall of the Scottish parliament, to stop water privatisation and to achieve independence in Europe'.[75] It showed, as the journalist Peter Jones later wrote, that 'the fundamentalism to which the SNP moved after the disappointments and failures of the gradualist approach of the 1970s still strongly grips the party'.[76]

The incident, meanwhile, clearly made little difference to Salmond's relationship with Sturgeon, for a few months later he appointed Sturgeon to his 'Cabinet' (itself a controversial innovation within the party) covering employment and women's issues, and within days she was warning that Scotland was 'suffering the penalties of being a branch economy',[77] while, later, accusing the Conservatives of doctoring unemployment figures. Salmond also appointed her to a four-strong team (the others being Neil, Fergus Ewing and the Labour defectee Dick Douglas) tasked with drawing up a four-year economic strategy and budget for an independent Scotland. In April 1996 Sturgeon also fronted an SNP campaign against what it called the 'London levy', attempting to argue that every Scottish taxpayer subsidised the rest of the UK to the tune of £10 a week.

Europe was also an issue that preoccupied Sturgeon and the SNP during the mid 1990s, particularly following the Maastricht debacle. Responding to European Commissioner Bruce Millan's comment about Sweden and Scotland enjoying a 'natural affinity', Sturgeon complained to the *Herald* that, while Sweden would 'play a full and direct part in decision making at the highest levels of the EU', Scotland would remain 'a second-class member of the EU, excluded from the decision-making process, hoping in vain that an often unsympathetic London Government will look after her interests'.[78]

And when, at the following year's SNP conference, the 'independence in Europe' policy (or rather slogan) came under attack from, among others, the future MSP John Mason, Sturgeon was critical of the main motion, tabled by Alex Neil and MEP Winnie Ewing, which called for legislative parity between the European Parliament and Council of Ministers. 'Europe is our flagship policy,' said Sturgeon, warning that the party's opponents would exploit the disagreement. 'It is far too important to be dealt with by a mish-mash of statements which leave us facing different directions at once.'[79] Sturgeon had no truck with the view that 'independence' was incompatible with membership of the EU (held by some in the party), arguing that Scotland would enjoy 'equality of status with other European nations and a direct Scottish voice in the decision-making bodies of the EU'. She also believed it was to the SNP's 'credit' that it was prepared to debate, 'openly and fully, the many complex issues arising out of the development of the EU'.[80]

Sturgeon was also kept busy in terms of domestic politics, contesting the Baillieston/Mount Vernon ward in Glasgow during the last elections, in May 1994, to Strathclyde Regional Council, soon to be phased out and replaced by several unitary authorities including one covering her adopted city of Glasgow (in the mid 1990s Sturgeon lived in a flat on Cathkin Road). The Labour Co-op candidate, however, beat her decisively by 4,908 votes to 2,140, depriving her of that well-worn rung on the electoral ladder – a stint as a local councillor. Sturgeon also stood in the following year's elections to the new Glasgow City Council for Bridgeton in the East End, a straight SNP/Labour fight between Sturgeon and Elaine Smith, later an MSP. Unknown to Sturgeon, the signature of one her nominees had actually been forged, prompting a police investigation and a heightened awareness of potential fraud in future contests.[81] Smith won.

Still, Sturgeon impressed contemporaries with her discipline. Future Liberal Democrat Scottish Secretary Michael Moore, who in 1995 had just been selected to fight Sir David Steel's

Borders constituency, recalled appearing alongside Sturgeon on a panel discussion the same year. 'Just as we went on air, in came Nicola, and even at that stage she was a professional politician to her fingertips,' said Moore. 'She wasn't particularly open to the rest of us but she knew what she'd come to do, and she was far and away the best prepared and the best performer.'[82]

There were, as ever, by-elections. When Kay Ullrich was chosen to fight the June 1994 Monklands East seat following the death of Labour leader John Smith, Sturgeon campaigned with 'great enthusiasm',[83] while in 1995 the death of the colourful Tory MP Sir Nicholas Fairbairn also led to a by-election in Perth and Kinross, once one of the safest Conservative seats in mainland Britain. The SNP had high hopes of capturing it with Roseanna Cunningham, who despite a 19-year age gap had become a close friend of Sturgeon, considered a frontrunner for the nomination. But when, during a vetting session, party president Winnie Ewing accused Cunningham of having had an affair with her daughter-in-law Margaret Ewing's then husband Donald Bain 18 years previously, Cunningham withdrew (she admitted to the affair, but not to having wrecked Ewing's marriage). It was a difficult situation, inevitably exacerbated by internal factions, but Sturgeon judged her friend to have 'acted with a great deal of dignity' in withdrawing.[84]

Cunningham, however, was later reinstated (most likely at the behest of Salmond, a fellow 79 Grouper) and went on to take the seat with an 11.6 per cent swing to the SNP and a majority of 7,311 over Labour's Douglas Alexander. Sturgeon worked as Roseanna's aide – or bag carrier, in political parlance – for the three-week campaign, which of course gave the party a valuable boost in the middle of that Parliament. Cunningham, Sturgeon and several others including Mary Picken, who worked at the STUC, and the journalist Susan Stewart, were regulars at Babbity Bowster, an atmospheric bar in Glasgow's Merchant City. Fiona Hyslop would occasionally join them, laughing and joking amid lawyers and other regulars.

By the mid 1990s Sturgeon was increasingly influential within the SNP's NEC, the party's governing body to which she had been elected in 1992. Cliff Williamson remembered her having 'a reputation for competence and steadfastness' and although others were ahead of her in the Nationalist pecking order (Hyslop, for example, had been elected to the NEC before Sturgeon), 'there was no doubt that by 1995/96 Nicola was a star and that if a plum [seat] became available then she would get it'.[85] 'She was seen as the best of her generation,' recalled another contemporary, 'viewed as a future member of the leadership, and eventually as a future leader in her own right.'[86]

Those outside the party, however, remembered Sturgeon rather differently. The journalist Iain Macwhirter later recalled 'a slightly mannish' young activist, someone who did not strike him as 'destined for glory or leadership', complaining to him at conferences about his coverage of the SNP,[87] although there obviously existed a lighter side. Much later, she recalled being in Australia at around this time on a political study visit with the Liberal Democrat MP Charles Kennedy:

> Perhaps my fondest memory from that visit – if perhaps a slightly bizarre memory – was of the two of us skiving off one day to watch *Trainspotting* in a Melbourne cinema. I think we were the only two Scots in the audience at that time, so we drew some very strange looks from other people as we were uproariously laughing at lots of jokes that nobody else in the cinema were even beginning to understand.[88]

Back in Scotland there remained tensions and, with a devolutionary tide apparently rising in Scotland, Salmond was determined to avoid the SNP becoming isolated from majority Scottish opinion (the party was formally opposed to a devolved Scottish Parliament). In early 1995 he began to move, saying that he favoured independence and devolution in that order, while at one NEC meeting he said he would reprise that line if asked by a journalist, a position supported by Sturgeon and Fergus Ewing. So-called 'fundamentalists' (which included, at that time, Alex Neil and Kenny MacAskill), however, warned that committing the party to devolution legislation it had not yet seen was foolish and might also undermine the SNP's independence message.

Salmond had (correctly) been anticipating the formation of a Labour government at the next election and therefore the likelihood of swift legislation for a Scottish Parliament, although navigating the pro- and anti-devolution wings of his party would prove sensitive. Sturgeon was firmly on the 'gradualist' wing, believing devolution to be a necessary stepping-stone towards the ultimate goal of independence. This did not stop her exploiting Labour's difficulty over the policy, particularly when Tony Blair surprised even his own party by committing to a two-question referendum rather than unconditional legislation in 1996. 'New Labour's proposed Assembly,' she charged, was 'now subject to a rigged referendum.'[89] That, of course, did not answer the question of how Nationalists would campaign and vote should that 'rigged' referendum to come to pass in a few years' time.

Despite her profile, Sturgeon was still only in her mid 20s, making her a natural poster girl for the SNP's pitch to younger voters. At the 1994 SNP conference, she was elected Vice-Convener for Youth Affairs (fighting off Henry Sloan and future MSP Kevin Stewart), a post she would retain for the next few years (although Stewart challenged her in 1996). By that point, the SNP had around 1,600 young members and more youth and student branches than any other political party in Scotland. 'As these young Scots reach the age of individual political power,' Sturgeon explained rather awkwardly in early 1994, 'their strong support for the SNP will help Scotland regain its national political power.'[90]

There was much discussion about young people being disillusioned with politics, and Sturgeon argued that young Scots were 'doubly disadvantaged' because 'they think they can't change anything as young people and they can't change things because they are Scottish'.[91] When, in late 1996, details began to emerge of Labour's planned education policies, it gave Sturgeon a convenient point of attack. She described plans to replace student grants with loans as 'the most disgusting betrayal of all by Tony Blair'[92] and reiterated the SNP's commitment to both grants and 'free education' for all students. This (the latter if not the former) would become an important – and consistent – Sturgeon theme over the next couple of decades. A poll in late 1996 showing that more than half of young Scots favoured independence also gave the SNP a boost. It demonstrated, argued Sturgeon, that Scotland had 'outgrown Westminster'. 'Rather than staying tied to a London-based system which is utterly unrepresentative of their views and needs,' she added, 'a clear majority of young Scots see independence as being the best way forward for both themselves and their nation.'[93]

By the mid 1990s, the SNP had become both more professional and financially stable. In 1994 the ebullient Mike Russell was appointed chief executive and, in partnership with Salmond, gave effect to a series of reforms that owed more than either would have admitted to Peter Mandelson's transformation of the Labour Party a decade earlier. Salmond's economic case for independence also mirrored shifts in Labour thinking, not least the emphasis on a business-friendly agenda intended to promote economic growth. An economist called Andrew Wilson, like Sturgeon a bright young thing, joined party HQ in 1994 and, by the late 1990s, the SNP was deploying an awkward marriage of standard left-wing Keynesian economics and the corporate tax-cutting agenda favoured by New Labour. To this Salmond added a robust assault on the idea that Scotland could not afford to be independent.

There is no evidence Sturgeon was uncomfortable with these shifts, although it is likely Alex Salmond's efforts to reach out to both Catholic voters (following the traumatic 1994 Monklands by-election) and also Scots Asians, found greater favour, not least as both represented potential areas of support in the Govan constituency (see next chapter). Scots Asians for Independence (SAfI) for example, was formed in 1995 and was fielding candidates within two years. This was the beginning of a concerted push towards 'civic' Nationalism, and it chimed perfectly with Sturgeon's non-sectarian, internationalist and anti-racist instincts.

Amid all this stimulating political activity, meanwhile,

Sturgeon had spent an obligatory two years learning the ropes as a trainee solicitor at McClure Naismith, although during 1995 she began commuting to Stirling where the small firm of Bell & Craig had taken her on as an associate. Established by Fergus Bell and George Craig only a few years earlier, it mainly handled conveyancing work in Central Scotland, although Sturgeon was recruited to try to develop the firm's court business.

She did mostly matrimonial and civil court work, and also handled some criminal cases. Her employers employed her fully aware of her political ambitions and were initially happy to accommodate them. One of the partners was an SNP member and Sturgeon came with the recommendation of the late Tom Chalmers, who in 1995 was the party's national treasurer as well as chairman of the Glasgow SNP. Later, there were rumours that something had gone wrong in her legal career but, when asked about this in 2014, Sturgeon said simply, 'I've got nothing I want to confess.'[94] Besides, as a trainee, she would not have had enough responsibility to make mistakes, although that did not rule out an incident at the smaller Stirling firm.

Sturgeon was not the first lawyer to actively pursue a political career, and nor would she be the last. Winning election either to Westminster or the devolved Scottish Parliament she and her contemporaries hoped to see established was not just an enjoyable sideline – she was serious about it. Bell & Craig granted Sturgeon leave to contest the Govan constituency at the 1997 general election, an important contest that would have significant consequences for both her and Scotland in general.

Chapter 4

The battle for Govan

The Glasgow constituency of Govan has a special place in the history of the National Movement in Scotland. In November 1973, when Nicola Sturgeon was just three years old, Margo MacDonald won the seat in a memorable by-election, although went on to lose it just months later at a general election. Then, 15 years later, MacDonald's husband, the former Labour MP Jim Sillars, captured it in another by-election (in which Sturgeon helped campaign), holding it until the 1992 general election.

But its demographic make-up gave it an added significance. As a predominantly working-class urban constituency – in other words natural Labour territory – by-election victories there hinted at the breakthrough the SNP badly needed in order to advance both itself and its *raison d'être*. It was also to become central to Sturgeon's transition from activist to elected Parliamentarian. Indeed, two candidacies – one in May 1997 and another exactly two years later – would neatly bridge another transition, between pre- and post-devolution Scotland. And only at this point did the prospect of a career in the SNP become – for Sturgeon and many others – a serious prospect.

In November 1995, the SNP announced that the candidate for Govan would be a woman, following the selection of a short-list that happened to be all female rather than one contrived to that end. It comprised three prominent activists: Sturgeon, still

Vice-Convener for Youth Affairs and energy spokeswoman, Patsy Thomson, convener of the Glasgow SNP, and Shona Robison, an elected member of the party's National Council and also a close friend of Sturgeon. The Govan South branch – which included fellow YSNer Andrew Wilson – formally nominated Sturgeon.

At a meeting at Govan Cross on 6 November, Sturgeon emerged the winner, a selection ratified by the SNP's NEC five days later, following which she hailed the constituency as 'the most marginal in Glasgow' as a result of boundary changes as well as 'one in which the SNP has a tradition of support'.[1] Several newspapers noted that she might benefit from an ongoing battle between a local councillor, Mohammad Sarwar, and the Glasgow Central MP Mike Watson for the Labour nomination (Sarwar eventually won). At the 1992 general election, meanwhile, Labour had regained the seat from Jim Sillars with a healthy majority of 4,125.

It was an electoral contest that looked eminently winnable; indeed, the selection of Sturgeon demonstrated precisely how seriously the SNP leadership took Govan. Profiling the constituency in *The Sunday Times*, political scientist James Mitchell wrote (with personal insight) that the young lawyer was 'regarded by some as the most able SNP member of her generation',[2] while *The Times* noted that she was 'bright, articulate, and tipped as a future party leader'.[3] Her appointment as the party's energy spokeswoman in the autumn of 1996 boosted Sturgeon's media profile further, giving her a platform to rail against rising electricity prices, safety at Dounreay and, of course, Westminster's handling of North Sea oil revenue, while the issues at play in Govan – housing, poverty and unemployment – also played to her policy strengths.

Despite its name, however, Glasgow Govan was largely a new seat, comprising parts of the old Govan, Pollok, Central and Cathcart constituencies. Sturgeon moved to Camphill Avenue for the duration of the campaign, and the media took a keen interest in both her candidacy and the wider battle. 'Neat, dark-haired (with just one or two white hairs appearing prematurely – an advantage perhaps?),' observed the *Herald*, 'she talks with quiet control, reasoned logic, and sincere but measured passion.'

Instead of simply bashing Labour (in the way it tended to 'bash the Nats'), Sturgeon took a subtler approach: criticising Labour for arrogantly assuming Govan was theirs for the taking. She also drew a distinction between her motivation and that of Mohammad Sarwar. 'He wants Govan because he wants to be Britain's first Muslim MP,' she said. 'I want Govan because I want to do whatever I can to help the people of Govan.'

Sturgeon was unapologetic about retaining most of the idealism that had originally led her to the SNP aged 16. 'One of the sad things about politics in this country is that there is a lack of any real vision, a lack of aspiration,' she lamented. 'There is a sterility about political debate in this country. It is healthy to have a degree of idealism, so long as it does not cloud your judgment. You have to have an idea of the kind of society you want to live in.'[4]

Govan was, of course, a useful backdrop when it came to articulating that vision, while also a challenge in campaigning terms. Pivotal in this respect was a talented Nationalist organiser called Allison Hunter, more of a traditionalist than Sturgeon but the sort to take young hard-working activists under her wing. She had served as election agent to Jim Sillars at the 1988 Govan by-election and would remain an important figure in the Glasgow SNP until her death in 2013, after which Sturgeon paid tribute to a 'mentor' who had been a 'constant source of advice and support' during her candidacies in the city, although, in reality, their relationship had been more necessary than warm.[5] But while the SNP's candidate was undeniably slick, one Labour activist remembered getting the impression that 'underneath it all it was a bit of a shambles'. 'However bad things were for us,' he added, 'we knew where our vote was and that we'd be able to get it out.'[6]

In 1997, Sturgeon was frank in admitting that in past campaigns the SNP had not made 'enough effort to become involved in different sections of the community' thus allowing opponents to 'spread scare stories'. Via Scots Asians for Independence (launched at the 1995 SNP conference), this was a facet of the campaign Sturgeon tackled head on, even spending her 26th birthday at a mosque in the constituency. 'I do not accept that Mohammad Sarwar will get the votes of the Asian community en bloc simply because he is an Asian,' she stated, 'and I do not believe that I will automatically get the votes of the non-Asians.' And anyone thinking of voting for her out of 'racial motivation', added Sturgeon emphatically, should 'think again': 'I do not want the votes of people who are racist, narrow-minded or divisive.'

But above all in Govan Sturgeon once again demonstrated her capacity for sheer hard graft. Since being selected in late 1995 she had spent every spare minute in the constituency, devoting four evenings a week and every weekend to campaigning, in addition to attending internal party strategy meetings or meetings of the SNP's NEC (as well as energy spokeswoman, she remained Vice-Convener for Youth Affairs). 'I had to work hard, and my parents had to work hard to support me through university,' she said, providing an insight into her personal philosophy. 'I had to work hard at university and I have worked hard at the SNP to be where I am in the SNP. I am a great believer in the idea that nothing falls at anybody's feet. You have to work for success. That is what I am trying to do in Govan.'[7]

Hard work, however, was not always enough, especially in politics. Govan became a crowded field with an array of independent candidates, including three from the Asian community and even one from the British National Party, ensuring that race remained a live issue. Mohammad Sarwar also provoked strong reactions, the bitter nature of his selection leading several Labour activists (including Paul McKinney, later the party's Scottish director of communications) to privately back Sturgeon. When, in May 1996, John Smith House ordered a re-run of the selection contest following allegations of vote rigging and racism, Sturgeon naturally took full advantage of the uncertainty, telling the *Herald* that Labour's 'shambolic performance' showed they were 'unfit to represent the people of Govan and Scotland'.[8] Elsewhere she went even further, telling the June 1996 Bannockburn rally that Labour's 'rotten practices' in Govan had divided activists, MPs and the local community.[9] In July, meanwhile, Sturgeon vowed to pursue Sarwar throughout the constituency until he agreed to a public debate.

In early 1997, with the election just months away, Sturgeon ostentatiously tried to maximise support from Asian voters in Govan by publicly backing the battle for independence in Kashmir; businessman Humayun Hanif, the SNP's candidate in Sturgeon's old constituency of Shettleston, estimated that, of the 1,400 members of SAfI, around 400 were of Kashmiri origin. The SNP's campaign was also boosted by the defection of prominent Glasgow Asians including Abdul Majeed, former chairman of the Pollokshields Tory party association, former Labour supporter Haji Mohammed Sadiq, a past vice president of Glasgow's Central Mosque and, most prominently, Adil Bhatti, a former political ally of Sarwar himself. The 85-year-old John Macfarlane, who had canvassed for Red Clydesider James Maxton in the 1930s, also joined the Sturgeon bandwagon.

Sarwar's name featured prominently in much of Sturgeon's election literature, a clear attempt to exploit his local difficulties, while she unashamedly targeted the traditional Labour vote, apparently unhappy about Blair's move to the right, a pitch that attracted Labour councillor Yvonne Anderson and former Labour candidate Stuart MacLennan to Sturgeon's campaign. Sturgeon also took care to highlight more local concerns – the closure of a much-loved swimming pool, council tax increases of up to 22 per cent and housing, committing the SNP to transferring Glasgow's considerable local authority capital debt to central government. She even believed Tory supporters might vote for her tactically to keep Labour out, and modestly predicted with just weeks to go was that she stood 'a very good chance' of victory.[10]

Alex Salmond lent a helping hand, describing Govan as the 'cockpit' of the broader battle between the SNP and Labour,[11] and praising Sturgeon for articulating 'a strong Scottish message of social justice'.[12] Sturgeon was also present at the launch of her party's national election campaign, giving her a valuable profile in the closing weeks. Still there was trouble in the rival camp and, when hundreds of late entries were made to the electoral roll (200 of which came from Mohammad Sarwar's old council ward in Pollokshields), Sturgeon spoke of a 'cloud of suspicion' hanging over her Labour opponent.[13]

For the past year-and-a-half, Sturgeon had taken the fight to Labour with a tireless doorstep campaign that, at points, resembled a by-election contest. And, up against the somewhat wooden Sarwar, she had found it easy to shine, not just on the ground but increasingly under the media spotlight. As even Gerry Hassan (who worked on the Labour campaign) conceded, 'She ran a good campaign and demolished Sarwar in all of the public hustings.'[14] For once, Sturgeon could have been forgiven the belief – known as 'candidatitus' among politicos – that she might actually win Govan, particularly after senior Nationalists 'blitzed' the area in the final week. On polling day, however, it was not to be:

Labour	Mohammad Sarwar	14,216
SNP	Nicola Sturgeon	11,302
Conservative	William Thomas	2,839
Liberal Democrat	Bob Stewart	1,918
Scottish Socialist	Alan McCombes	755

Sarwar, however, held on with a majority of just 2,914, more than a thousand votes fewer than in 1992, making it close to a moral victory for Sturgeon who, although not an MP, was still well on her way to being one of Scotland's most prominent young Nationalists. Nevertheless, the breakthrough she and others had hoped for – much like in 1992 – had failed to transpire.

A major part of the SNP's strategy during the 1997 election campaign had been to depict New Labour as having abandoned its principles and thus deserted its core electorate, a point that

– in various forms – Sturgeon had been making since the late 1980s. As one campaign poster had it: 'New Labour = Old Tories'. This, however, had little effect, with Labour winning 56 seats (old and new) in Scotland and increasing its share of the vote by 6.6 per cent. The SNP doubled its seats with 22.1 per cent of the vote, only a marginal increase on 1992. Govan, however, had been the only Scottish seat to witness a swing *away* from Labour.

The battle for Govan, however, did not end with the 1997 general election. Within days of Sarwar becoming the UK's first Muslim MP, the new Labour government was engulfed in its first sleaze scandal, involving allegations of bribery, irregularities with expenses and electoral fraud, with the new MP having allegedly handed £5,000 to Badar Islam, who had stood as an independent Labour candidate, to prevent him actively campaigning against him, as well as separate charges of buying votes and manipulating the electoral roll.

'The allegations are serious and they give me serious cause for concern,' responded Sturgeon. 'Democracy has to be done and that doesn't seem to be the case in Govan.'[15] Under the Representation of the People Act 1983, however, a petition for a re-run had to be lodged within 21 days of the original election and it seemed unlikely the resulting police investigation would be completed in time. Sturgeon wrote to the Chief Constable of Strathclyde Police asking that it be concluded within that timescale while refusing to rule out legal action on behalf of the SNP. Labour also launched its own internal inquiry into the allegations and suspended Sarwar in the interim.

By late June, the SNP's Govan constituency association had formally called on Sarwar to stand down as the scandal(s) dragged on, with Sturgeon urging him to 'take the opportunity to go before he is pushed by Labour's chief whip'.[16] Against all the odds, however, Sarwar appeared determined to tough things out – Labour even retained his old Pollokshields East council seat in a by-election, albeit with a vastly reduced majority. 'Govan has effectively been unrepresented since May 1,'[17] said Sturgeon, making it clear she was prepared for a by-election which, she predicted, 'the SNP would win'.[18]

But, by the beginning of 1998, the whole messy affair began to peter out and in 1999, following a nine-week trial at the High Court in Edinburgh, Sarwar was acquitted and his suspension from holding office within the Labour Party lifted. Not only that, but the voters of Govan re-elected him in 2001, while in 2005, following further boundary changes, Sarwar fought and won Glasgow Central, a new constituency retained by his son Anas five years later. In the interim, Sarwar had become a popular chairman of the Scottish Affairs Select Committee and, in August 2013, he was sworn in as Governor of the Punjab in his native Pakistan, the events of the late 1990s a distant memory.

'Anyone who has been involved in election campaigning', wrote Sturgeon in a caustic review of John Williams' account of the general election, 'is only too aware of the highs and lows, the tensions and excitement, and the inevitable mood swings of the exhausted candidate.'[19] She spoke from recent (1997) and historic (1987 and 1992) personal experience while at the same betraying her obvious infatuation with the world of politics, a fascination that would be amply rewarded over the next two years, first via Labour's promised two-question devolution referendum and subsequently in elections to the Scottish Parliament that a plebiscite would create.

In early August, SNP activists overwhelmingly backed Alex Salmond's recommendation to campaign for a Yes-Yes vote the following month, the culmination of his long-standing efforts to persuade his party to learn to stop worrying and love the halfway house of devolution. In another significant development the party was also to campaign alongside Labour and the Liberal Democrats via the cross-party 'Scotland Forward' organisation established by the businessman Nigel Smith. Sturgeon's friend Kay Ullrich joined George Reid and Alex Neil, a mix of gradualists and fundamentalists, to represent the SNP on its executive (Sturgeon herself had been tipped).

The cross-party nature of the campaign meant the SNP was restricted, at least between May and September, in terms of exploiting Mohammad Sarwar's high-profile difficulties in Govan, where Sturgeon had clearly distinguished herself. In the *Observer*'s judgement, she had come 'across as fresh, gutsy and highly talented', representing the 'rational and liberal face of the party'.[20] Others began to appreciate a more human side seldom seen in the heat of political battle. The journalist Gerry Hassan, who had campaigned for Sarwar at the general election, recalls organising a conference on the UK Government's devolution White Paper that summer, after which Sturgeon spent an entire evening with him and another Labour activist at Glasgow's Tron Bar 'talking about the highs and lows of the Govan campaign'. 'That made me feel there was a human being in there,' he said. 'Her preparedness to spend time with a couple of Labour activists showed her in a good light.'[21]

Senior Nationalists agreed, admiring both her professionalism and obvious dedication, and, at the SNP conference that followed the successful referendum, Sturgeon climbed the party ladder further on being elected Vice-Convener for Publicity, a prominent post once held by Salmond and one tailor-made for her growing talent as a political communicator. Indeed, Salmond had turned it into one of the party's most important positions.

Shortly after conference, Sturgeon also became education spokeswoman in the SNP's 'shadow cabinet', allowing her to campaign against the Labour government's plans to introduce university tuition fees and scrap grants, something she said would create 'yet another barrier between young people and higher education'.[22] Sturgeon also predicted the policy would have 'a devastating impact on Scottish higher education, Scottish students and Scottish families', adding that the forthcoming Scottish Parliament ought to 'defend the crucial principle of free access to our colleges and universities'[23] and highlighting the fee-free systems in Ireland, Finland and Norway.

In particular, Sturgeon targeted the Scottish education minister Brian Wilson, long a *bête noire* of Nationalists due to his penetrating critiques of the SNP, accusing him of not only adopting a Tory education agenda but actually extending it further. Towards the end of 1997, when statistics showed Scottish universities were experiencing significant reductions in applications, she held Wilson personally responsible for deterring not only poorer students but 'those from middle-income backgrounds',[24] evidence the SNP was learning to pitch its message more broadly. When it came to secondary education Sturgeon also opposed what she described as 'creeping privatisation' via the controversial Private Finance Initiative (PFI), although she cautioned against becoming blinded by 'tradition or ideology'. 'State schools are built for the benefit of children and local communities,' she wrote in the *Herald*, 'and for many it is hard to accept that in future they may serve to line the pockets of private developers.'[25]

Beyond her education brief, Sturgeon not only appeared on the BBC's flagship current affairs programme *Question Time* but spoke for the SNP as it appeared to be on a roll in the political no-man's land between the 1997 general election and forthcoming 1999 Scottish Parliament campaign. According to opinion polls, Labour's lead over the SNP was down to just 11 per cent. 'Labour said devolution would kill support for the SNP stone dead,' Sturgeon told journalists before a March 1998 meeting of the party's National Council in Stirling, 'but the polls show the opposite is proving true.'[26]

A few days later, a System Three poll put the SNP within one point of Labour in terms of voting intentions the following year. 'If we have a majority as we expect, we shall form the Scottish government,' stated a confident Sturgeon, 'and if we form the Scottish government we shall call a referendum on independence in the first term of that government.'[27] Importantly, that referendum pledge was yet to become formal party policy, although Sturgeon was prominent in backing Salmond when he revived the plebiscite policy in the wake of the party's buoyant performance in the polls, later citing a private poll (showing that 8 in 10 Scots wanted a vote on independence as soon as the Scottish Parliament was established) as vindication of the SNP's position 'of offering the referendum as part of our package for governing Scotland'.[28]

The good news continued into May 1998, when one poll even put the SNP ahead of Labour. 'For the first time ever we have the level playing field,' commented Sturgeon, 'and that is all we have ever asked for.' She also unveiled her party's campaign slogan: 'Scotland's Parliament needs Scotland's party'. When Mike Russell, the SNP's chief executive, said the party must 'pace' itself over the next 12 months, Sturgeon took the cue by adding, '[W]e are now in training for a marathon not a sprint.'[29] But this poll bounce, judged SNP historian Peter Lynch, was 'based on nothing concrete' and indeed privately the party leadership did not take it seriously.[30]

The promotion of Sturgeon by the SNP allowed it to counter long-standing charges that it was little more than a 'one-man band', with her and the economist Andrew Wilson, who was also 27, regularly punted to the media as future leadership contenders, although internal research later revealed that Sturgeon, John Swinney et al. were practically unknown to the electorate. Alex Salmond even claimed his party had 'almost all the Scottish political talent below the age of 30',[31] frequently singling out Sturgeon for particular praise, while in May he put her in charge of a policy review committee to cost and test the party's manifesto commitments ahead of the election.

This inevitably led to jealousy, with one colleague commenting that however talented she needed 'to loosen up a bit'.[32] Others referred to 'Her Master's Voice',[33] betraying a perception that 'other talented people' were being 'overlooked'.[34] Privately, however, Sturgeon was anything but buttoned up. 'She's always been very funny, personally kind and considerate,' recalled someone who socialised with her in the mid 1990s. 'I think the thing about Nicola is she became prominent in politics very young, so she struggled to be taken seriously and because of that, consciously or unconsciously, she adopted a more po-faced persona than she needed to.'[35] In a 2014 interview, Sturgeon reflected that when she first came into politics the pressure was 'to conform to the male model of doing politics . . . to go along with the adversarial element of it. That's how you are conditioned to be. But then you get criticised because you're not being female enough. But if you then become all female about it, you get criticised for not being serious enough. So you are kind of caught in the middle.'[36] Getting that balance right was something that would evolve over time, while others, far from being 'overlooked', were aware that they had been given positions as a result of quiet lobbying by Sturgeon. Kate Higgins, for example, became the SNP's equality spokeswoman in 1998 on the basis of her recommendation, a demonstration of how close she was to the party leader even at that stage, and indeed of his willingness to follow her advice.

Sturgeon, rather than Salmond, often led the charge against Labour. When Tony Blair appointed a group of ministers to lead a 'fightback' against the Nationalists, she mocked them as 'the London expeditionary force' and Labour as 'a hand-me-down party taking orders straight from London',[37] something that was to become a prominent SNP theme along with New Labour's supposed similarity to the Conservatives.

Naturally, Labour fought back, with Blair charging veteran Nat-basher Helen Liddell with the task of keeping the SNP in check, although that appointment simply provided Sturgeon with further evidence that New Labour was 'a London-controlled party, out of touch with Scotland', quoting, for good measure, Liddell's reported protest that she would have to be 'dragged kicking and screaming' from London back to Scotland.[38] Liddell was another Nationalist bogey-woman and Sturgeon would have fun shadowing the Deputy Scottish Secretary, taking her on not only in terms of the forthcoming election but also as the new education minister at the Scottish Office.

Sturgeon was due to unveil the SNP's education policy document at the September 1998 conference, and it was expected to focus on three main areas: arrangements for pupils transferring between primary and secondary, the new Higher Still exam (which she did not rule out scrapping) and the most high-profile – student tuition fees. At conference a left-wing activist called Calum Miller also came close to ousting Sturgeon

71

as Vice-Convener for Publicity, apparently a consequence of disquiet about the SNP's increasing professionalisation.

Indeed, although relentlessly critical of New Labour and 'Blairism', both Salmond and Sturgeon were at the heart of a similar modernisation project, moderating the socialist and republican voices (which had, not that long ago, included her) in a party traditionally to the left of Labour. And, like Blair, critics of Salmond accused him of having autocratic tendencies. At around this time, the SNP backed lower Corporation Tax, implicitly endorsed low-tax economics and abandoned demands to reverse certain Thatcher-era privatisations, all policies that would have troubled Sturgeon a decade earlier. She also trod carefully when it came to whether her party would use the Scottish Parliament's tax-varying powers. That, said Sturgeon as if beholden to New Labour-style focus groups, would 'take into account a variety of factors, including expressions of public opinion'.[39]

But the Sturgeon of 1998 was more ideologically pragmatic and, above all, loyal to the leadership. While claiming that Scots had clocked Blairism as 'just an extension of Thatcherism',[40] she also espoused the SNP's 'ideology' of 'Enterprise, Compassion and Democracy' which, of course, sounded distinctly Blairite in its triangulating vagueness. Instead, Sturgeon preferred to emphasise her party's 'democratic civic nationalism' as 'progressive and inclusive'. 'It reflects', she explained, 'Scotland in all its diversity and aims to speak to and represent all of Scotland.'[41] And when it came to independence, Sturgeon believed it to be merely a matter of time (the decline of Labour) and demographics (the youth vote). Scotland, she said, was already 'in a process of independence', the 'pace' of which would be set 'by the people of Scotland'.[42]

Sturgeon's education brief also highlighted these ideological and presentational shifts, as well as increasing realism now that the SNP was bidding to run a devolved Scottish Executive. At conference, it became clear the SNP was rolling back from its 1997 manifesto commitment to restoring student grants ('a return to maintenance grants at the 1990 equivalent, index-linked for successive years'), a pledge missing from its draft policy document 'Towards the Scottish Parliament'. Instead Sturgeon argued that 'when we have got the resources of independence then we will restore student grants',[43] although later she was even more cautious, saying an SNP administration would merely 'try to bring the grant system back'.[44] Interestingly, she applied the same logic to scrapping tuition fees, another long-standing pledge, while promising that, if necessary, an SNP government would pay the fourth-year tuition fees of English, Welsh and Northern Ireland students in order to end the so-called 'Scottish anomaly' arising from the traditional four-year degree north of the border, and thus cleverly combating charges of being anti-English.

Inevitably, this backtracking did not escape the attention of students, one of whom literally waved the 1997 SNP manifesto in the direction of Sturgeon as she spoke at a 'People's Assembly' intended as a consultation on its education policies. 'Whatever government is elected next May,' she admitted at that Edinburgh gathering, 'will have the same amount of money for Scottish education,' and, although tax-varying powers might raise more revenue, the SNP had still not decided whether to include a tax hike in its manifesto.[45]

More broadly, Sturgeon promised an SNP government would end the 'ideological meddling' she believed had characterised the Conservative and Labour approach to education policy over the last 20 years (this assumed the abolition of tuition fees was somehow non-ideological), instead replacing the 'top down, talk down' attitude of Helen Liddell with a 'bottom up' approach involving key stakeholders.[46] Here, too, Sturgeon was no militant, even calling on the Scottish Secondary Teachers' Association to pull back from industrial action during the Christmas of 1998.

Again, pragmatism was the order of the day, although often smothered with left-wing rhetoric, a balancing act that would be a consistent feature of her political career. Media watchers, however, were generally impressed. When the *Herald* journalist Murray Ritchie introduced his editor Harry Reid (a former education correspondent) to Sturgeon, 'the two of them become involved in a series of spirited exchanges, with Harry, in mischievous mood none too subtly testing her knowledge and debating skills'. 'Nicola', he recalled of their encounter, emerged 'unscathed and Harry pronounces himself greatly impressed. She permits herself just the hint of a smile of satisfaction as we say goodbye.'[47]

Following the 1997 general election, meanwhile, it had become clear that Sturgeon, then commuting to Stirling for her day job at Bell & Craig, needed to be nearer her potential constituents in Glasgow while the small (but expanding) legal firm needed a solicitor who could commit more time to their clients and the business in general – both goals could not be fulfilled. The lifestyle associated with a corporate law firm, she had quickly discovered, was not for her. As one political contemporary recalled, 'she clearly didn't feel comfortable in that environment'.[48]

During 1996, Sturgeon had already started volunteering at the Legal Services Agency, an advice centre based in Glasgow since 1989, where she helped research a short book entitled *Home loss and disturbance payments*, chiefly written by Sarah Craig, Simon Collins and Paul D. Brown, who would become a long-standing associate. An 'authoritative and practical guide' to legislation covering 'home loss' payments, which usually took the form of compensation for a person's compulsory removal from their home, the book also offered advice to lawyers working on landlord/tenant disputes.

This was law with a social justice tenor and therefore of real interest to the practical and fair-minded Sturgeon. The book's acknowledgements, however, credited several people with having 'wrestled' with the provisions of the 1973 Land Compensation (Scotland) Act, including 'Nicola Spurgeon', a misspelling that became a running joke between Sturgeon and Paul Brown.[49] Nevertheless, it brought her to the attention of Jim Gray, a solicitor and welfare rights manager who had established the Drumchapel Law and Money Advice Centre in 1992, the consequence of a merger between a Money Advice Centre that had opened in 1989 and a separate project involving a solicitor to meet 'unmet' legal needs in Drumchapel. Initially it had two solicitors (including Gray) but, as funding and income permitted, by 1997 there were four.

Sturgeon initially joined as maternity cover shortly after her electoral near miss in Govan, Paul Brown having acted as her referee, but so impressed were Gray et al. that means were found to keep her on permanently. Although law centres were firmly part of the voluntary sector, they also employed solicitors, like Sturgeon, and operated as a legal partnership in much the same way that a private law firm would and were regulated, as per statute, by the Law Society of Scotland. More to the point, the location and working patterns of the Drumchapel Law Centre were much more amenable to Sturgeon's political aspirations.

Although Jim Gray came from a different political viewpoint (he had once stood as a Labour candidate) he quickly came to respect his new employee's ability as well as her motivations. 'She was very bright and very able,' he recalled, 'and she was very committed to the work. It was not the sort of work you'd go into for money or the profile, so she clearly wanted to do it – to help people.' The work included housing, debt issues, social security payments and criminal injury compensation – matters, in other words, which were not very attractive to private sector lawyers.

As with others who had encountered Sturgeon in her teens and twenties, Gray also remembered her initially being quite reserved, taking a 'while to open up with people', although that was something he recognised as 'perfectly normal for those involved in politics'. At the same time, in other familiar descriptions, she was 'driven'. 'She was also quite an effective advocate and I used to get good feedback from people she represented,' recalled Gray. 'Nicola often got good results for her clients – she had a forceful although not aggressive style.'[50]

Sturgeon became a fixture at what was known as the evictions court, which sat in Glasgow Sheriff Court a couple of times a week (more formally it was called the Heritable Court). The lawyer Mike Dailly who, like Jim Gray, was not of a Nationalist persuasion, remembers watching her at work and coming, again like Gray, to respect her qualities as an advocate for those who would otherwise have struggled to find legal representation. 'It was a very busy court with private and social sector clients all subject to eviction action,' said Dailly. 'She was very able and certainly very principled – and very committed.'[51]

The *Herald* journalist Frances Horsburgh judged that Sturgeon was 'much happier' working at Drumchapel than she had been in Stirling.[52] As a party contemporary observed, the Law Centre job would have 'paid peanuts by comparison' with her previous employment, 'but that's where she felt comfortable and that said a lot about her. She chose to do that; she walked away from private sector where she could have made a lot of money.'[53] But this was the frontline of 'social justice' and an experience that would later give her an affinity with figures like Noel Dolan, formerly of the housing charity Shelter, as well as influence her policy agenda as a minister, for example on social housing and abolition of the 'Right to Buy'. (Sturgeon's university friend Claire Mitchell also worked at Castlemilk Law Centre.)

'I found it really, really satisfying', reflected Sturgeon in 2003, 'and also really difficult sometimes because the conditions, the circumstances in which so many people in that community lived, were just appalling. But it was good work to do and in many ways it stood me in good stead for the job I do now.'[54] She meant, of course, the surgery work associated with the work of a constituency MP or rather MSP – Member of the Scottish Parliament. By the beginning of 1999, the SNP was firmly on an election footing and Sturgeon left the Drumchapel Law Centre after nearly two satisfying years in order to have a second go at winning Govan, this time for a legislature much closer to home.

The Labour politician Malcolm Chisholm recalled debating with Sturgeon at the Strathclyde University Union in 1996 (she was, he said, 'outstanding') and saying in parting: 'See you in the Scottish Parliament,' for it was clear to him that was where both were headed.[55] Indeed, as early as October 1997 (a year and a half before the first elections were due), Sturgeon was speculating as to what life would be like in the new Scottish Parliament. 'The idea of having to go to London to an institution which was created for and by men and is dominated by them would for me be going into an alien culture,' she told the *Herald*. 'I stood for Westminster, but I should say quite honestly that the prospect of going to Westminster if I had been elected would not be something I would have looked forward to. By contrast, an Edinburgh parliament, because it is a new institution, being created in the late twentieth century, hopefully is going to be much more friendly, not only to women but to people of ethnic background.' She dwelled a little more on part of her final point: 'Women are generally speaking more practical than men, and the idea of being able to be an MP without the physical necessity of having to go away from home is appealing, even to someone like me who is single and has no family.'[56]

Scottish politics, added Sturgeon, was 'littered' with women who did an 'excellent job at their own level but stop themselves going any higher',[57] therefore the 'question of role models' mattered. 'I often talk to younger women who say that there are no women in politics, so politics is not for them,' she told the *Guardian*. 'That is bound to change.'[58]

Sturgeon had spoken out publicly in favour of the SNP adopting a policy of gender balance when it came to selecting candidates for the Scottish Parliament but the party decided otherwise. In the event, however, the choices of local constituency associations meant around 40 per cent of the party's MSPs were likely to be women. Sturgeon also argued that the SNP, unlike Labour, had not 'drawn up a list notable by its exclusions'. 'We have candidates who know Scotland and who want to make it better,' she said, 'not people who listen to Millbank and do what they are told.'[59]

This list included several long-standing Nationalists and Sturgeon associates such as Roseanna Cunningham and Fiona

Hyslop, but also first-time candidates like Kate Higgins (who had succeeded Sturgeon as Vice-Convener for Youth Affairs) and Kaukab Stewart (standing in Glasgow Anniesland), the latter a confidante of Sturgeon and also her deputy in the education brief. Naturally, however, there were also tensions, with the *Daily Record* reporting in June 1998 that Cunningham and Sturgeon had been charged with blocking Margo MacDonald's return to frontline politics, a result of the continuing feud between her husband (Jim Sillars) and Alex Salmond. Although Sturgeon's hands were largely clean of Machiavellian scheming, she was not beyond doing the leadership's dirty work.

At the beginning of 1999, the *Herald* assessed the 28-year-old Sturgeon's strengths and weaknesses. The former included looking good as a 'vigorous, young, high-profile party figurehead' capable of 'wrong-footing older opponents' while the latter touched on perceptions that she was ('perhaps wrongly') a 'cold fish', seriously burdened 'for one so young and now being put into bat against Labour at highest level'. In terms of prospects, Robbie Dinwoodie concluded that she had to take Govan second time round or the SNP would 'have flattered to deceive, again'. Nevertheless the general verdict was positive: 'Will grow in political stature, and [has] leadership potential.'[60]

Sturgeon had already been unveiled as one of what Salmond called the SNP's 'Scottish Parliament ministerial team', still in charge of education and, in addition, culture. A few weeks into the New Year, meanwhile, she also topped the party's regional list for Glasgow (the new Parliament was to have a mix of first-past-the-post and PR members), virtually guaranteeing her a seat even if she failed to take Govan by traditional electoral means. At the constituency level Sturgeon was to be one of three lawyers contesting the seat, the others being Gordon Jackson QC, another regular at Glasgow's Babbity Bowster bar, and the Conservative Tasmina Ahmed-Sheikh, a Scots–Pakistani Muslim who later joined the SNP. As the *Herald* political editor Murray Ritchie judged, Govan would probably be 'the most closely watched result on May 6 because if the SNP and Nicola don't take it from Labour, the Nationalists can forget the whole election'.[61]

The future of the Kvaerner shipyard soon emerged as perhaps the key local issue when its Norwegian owner announced it was pulling out, thereby threatening 5,000 jobs, although it also had national resonance. 'If Kvaerner goes we are looking at the end of shipbuilding in Scotland,' warned Sturgeon. 'We have the opportunity to save the shipbuilding industry over the short and the long term.'[62] She urged the Ministry of Defence to award a £250-million order for roll-on/roll-off ferries to make the yard more attractive to any potential buyer and made sure the shop stewards knew she was on their side, particularly when the Swan Hunter yard made a bid that would have involved the loss of hundreds of jobs.

At the same time, Sturgeon was careful not to make too much political capital out of the situation, expressing again and again her support for the UK government task force set up to find a buyer thus letting the saga speak for itself. But her swift action in meeting workers at the yard undoubtedly impressed the Kvaerner shop stewards, one of whom, Jamie Webster, described her in a newspaper article as 'a nippy sweetie'.[63] Although this was intended as a compliment to Sturgeon's tenacity, it thereafter was more frequently used pejoratively. 'I actually called her "a nippy sweetie and an able yin",' recalled Webster. 'It's very Glaswegian. "Nippy sweetie" means "right in your face" and "able yin" means "right up for it". It was a compliment and I stand by it.'[64]

Party colleagues were impressed with Sturgeon's judgement ('Going into the shipyards as a young woman can't have been easy,' commented one.[65]), as they were with her involvement in the SNP's national campaign as education spokeswoman, and continued to major on her party's policy of scrapping tuition fees, this time pledging to spend £150 million on abolishing all tuition fees for domestic students and restoring grants of £500 a year for 20,000 students from low-income families. In doing so, she argued in the *Herald*, 'we will demonstrate the real difference between the SNP and New Labour. The

SNP – Scotland's party – is not just the party of education in Scotland. The SNP is the party of free education.'[66]

Importantly, this policy meant the SNP was no longer claiming that its promises regarding tuition fees and grants could only be delivered with independence; rather Sturgeon was highlighting that the party was determined to prove progress could be made even within the devolution settlement (she also proposed to spend £20 per school pupil on textbooks while reducing maximum class sizes from 33 to 30 within six years). A plan to scrap the National Grid for Learning (which would have linked every school to the Internet) was less successful, with Labour accusing Sturgeon of being a Luddite who wanted to take classrooms back to the days of slate and chalk.

All of this was consistent with a strategic review Sturgeon, as Publicity Vice-Convener, had set out a few months before, objectives and tactics including 'building confidence, maintaining the momentum, stating the case for independence, attacking Labour and probably the most important, presenting the Party as a responsible government'.[67]

There had been speculation the SNP planned to fund its spending commitments by making use of the so-called 'Tartan Tax', the Scottish Parliament's ability to vary the basic rate of income tax by 3p. At the party's pre-election conference in Aberdeen, this was finally confirmed, with Alex Salmond deciding at the eleventh hour to spend what he called 'a Penny for Scotland' on higher public spending should the SNP form the first Scottish Executive. Key figures, including Sturgeon, spoke in favour of the policy from the conference podium and, although they did not realise it at the time, the policy and its (perceived) electoral consequences would mark a significant shift in the party's fiscal thinking.

The policy, argued Sturgeon unconvincingly during the campaign, was a 'big winner' with voters, particularly the additional £700 million it would release for spending on health, education and housing. 'If we are to improve education we have to invest,' she reasoned, 'and to do that we must forego the Chancellor's tax "bribe".'[68] Sturgeon also flanked Salmond when he launched the formal SNP campaign on 6 April, publishing a New Labour-style pledge card containing '10 promises from Scotland's Party for Scotland's Parliament', which attracted some flak when it emerged that only the tenth and final pledge mentioned independence. When Labour published its five pledges the following day, Sturgeon dismissed them as 'cauld kail rehet'.[69]

When the *Herald*'s Frances Horsburgh asked Sturgeon if she had a 'talent for politics', she recording the candidate's rather testy response. 'I'm not in it for the mechanics,' she said. 'Politics is something I am passionate about. Politics is about achieving something for people. I want to be able to help achieve an independent Scotland which I think will be a much fairer Scotland and a better place to live.'[70]

Although this was undoubtedly sincere, Horsburgh had probably touched a nerve, for Sturgeon's life increasingly revolved around politics, and to some extent had always done since joining the SNP 12 years earlier, her only escape being books and her legal work, although both were also political in nature. She even enthused to a journalist about what good fun the SNP conference was. 'It's still a much better social occasion than any of the other parties' conferences,' she explained. 'People will be up to the early hours of the morning enjoying themselves.'[71] Even her proposal that Scotland should have a separate Eurovision entry was cast as the 'serious' business of 'projecting the image of a country'.[72]

During the campaign, Sturgeon was living in Scotstoun with her new partner Stuart Morrison, described in the *Herald* as working in IT at Glasgow University but also, like Ricky Bell, a fellow SNP activist. 'So assiduous is she in her politicking', noted the *Sunday Herald*, 'that although she lives on the other side of the river in Scotstoun, she shops in Govan.'[73] Joan Sturgeon, Nicola's mother, was also standing in local authority elections to be held on the same day as those for the Scottish Parliament, hoping to win back the marginal Dreghorn ward from Labour (she lost, but was successful in 2007). 'She asked me what I thought and I said she should stand because she will be just brilliant,' said Joan's daughter, 'no doubt about it.'[74]

Rather than a parent politicising their children, the Sturgeons had done it in reverse. (Later, in August 2016, Joan's husband Robin would also unsuccessfully contest a by-election for North Ayrshire Council.)

The campaign, meanwhile, was not a happy one for the SNP, finding itself torn between arguing on two different levels, devolved and independent, which proved confusing. If it majored on independence it was attacked; if it did not it was accused of trying to hide its true agenda. And with ten days until 6 May it went into meltdown, polls putting the party a full 20 points behind Labour, in response to which an off-form Alex Salmond scrapped the party's daily press conference, launched a special newspaper – the generally embarrassing *Scotland's Voice* – and took to the streets in an attempt to regain momentum. Reports even suggested Sturgeon was being lined up for a leadership challenge after the election, although Salmond loyalists quickly closed that down. 'To challenge for the leadership,' said one pointedly, 'you have to have leadership qualities.'[75]

Two of the issues identified as having been 'unhelpful' in campaigning terms had impacted upon Sturgeon in Govan – chiefly Salmond's condemnation of Allied bombing in Kosovo (many local Asians supported military action in defence of Muslim Albanians) and a strategic decision not to use Kvaerner as a political weapon. That said, many observers noted that, however talented she was, Sturgeon had not enjoyed the best campaign herself. Although hugely experienced for her age, having fought two general elections, that proved scant preparation for a national campaign under the relentless glare of a well-oiled New Labour machine, thus Sturgeon (and other Nationalists like John Swinney) found her carefully planned agendas hijacked or simply ignored by the media.

The BBC journalist Brian Taylor later observed that lack of money and staff had been to blame, with one source telling him the SNP had been 'out-resourced, out-gunned and driven into the ground' by their Labour rivals. 'It was left to a tiny core team to direct the party's strategy – with that same team then broadly expected to implement that strategy on the ground,' wrote Taylor. 'According to insiders, that accounted for a lack of readiness, a lack of sharpness in the campaign.'[76]

Worse, senior SNP figures often appeared unable to answer simple questions relating to their own briefs. When, for example, Sturgeon proudly proclaimed that the SNP wanted foreign languages to be taught in primary schools, an inquisitive journalist enquired, perfectly reasonably, 'Which ones?', to which all she could manage in response was 'Er, um.'[77] Party chief executive Mike Russell rescued her, after a fashion, by reeling some modern languages off the top of his head. 'This was their main policy announcement for the day,' observed Taylor, 'and yet they had not worked through the elementary details.'[78]

Given the sort of politician Sturgeon was, she would have endeavoured to learn from the experience rather than get upset about it, while there was also evidence of an attempt to soften her hard-faced image. A memorable photograph in *The Times* showed her cradling two children during a visit to the Rooftops Nursery in Edinburgh, looking entirely natural; she affected an affinity with Ayr United while one newspaper reckoned 'the Nats' were about to play the glamour card. 'Nicola Sturgeon', it reported, 'has been spotted wearing lippy.'[79]

As in 1997, Govan was considered a bellwether constituency, an indication of whether the SNP would succeed or fail nationally, although – perhaps revealingly – Sturgeon sought to play this down, denying it would constitute a 'disaster' if the party did not take the seat. But apart from the four-way marginal of Inverness East, Govan – which required only a 4.5 per cent swing – represented the SNP's best chance of taking a constituency it did not already hold at Westminster.

Ever the loyalist, Sturgeon also cautioned against writing off the SNP and its leader. 'We've done our best,' she explained, 'as underdogs.'[80] In late April Salmond hit the campaign trail with Sturgeon and, with several Labour figures privately conceding defeat, it looked as if she might have done it when polls closed on the evening of 6 May. Indeed, early editions of the *Daily Record* reported that Sturgeon was confident of success and had even begun 'early celebrations'.

But again, as with two years earlier, it was not to be. The result was:

Labour	Gordon Jackson	11,421
SNP	Nicola Sturgeon	9,665
Conservative	Tasmina Ahmed-Sheikh	2,343
Liberal Democrat	Mohammed Aslam Khan	1,479
Scottish Socialist	Charlie McCarthy	1,275

Although Sturgeon had increased her share of the vote compared with 1997, it still was not enough to dislodge Labour. At the count, Gordon Jackson's supporters roared with relief. 'What on earth,' asked a Labour source, 'do we have to do to lose Govan?' Sturgeon must have been asking herself the same question, although ever the professional she put a brave face on the outcome, saying results from around the country showed 'the SNP vote is up and the Labour Party's vote is down'.[81] Later, however, she blamed negative campaigning and 'scare-mongering', observing that perhaps the 'goings-on in Govan' had 'made people fed up with the whole political process'.[82]

Sturgeon could be forgiven for feeling bitter in defeat, for she and her party had invested a huge amount of time and resources in fighting a constituency it had held twice in the past and against an opponent who often looked like he was trying very hard to lose. But there was 'no sense', recalled a contemporary, that losing Govan for the second time had done Sturgeon 'any damage'. 'She had the burden of great expectations from an early age, because she shone early on she had a lot to live up to.'[83]

Gradually, however, Sturgeon would reconcile herself to the thought of the SNP becoming the main opposition party in the devolved legislature, itself remarkable progress for a hitherto fringe political force. 'The SNP has fought a wonderful campaign,' Sturgeon told *The Scotsman*, 'and . . . the SNP will play a full part in the Scottish parliament.'[84] And although she would be a list MSP rather than a constituency one, Sturgeon was finally an elected member of parliament.

Chapter 5

'Nippy Sweetie'

On the morning of Friday 7 May 1999, the SNP leader Alex Salmond gave a characteristically upbeat performance at the Holiday Inn hotel on Queensferry Road in Edinburgh. Flanking him at the packed press conference were Nicola Sturgeon, party chief executive Mike Russell and John Swinney. Salmond was putting a brave face on a disappointing result, in which not one of his target seats – including Govan – had been won in a head-to-head contest with Labour.

As one of Salmond's famously tight 'inner circle' during the election campaign, not to forget one of its highest-profile public faces, Sturgeon bore her share of responsibility for the outcome, although on her part it had not been for want of hard work. Now poised to take up her place in the new cradle of Scottish democracy as a list member, she would also be the youngest female member of the devolved Parliament and, as ever, spoken of as a 'possible future party leader'.[1]

The first 'class' photograph in what would be the temporary debating chamber on Edinburgh's Mound, borrowed from the Church of Scotland, shows a serious-looking Sturgeon standing at the back flanked by Shona Robison and Roseanna Cunningham, the former a long-standing friend from the Young Scottish Nationalists, the latter a more recent confidante following the 1995 Perth and Kinross by-election. 'Republican Rose' was also a well-known opponent of the UK's hereditary monarchy and responsible, therefore, for committing the SNP to a referendum on Scotland's head of state once it became independent. On being sworn in as Members of the Scottish Parliament (MSPs), Sturgeon joined Cunningham and several others in 'solemnly affirming' (rather than swearing an oath on) her allegiance to Queen Elizabeth, Alex Salmond (although himself a monarchist) having spoken on behalf of the SNP parliamentary group in stressing the sovereignty of the Scottish people.

For those who experienced it, the fledgling months of the Scottish Parliament were optimistic as well as frustrating, with heightened expectations inevitably dampened by the more humdrum reality and early scandals relating to a proposed new home for the devolved legislature. Sturgeon had 'grave reservations' about the proposed site at Holyrood, particularly its projected cost (then a modest £10 million). 'Where we are now is ideal,' she said a few weeks into the job, 'and I can't see why we can't stay.'[2]

Beyond logistics the new Glasgow list MSP planned a member's bill to crack down on money lenders and their 'exorbitant' interest rates,[3] while focusing – in her continuing capacity as spokeswoman on children and education – on the new Labour–Liberal Democrat coalition's negotiations regarding tuition fees. Even before polls had closed, the Scottish Secretary Donald Dewar had signalled his willingness to negotiate, and in Sturgeon's first speech as an MSP she reminded the Liberal Democrat Nicol Stephen – recently appointed Deputy Minister for Enterprise and Lifelong Learning – of his promises during the campaign to 'abolish tuition fees'. 'I believed him,' she added. 'I think his constituents believed him as well.' The Labour–Lib Dem negotiations had hinged not so much on outright abolition of fees but their replacement with a set amount paid upon graduation and once earnings reached a certain threshold. 'A two-thirds majority of this Parliament was elected on a promise to abolish tuition fees,' continued Sturgeon in her speech. 'The fact that Jim Wallace [the Scottish Lib Dem leader], who before the election declared the abolition of tuition fees to be non-negotiable, is now prepared to barter that majority for a position of power . . . will [I think] be unacceptable to the people of Scotland.'[4]

Indeed Sturgeon would view this, over the next decade, as unfinished business. As education spokeswoman, meanwhile, Sturgeon appeared to enjoy a lot of influence over the choice of deputy, something she used to advance individuals she believed had something to contribute. The West of Scotland list MSP Fiona McLeod, for example, was not an obvious choice as her number two, but Sturgeon pushed for her appointment (15 years later McLeod would help run her leadership campaign following Alex Salmond's resignation).

The media view of Sturgeon, meanwhile, remained that of a rather po-faced yet talented young politician. Even so, *Scotland on Sunday* ranked her 49 in its most-eligible list ('Hard shell to crack. Denies all accusations of romanticism'[5]), although following the election she was still seeing IT consultant Stuart Morrison. The pejorative interpretation of the 'nippy sweetie' moniker became established early on. On election night Labour MP Brian Wilson had railed against Sturgeon's 'whingeing' and 'carping' ('I've never heard that woman say a positive thing in her life,' he opined[6]), while in early 2000 the Conservative MSP Brian Monteith described her as being 'in a particularly sour mood', advising that 'she really should learn to bite her tongue and smile more',[7] something later echoed by journalist Lorraine Davidson who recommended 'lessons on how to smile so she can stop being outraged all of the time'.[8] Her public persona, recalled a frontbench colleague, was 'very one sided'. 'It had got to the stage that it had become the dominant narrative about her and I got the impression that a) she felt the nippy sweetie tag was unfair, and b) she had to convey something else in order to combat it.'[9]

There was, however, clearly a more aggressive edge to Sturgeon, as illustrated by a bizarre incident towards the end of 2000. After the Liberal Democrat MSP (and convener of the Health Committee) Margaret Smith attempted to block an SNP debate on community care, witnesses claimed to have seen

Sturgeon and fellow SNP MSPs Tricia Marwick and Shona Robison surround Smith in a corridor outside the debating chamber and start shouting at her. Sturgeon was said to have had her face 'quite close' to that of Smith, with the row growing so heated that a security guard was compelled to intervene.

Mary Scanlon, a Conservative MSP, also claimed to have had her 'brush with the heavy mob', by which she meant Sturgeon and Robison. As a witness recounted, it had 'looked very intimidating . . . reminiscent of what happened to people who went into the toilet when the third-year girls were having a fag'. Sturgeon played it down, echoing Robison and Marwick in claiming it had been nothing more than 'an exchange of views'. As for having been intimidating, she said, nothing 'could be further from the truth'.[10] The trigger for the incident was not clear, although perhaps the forthcoming double by-election in Glasgow Anniesland (caused by Donald Dewar's death) had raised the political temperature on the Mound.

Yet this 'storm in a teacup',[11] as Sturgeon called it, and journalistic impressions did not quite capture her character in the round. Writing in *The Scotsman* towards the end of 1999, the teacher Hugh Reilly recorded a visit made by Sturgeon to his modern studies students and, although conscious of the 'nippy sweetie' image, he observed that this 'was not evident on her visit'. He continued, 'She arrived at the classroom punctually and alone; when de facto minister Clare Short from Westminster visited she brought an entourage. She chatted informally with the department before addressing her audience, straight away establishing street cred by making light-hearted comments about the age of teachers before launching into her lecture. Lecture is perhaps an inappropriate word because she spoke eloquently, without notes, making good use of humour and self-deprecation as she covered some of the key issues concerning young people. Unlike others, she used a level of vocabulary appropriate to her audience.'[12]

So there was clearly a gap between Sturgeon's parliamentary and semi-public personas; the former could be relatively severe (though probably this owed more to Sturgeon's shyness than many realised), the latter warm and engaging. She was also consistent (attending a march against NATO action in the Balkans shortly after becoming an MSP) and passionate (her 'shyness and softly-spoken manner', observed one journalist, 'conceal a fire'[13]). When it came to equality issues, Sturgeon was consistent in her commitment, joining the Scottish Parliament's Cross-Party Group on Women and condemning Section 28 (or Section 2a in Scotland), which banned the 'promotion' of homosexuality in schools, as 'despicable'.

On this, a row that dominated the Parliament's first year, the SNP was somewhat equivocal, supporting repeal while criticising the Scottish Executive for not doing enough to assuage public concern. Sturgeon's instincts, however, were clear from her public statements. 'The natural desire we all have to protect children', she said in April 2000, 'must not become confused as support for a piece of legislation that legitimises intolerance.'[14]

Michael Torrance, then a sabbatical vice president at Aberdeen University, recalls attending an SNP meeting on campus at which a party member complained to Sturgeon about his daughter being taught about gay lifestyles at her school. 'She quickly slapped him down', he recalled, 'by saying firmly that the legislation had yet to be amended so it couldn't possibly relate to his child's lessons.'[15] Sturgeon was not a politician inclined to tell people, even SNP members, what they wanted to hear.

As education spokeswoman, Sturgeon also did her best to trip up education minister Sam Galbraith, a capable and laconic former brain surgeon, but only really succeeded when he was under fire for an exams crisis involving the Scottish Qualifications Authority (SQA). 'The SQA crisis,' recalled a parliamentary colleague, 'was a good opportunity for Sturgeon to make her mark early on in the new Parliament.'[16] In terms of policy, she reprised an election theme in calling for improvements to how modern languages were taught, particularly at primary schools, her concern being that 'with more business links being developed with Europe, Scottish kids are going to be left behind when it comes to finding jobs'. Sturgeon admitted herself that she had 'no languages' despite having studied French at Greenwood Academy.[17]

Teasing Sturgeon during an SNP-initiated debate on the McCrone report into teachers' pay and conditions in June 2000, the Liberal Democrat MSP Ian Jenkins likened his Nationalist counterpart to 'one of those kids that we used to get in school', sometimes 'a wee bit surly' but 'bright and intelligent'. The only problem, he added, was that she did not fancy anyone else getting in on any act. After a main part in a play she would say, 'I'm not in it for another 10 pages – can we get on to that bit?'[18]

Jenkins had detected a certain impatience in the almost 30-year-old shadow education minister for Sturgeon was, after all, a young woman in a hurry, just as Alex Salmond had been a young man in a hurry a decade earlier. The Scottish Parliament gave her a greater chance to shine in a more high-profile setting. Kay Ullrich, now also an MSP and health spokeswoman, watched the woman she had inducted into the SNP 'just blossom and blossom' in those early years of devolution,[19] while another frontbench colleague said she 'developed very quickly from just a spokeswoman into someone who was taken seriously'.[20]

But at the same time Sturgeon, whose star had shone so brightly since the mid 1990s, now had to share the parliamentary limelight with many other bright young things, including Andrew Wilson and Duncan Hamilton. Evaluating the Scottish political scene in April 2000, the *Sunday Herald*, as a consequence of this dynamic, even classified her as having had the 'most stalled career'.[21]

Then, on Monday 17 July 2000, Alex Salmond sent a letter to each SNP MSP informing them of his resignation and rumours swirled as to his motivation. However, a combination of fatigue, a feeling he was not quite getting into his stride in the Scottish Parliament and a suspicion that he was beginning to hinder the National Movement rather than help it was the more mundane, but more accurate, explanation.

There had been grumbling about Salmond's leadership within months of the 1999 elections, and noses were further put out of joint after he committed the SNP to joining the pro-single currency 'Britain in Europe' campaign with minimal consultation. This was very much Salmond's style – which some called 'dictatorial' – and, by the summer of 2000, the long-running tension between so-called fundamentalists (those who desired independence, nothing less) and gradualists (those who favoured taking things slowly via devolution) had reached a crescendo. Sturgeon was a leading Salmond loyalist alongside deputy leader John Swinney and chief whip Bruce Crawford.

But, when Salmond dropped his resignation bombshell, it was simply too early in her parliamentary career for Sturgeon to consider standing as his successor. Instead Swinney entered the race and appointed Sturgeon his campaign manager (interpreted at the time as a snub to business manager Mike Russell), giving him a valuable west-of-Scotland base to balance his Tayside constituency. The appointment was also a vote of confidence by Swinney in her organisational ability and capacity for hard graft. Sturgeon's close friend Roseanna Cunningham, meanwhile, put her name forward for the deputy leadership.

There was, however, little prospect of Swinney losing the contest (Alex Neil also stood). Indeed, reports even suggested Sturgeon was determined to go to France for a week's holiday in August, so relaxed was she about the outcome. Peter Kearney, another candidate for the deputy leadership, criticised Sturgeon's refusal to support a no-confidence vote in education minister Sam Galbraith (then under pressure over an exams crisis), suggesting that this put her at odds with the wider party, but she dismissed it as a 'mythical split' and pointed out, bluntly, that 'in the real world someone has to take a final decision'.[22]

This was a minor distraction, for on 23 September 2000 John Swinney was elected leader with a decisive 67 per cent of delegates' votes at the SNP conference in Inverness, while Cunningham became deputy leader by a similarly large margin. A few days later the new leader reshuffled his front bench team and rewarded Sturgeon with promotion to the health brief, where she replaced her friend Kay Ullrich (who became chief whip). Fiona Hyslop, another key figure in Swinney's campaign team, remained shadow housing minister.

Sturgeon quickly became part of Swinney's 'inner circle', the most prominent of his frontbenchers. Indeed, it is likely Salmond encouraged the two to work closely together, to form the starting point for a leadership 'troika' – past, present and future – that would dominate the SNP for the next decade and a half. Like Sturgeon, Swinney had joined the party as a teenager (aged 15, a year younger than she had been on signing up) and they worked well together – particularly in terms of preparation for the weekly First Minister's Questions – despite being from different wings of the party; although only six years older than Sturgeon, in the late 1980s the YSN would have regarded Swinney, then national secretary, as part of the leadership 'Establishment'. The fact that Sturgeon had not supported the leadership bid of Alex Neil, whom she had been closer to at that time, illustrated how far she had shifted within the SNP. 'I wouldn't say John and Nicola were friends,' recalled a parliamentary colleague, 'but there was certainly mutual respect.'[23]

There remained less than a year to go until the 2001 UK general election, the first of the devolution era and Swinney's first electoral test as Alex Salmond's successor. Sturgeon got to grips with her new portfolio, advocating a ban on tobacco advertising, taunting First Minister Henry McLeish over free personal care for the elderly and developing manifesto pledges (even though health was a devolved area) including freezing (and, if possible, abolishing) prescription charges and providing free fruit to every primary school pupil in Scotland. 'Scotland has one of the worst health records in Europe,' she said on launching 'A Prescription for Better Health' in early 2001, continuing, 'We have fewer nurses in our hospitals now than in 1997; patients are waiting longer for treatment; the care received by patients too often depends on where they live; and New Labour has failed to deliver on its key election pledge to reduce waiting lists . . . The SNP will take action to end post-code treatment by making assessments . . . binding on health boards, and empowering our proposed National Health Care Commission to root out and work to eradicate inequalities.'[24]

As the general election approached, Sturgeon also formed part of the SNP campaign team (she was co-ordinator) at its McDonald Road HQ, which also included former Salmond aide – and future Mr Sturgeon – Peter Murrell. Westminster, however, was no longer the primary means by which the party could gain power and, more to the point, make progress towards independence. Thus the campaign was deliberately low key; all eyes were instead on the next Scottish Parliament contest in May 2003.

Nevertheless, the election on 7 June 2001 (which resulted in a second landslide for Tony Blair's 'New' Labour Party) represented a further setback for the SNP, which won just 20 per cent of the vote (its target had been a quarter), losing one of its six MPs (to a Conservative, which made it look worse than it was) and coming within a few dozen votes of losing a second. There was the usual, though increasingly less convincing, attempt to put a positive spin on the result, with Sturgeon arguing that far from the party being irrelevant in a Westminster context more Scots had voted SNP than the Liberal Democrats or Conservatives 'so we are more relevant than either of them'.[25]

The post-mortem that inevitably followed rested upon 'fiscal autonomy', a constitutional option short of independence advocated by finance spokesman Andrew Wilson prior to and during the general election campaign. Sources close to Sturgeon implied that he was to blame for 'distorting' the election campaign when the focus ought to have been on bread-and-butter issues like jobs, schools and hospitals, while Wilson's camp believed not enough had been made of their 'big idea', accusing Sturgeon, Hyslop et al. of being overly focused on events on the Mound; there was also resentment that television coverage had been dominated by the trium-virate of Swinney, Sturgeon and Hyslop,[26] while Sturgeon also came in for criticism over her handling of party election broadcasts.

Briefing against colleagues was not something Sturgeon often indulged in, but in this case there was obvious frustration with both the campaign itself and its outcome. Party morale was generally low, with fears that, up against a superior Labour campaigning machine in 2003, George Robertson's prediction about devolution killing Nationalism 'stone dead' would begin to look uncomfortably accurate. Swinney, meanwhile, attempted to shore up his position, pleading for discipline (his critics had a predilection for television cameras) while announcing three internal reviews covering organisation, policy and campaigning; Sturgeon handled organisation, giving her experience of party management for the first time. He also reshuffled his shadow cabinet, appointing Alex Salmond leader of the SNP's Westminster group (he had chosen to quit his Scottish Parliament seat) and keeping Sturgeon at health.

She was also charged with professionalising the SNP's campaigning machine in the run-up to the more important devolved elections in 2003, and quickly formed a tight circle with the new leader and Fiona Hyslop, the latter now in charge of policy. This attracted more resentment from both internal critics, who argued they were cutting Swinney off from the rest of the party, and tabloid ire. 'The only people Swinney listens to are Nicola Sturgeon and Fiona Hyslop,' commented the *Daily Record* a few weeks after the leadership election, 'the two nippiest sweeties in the Parliament. Charm-free and angry, their approach is to berate the Scottish public into voting for the SNP.'[27]

The real strategy was rather subtler. The SNP's NEC had met shortly after the general election to 'lay the groundwork' for the 2003 campaign by reviewing policy, election tactics and headquarters' organisation. In her introduction to a strategy paper circulated that August, Sturgeon wrote of identifying 'what steps must be taken to create an electoral machine capable of winning political leadership in Scotland', highlighting in particular the SNP's 'brand image' and the need for 'a culture of continuous campaigning' in order to take account of 'increasingly sophisticated voting patterns' among the electorate,[28] all of which would become hugely important over the next decade.

On the domestic front, Sturgeon promoted her Tobacco Advertising and Promotion (Scotland) Bill, intended to ban billboard and point-of-sale advertising of tobacco products together with adverts in Scottish (and Scottish editions of UK) newspapers and magazines. This won the support of the British Medical Association, the Royal College of Nursing in Scotland, ASH Scotland and cancer charities. Sturgeon, however, made it clear that she would withdraw her (private) member's bill if Westminster opted to introduce a UK-wide ban.

Sturgeon also developed a reputation as a skilful parliamentarian, winning the Donald Dewar Debater of the Year Award in November 2001 and when, in March 2002, MSPs had to vote on a controversial pay increase, she joined other SNP MSPs in opting to accept the extra cash but donating it to charity. This was obvious fare for the press pack at Holyrood, generally keen to repatriate not only political responsibility from Westminster but cynicism too. The *Mail on Sunday* attacked MSPs like Sturgeon for receiving external income in addition to their parliamentary salaries of £50,000 (she received £7,800 a year for a column in the Glasgow *Evening Times*), while the *Daily Mail* accused her of nepotism, for employing her sister Gillian part-time in her Glasgow office (her mother Joan also worked for Mike Russell).

The *Sunday Express*, meanwhile, accused Sturgeon of 'reneging' on her pledge to vote against the pay rise. A few days before the vote she had said she could not look her 'constituents in the eye and justify an 11 per cent pay rise for already well-paid MSPs, when so many hard working folk struggle to make ends meet', while on the day of the vote she actually abstained on the main motion and instead backed an amendment limiting the pay rise to the level of inflation. 'I am going to give it to charity every month after the tax has been deducted,' she explained, with the first few hundred pounds going to the Maggie's Centre in Glasgow.[29]

In Scotland's largest city, meanwhile, 82,000 council-house tenants were asked (in a referendum) to accept or reject the transfer of their homes to a housing association in return for £4 billion of investment. Despite earlier enthusiasm, Sturgeon – together with fellow Glasgow list MSPs Sandra White and Dorothy-Grace Elder – campaigned for a 'no' vote, leading to a split with local government spokesman Kenny Gibson, who was inclined to support a 'yes'. Glaswegians, meanwhile, backed the transfer.

Rows and splits in the SNP, usually played out in public, remained the order of the day. In May 2002, Elder quit the party, accusing the leadership of 'bullying behaviour' in a 15-page resignation statement that also blamed Swinney and Sturgeon for driving her out of the party, matters having come to a head when her colleagues (led by Sturgeon and Shona Robison) voted by 25-1 to have Elder removed from the Scottish Parliament's Health Committee.[30]

There was also endless speculation over Swinney's future as the SNP continued to languish in the polls. Reports suggested Alex Salmond was planning a comeback to sort everything out, something Sturgeon dismissed as 'ludicrous'. 'John Swinney is the leader and doing an extremely good job,' she added. 'We are better prepared for an election than we have ever been.'[31] Within weeks, however, Swinney had been forced to issue a back-me-or-quit ultimatum to MSPs and activists, bluntly telling them to get their 'tanks' off his lawn. Sturgeon, as ever, was mentioned in reports as a likely successor if the 2003 election did not go to plan.

There was further trouble when, in mid June, details emerged of the SNP's list rankings for top-up parliamentary seats in that all-important election, something then in the gift of associations rather than individual members. Some, such as Mike Russell, Andrew Wilson and George Reid, were all ranked so low as to be virtual goners in political terms, while even Sturgeon came second to Sandra White in Glasgow, although that was sufficient to see her returned even if she failed to win Govan for a second time.

The most high-profile casualty of this process had been Margo MacDonald, who subsequently quit the SNP despite an offer of additional resources from Sturgeon in her capacity as the party's new election director. Despite the Govan connection, there was little affinity between the two. One journalist recalled standing with the duo in a Parliament lift: 'A roaring silence fills the tiny cabin. Sturgeon cracks first, enquiring if Margo is not on her holidays yet? "No," comes the terse reply. An eternity passes before the lift doors open with a grateful ping. "That's the first time she's ever spoken to me," Margo whispers.'[32]

Later matters got personal when someone leaked the fact that MacDonald was suffering from Parkinson's, a clumsy and unpleasant attempt to damage her chances as an independent candidate the following year, something Sturgeon branded 'despicable' while pointing out there was no proof it had actually been a leak.[33]

Meanwhile, Sturgeon was busy attempting to give both herself and the SNP a makeover. In terms of the latter this involved replacing the yellow-and-black colour scheme with pastel shades ahead of the election. 'Yellow and black is fantastic for window posters but research says it looks quite harsh on TV,' explained Sturgeon. 'We'd like to soften it up a bit, but I don't think we'll be getting rid of the yellow altogether.' She also acknowledged that internal polling showed the SNP was perceived 'to be quite a male party' with a 9 per cent gap between support from male and female voters.

And although Sturgeon did not mention herself, the *Mail on Sunday* believed that senior Nationalists such as her and Mike Russell were 'in need of an image boost'.[34] To that end Sturgeon had joined the recently formed Parliament Weightwatchers group, which met in a committee room every Wednesday at the behest of her former sparring partner Margaret Smith. 'I'm not in politics to talk about my weight,' explained Sturgeon rather reluctantly, 'but it's important we show the public we practise what we preach about healthy eating and hopefully encourage others to do the same.' Since January she had been following the so-called 'Carol Vorderman Detox' diet, which involved abstaining from alcohol, wheat, dairy products and caffeine, and had lost about a stone and a half as a result. 'The diet gives you plenty of fruit and vegetables and lots of water,' observed Sturgeon. 'You find you lose your taste for the bad foods after a while. My eating habits changed radically.'[35]

When it came to fashion Sturgeon was similarly reluctant to indulge in what she presumably saw as the frivolous, if not sexist, concerns of the media. 'I don't enjoy clothes shopping and I only go when I need to,' she had told the *Daily Mail* a year earlier. 'In my job it is important to look smart but you are on the go all day so clothes need to be practical, too. There is no way I can wear 6in[ch] heels I have to be able to walk about in them.' And when she did buy clothes, she added, she went 'for High Street shops and d[id]n't buy designer labels'.[36] That, of course, would change over time, but even two years into life as an MSP Sturgeon was clearly conscious it might be something she had to tackle. When a spoof correspondent called 'Dr Rosemary Hannay' emailed offering 'weekly reports' on how she was 'coming across on TV', Sturgeon replied chirpily: 'Weekly reports would be great and I await them with trepidation!!' In another exchange she wrote, 'I do appreciate objective comments but given the nature of yours, I fear that I may be beyond help in your eyes. In some respects I think we may just have very different tastes – for example, some of the people that you have held up to me as screen role models are people that I think look ghastly on TV . . . before I agree to take advice from your hairdresser, perhaps I should ask to see a photograph of you!!!'[37]

Sturgeon continued to holiday in France, although she was also known to be keen on the Western Isles. She was, of course, a political animal to her fingertips and, in the nine months leading up to the next Scottish Parliament elections, Sturgeon focused relentlessly on the politics of health, railing against the use of PFI for modernising hospitals, campaigning to suspend the planned closure of Stobhill and the Victoria Infirmary in Glasgow (Sturgeon's parliamentary bid was only narrowly defeated), promising nurses an 11 per cent pay rise, opposing private sector involvement in healthcare and relentlessly questioning the Scottish Executive's record on hospital staffing and cancelled operations.

Sturgeon's jousts with Health Minister Susan Deacon had often been memorable while Deacon's successor, Malcolm Chisholm, at first 'used a patronising and then a relaxed style to get the better of [Sturgeon's] serious, brittle approach'.[38] For her this approach paid dividends: she could claim a degree of credit for keeping up the political pressure that resulted in the introduction of free personal care for the elderly, while she also worked hard to expose 'deferred' (in other words hidden) hospital waiting lists, something the Executive was forced to end.

By the time delegates met for the September 2002 SNP conference, the last before the election, a new colour scheme (heather) was in place and the party was in a better place than it had been earlier that year. As campaign co-ordinator, Sturgeon told journalists that the party intended to 're-claim the arguments for independence'. 'In 1999 we allowed Labour to take control of the issue of independence,' she explained. 'This time we want to debate the issue on our terms. We want Labour and the other Unionist parties to explain what they think is wrong with Scots that we can't run our own affairs.'[39]

And by January 2003, with opinion polls being a little kinder to the Nationalists, Sturgeon was even more upbeat, arguing that, while the 1999 election had (understandably) been about devolution, the one to be held in May would focus more on independence. 'This is the first election we will be able to say, is the parliament doing what we want it to?' Sturgeon told the *Guardian*, 'Does it have the powers it needs?'[40] At this stage, however, SNP campaigning often remained crudely negative. One leaflet, showing the First Minister Jack McConnell being stubbed out in an ashtray, attempted to play on New Year resolutions, breaking old habits and therefore, as Sturgeon argued, 'tapping into the mood of the public at this time of year'.[41]

Early 2003 was also dominated by the looming war against Iraq, a controversy that was to dominate the next few years in UK politics and arguably aid the SNP's growth ahead of not the 2003 election, but the one after that. Sturgeon was almost instinctively opposed to the conflict and used her *Evening Times* column to set out her tightly argued reasoning. She rejected the argument made by some that a devolved parliament had no place debating foreign affairs ('At times of international crisis, the Scottish Parliament doesn't just have the right to be heard – it has an obligation to be so') and made it clear she was no 'apologist' for Saddam Hussein ('a murderous dictator that the world would be better off without') while flagging up inconsistencies (North Korea had expelled weapons inspectors while Hussein had let them in) and maintaining that any action against Iraq 'must be taken in accordance with international law'. She continued: 'The alternative is to allow the US to wage war at will just because it can. Might becomes right and principle, consistency and the rule of law go out the window. That's not the kind of world I want to live in. A war against Iraq might get rid of Saddam Hussein but who knows who would be installed in his place. It's not that long ago, after all, that Saddam himself was, in the eyes of the US, a good guy who should be plied with arms. What a war in Iraq will not do is bring about peace in the Middle East or end the injustices that feed resentment and breed terrorists. That will only happen when the UN resolutions demanding justice for Palestinians are enforced just as resolutely as those demanding the disarmament of Iraq.'[42]

The passion was obvious, while Sturgeon's position also harked back to an interest in international affairs first shown as a student in Glasgow, a city that played host to an 80,000-strong march against a potential war in Iraq in the middle of February. 'I know there are times when leaders have to stand up to public opinion and do what they believe to be right,' she wrote in another column. 'But there are other qualities of leadership just as important as the ability to take tough and unpopular decisions – the insight to know when you're wrong and the guts to admit it.' The case for war, argued Sturgeon, had 'not been proved'. She continued, 'We all face a choice right now beyond the immediacy of what happens in Iraq. We must decide what kind of world we want to live in. Is it one based on the rule of law and collective security, or one where might is right and the US, backed by the UK, gets to do what it wants just because it can? Six million people made that choice on Saturday. For all our sakes, we can only hope Blair was listening.'[43]

Sturgeon also revealed a personal facet to her concern. 'One of my cousins is in Kuwait with the Army,' she wrote in the *Evening Times*, 'so for me, like so many others, there is a real reason to be apprehensive about what lies ahead.'[44]

Foreign affairs, however, was not the SNP's strong point and, under pressure from an embattled Labour Party, it was compelled to spell out a clearer policy beyond outright opposition to war. Speaking at a debate in Glasgow's Royal Concert Hall, Sturgeon said her party would only contemplate a second United Nations resolution if it believed it to be based on evidence and if it specifically mandated war. Swinney had used his conference speech following the events of 11 September to take an ostentatiously pro-US stance, while now the SNP had legitimate concerns that war in Iraq might make it more difficult to prise moderate Arab opinion away from Islamic fundamentalists, on which, of course, it and Sturgeon had a point.

But while war was hell, it was also good politics for, unlike in 1999 when Alex Salmond's position on Kosovo was clearly at odds with Scottish public opinion, this time the SNP was confident it had made the right (as well as the most principled) call. With an election approaching, it hoped that popular mobilisation against Labour's actions would boost their support, as did the Liberal Democrats across the UK. In Govan anti-war feeling was also running high in the Muslim community, which cannot have escaped the SNP candidate's attention.

In the run-up to polling day, the SNP went for Labour,

determined to expose what Sturgeon melodramatically called 'the sleaze at the heart of Jack McConnell's Labour Party',[45] accusing it of breaking the law when the Electoral Commission upheld three complaints about unregistered donations, while also hinting at court action over Chancellor Gordon Brown's decision to deliver his Budget statement during the formal campaign (it had been delayed from March due to events in Iraq).

The 'I' word (independence), however, was still conspicuous by its absence. Although at the SNP's spring conference Sturgeon had promised to put it 'at the heart of our campaign', when senior Nationalists unveiled several campaign posters in March it was nowhere to be seen, with Sturgeon saying the 'dominant issue of the Scottish general election' would actually be 'Labour's record on public services',[46] suggesting there still existed doubts about overdoing it when it came to the party's *raison d'être*.

Nevertheless, as a consequence of Swinney's internal reforms and professionalisation of the party, the SNP was confident it was better equipped to fight this election than it had been in 1999. This time there would be no eleventh-hour announcements like those on Kosovo and the 'Penny for Scotland', and this time most manifesto pledges had been fully costed and trouble-proofed to avoid embarrassing incidents at press conferences. And although Swinney privately insisted victory was possible, more realistic Nationalists suggested an SNP group of more than 40 and a Labour tally of less than 50.

Leaving the Scottish Parliament was Kay Ullrich, whom Sturgeon often referred to as her 'mentor', signing her leaving present 'from one Dreghorn girl to another' and expressing disbelief that 16 years had passed since offering to help with her campaign in Ayrshire. Even more significant in personal terms was Sturgeon being 'thrown into a working relationship' with Peter Murrell, her campaign director. Only after the election, however, did they both realise 'there might be something else'.[47]

'This is the most sophisticated voter turn-out effort any

Scottish party has ever deployed,' said Sturgeon as she unveiled the then novel plans to email and text swing voters. 'We will engage directly with voters in key seats as never before.'[48] Labour, however, basically re-ran its 'divorce is an expensive business' campaign from four years previously, warning voters of the 'costs of divorce' in a hard-hitting election broadcast. Once again, given the SNP's failure to articulate what it saw as the consequences of independence, Labour plugged the gap, and not in a positive way.

In Govan, meanwhile, Sturgeon must have been conscious that a win – on her third attempt – was important for her political credibility, and perhaps even her leadership ambitions should Swinney stand aside. But again she was disappointed:

Labour	Gordon Jackson	7,834
SNP	Nicola Sturgeon	6,599
Scottish Socialist Party	Jimmy Scott	2,369
Conservative	Faisal Butt	1,878
Liberal Democrat	Paul Graham	1,807

Gordon Jackson had held on (despite a modest 0.41 per cent swing to the SNP), with a majority of 1,235, despite having taken a well-publicised holiday in Spain halfway through the campaign. While Labour's majority was down, so was Sturgeon's share of the vote, by five points to 31 per cent.

Sturgeon was resolute but rather ungracious in conceding defeat. 'I won't keep you for long,' she told her supporters. 'I know Gordon Jackson has court in the morning. This is a great result for the SNP. We have reduced Labour's majority. I think this might be the last time Gordon Jackson goes on holiday during the campaign. Govan will be ours.'[49] Later she told this author there was nothing 'more soul destroying' than putting 'your heart and soul into something and not quite pull[ing] it off'.[50]

Sturgeon, once again, was re-elected via the Glasgow list, but, once again, her failure to take Govan spoke to deeper problems for the SNP in the West of Scotland and, indeed, nationally. Instead of winning 40-plus MSPs, it had secured just 27, losing ground to the surprisingly buoyant Scottish Socialist and Green parties, both of whom had focused on the regional list vote to increase their support and representation. Although bad overall, there was a chink of light in that for the first time the SNP had started making inroads into urban Labour seats – Sturgeon's friend Shona Robison, for example, narrowly gained Dundee East – something that would be a feature of future Holyrood elections.

But, inevitably, the outcome increased the pressure on John Swinney, who had now presided over two unremarkable election results, this one having been an electoral rejection of him as First Minister. Instead, Jack McConnell formed another coalition Scottish Executive with the Liberal Democrats and Swinney had a reshuffle in order to try and keep his beleaguered team on their toes. Sturgeon switched from health to justice, a comfortable move given her legal background, while Shona Robison took over as health spokeswoman.

In July it fell to Sturgeon to encourage her colleagues to give £3,000 from their salaries to boost party coffers, arguing that 'as a matter of principle' representatives of the party ought to contribute 'to get more of us elected and achieve our aim of an independent Scotland',[51] but such a demand obviously caused resentment (in the event only Sturgeon and a few others paid the £250-a-month levy). Then, in late July, a little-known SNP activist called Bill Wilson announced he would be standing as a 'grassroots' candidate against Swinney at the September conference.

Despite suspicions at the time that her defence of the party leader was not as high profile as it might have been, Sturgeon responded to Wilson's intervention at length in an article for the *Sunday Herald*, praising him as someone of 'ability' if mistaken in his quixotic bid for the SNP leadership. On 27 September, she predicted, Swinney would be re-elected, but whether the party emerged 'from the contest as a stronger or weaker force in Scottish politics will depend entirely on the nature of the debate that we engage in over the next two months'. She continued, 'If we turn inwards to fight old battles, we will have no-one but ourselves to blame should the public doubt our ability to govern. But if we grasp the opportunity to have a genuine debate about the future of our party and the country we aspire to lead, we might yet take a decisive step forward.' She rejected claims that the party grassroots had been 'shorn of influence' (Wilson's 'very candidacy belies this argument') and also the charge that the SNP was 'New Labour in the making'. 'Yes, we have become more professional in our operations and not before time. There is nothing wrong with striving to be at the cutting edge of modern campaigning techniques, or to be better than our opponents at showcasing our message. But professionalism should be taken for granted, not celebrated as an end in itself. One lesson we should learn from New Labour is that trying to replace the substance of politics with spin no longer washes with a public that sees straight through it. Our values, our principles, our policies and our vision for Scotland are what matter.'

Sturgeon acknowledged that an 'unintended consequence' of the party's 'necessary and successful focus' on establishing 'strong economic credentials' was a perception that the SNP was 'slightly adrift' from its natural centre-left territory. This, however, had 'no basis in reality', and she went on to define her political philosophy: 'Our kind of Scotland is one where government is neither the enemy of the people nor the easy answer to every problem, but a progressive force for change. It is a Scotland where wealth creation is not merely an end in itself but a means to equality and social justice and is tempered always by the need to protect our environment for future generations. And on the world stage, our kind of Scotland would be a voice for peace, justice and human rights rather than narrow self-interest.'

Furthermore, Sturgeon argued that the idea independence had been put on the back burner was something 'the SNP needs to get over'. 'Independence is at the heart of what the SNP is and always will be about. It is what made me join when I was 16 years old and it is why I am still a member today. The referendum policy does not dilute our commitment to independence – it is simply the route by which we get there. But arguments about how we get to independence are academic until we persuade people why Scotland should be independent.' Doing that, she added, would not happen 'by arguing with each other about whose commitment to the cause is purest'. Sturgeon also dwelled on the European dimension with elections to the Brussels (and Strasbourg) parliament due the following year. The SNP, she said, had to 'resist the temptation to flirt with Euroscepticism', Scotland's problem being not Europe but its 'lack of status' in the EU, whose enlargement demonstrated 'the sheer normality of independence in Europe for small nations'. 'As Europe develops as a confederation of small states, do we in Scotland really want to be left on the sidelines? Because if enlargement demonstrates the normality of independence in Europe, the draft EU constitution is testament to its necessity. Under the new constitution it is Member States that matter. Member States confer powers on EU institutions and they are the collective decision-makers on policy. Regions and regional parliaments – and that's what Scotland and the Scottish parliament are in the eyes of Europe – are second-class citizens. Geography and the realities of the global economy mean that Europe's influence over Scotland is a fact of life, whether we are in or out, a Member State or just a region. But it is only when Scotland becomes an independent Member State that influence will become a two-way street.'[52]

Sturgeon's article was a powerful defence of the SNP's long-standing slogan 'independence in Europe' and could even be interpreted as a compelling personal manifesto for the leadership should Swinney fall on his sword, although obviously – at this point – it was intended to shore him up.

Her defence of her party's economic stance, however, was less convincing; with the small 'c' conservative Swinney generally in thrall to Salmondite principles of low Corporation Tax and Brownite fiscal prudence, Sturgeon glided over the obvious tensions between Laffer Curve economics and the party's more progressive goals. It was not clear how cutting corporate taxation, with a consequentially lower tax take, would provide a 'means to equality and social justice'.

Economics, generally speaking, did not seem to be a strong point. In a column for the *Evening Times* a few months earlier, Sturgeon had urged those in power to stop 'spending time and money simply confirming how bad things are in parts of Glasgow' and instead concentrate 'on doing something about it'. Yet her proposed solution was the fairly orthodox one of equipping Glaswegians 'with the training and skills to take up job opportunities',[53] which, of course, was a policy any party from left or right could have signed up to.

Sturgeon, meanwhile, supported much of the Scottish Executive's attempts to tackle anti-social behaviour but otherwise took a generally liberal line as SNP justice spokeswoman, criticising the First Minister for instructing police officers to continue arresting offenders for possession of cannabis (she confessed to 'doubts' about legalising it[54]), while she stood up to members of her own party who urged caution when it came to civil partnerships (and their extension to heterosexual couples). 'Marriage has and always will have a special place in our society,' she said in a speech at the 2003 SNP conference, 'but you don't value marriage by devaluing other forms of relationship.'[55] Scotland's Dungavel detention centre, meanwhile, was denounced as 'inhumane' (Sturgeon investigated an alternative 'open hostel' model in Brussels),[56] and the UK Asylum and Immigration Bill as 'odious and Draconian'.[57]

A story that dominated the domestic news agenda during April and May 2004, meanwhile, ensured Sturgeon a high profile. Justice Minister Cathy Jamieson came under sustained pressure when it emerged the private security firm Reliance had committed a string of blunders including the mistaken release of a convicted killer. Sturgeon not only blamed the decision to privatise the prisoner escort service but also called on Jamieson to resign. She also attacked Colin Boyd, the Lord Advocate, over plans for a UK Supreme Court, arguing that sending Scottish civil cases to the House of Lords (and now a separate court) 'was a practice set up to deal with the constitutional landscape of the eighteenth century' and therefore had 'no place in a modern legal system'.[58]

And although exceeding her brief, Sturgeon also argued that taxpayers should not 'subsidise the private decisions taken by individual parents' in relation to private education,[59] a view shared by the Scottish Socialist Party and some Labour MSPs who wanted to use legislation to compel independent schools to demonstrate a benefit to society as a whole in order to justify their charitable status (and resulting tax breaks). Sturgeon was also an early advocate of banning smoking in public places, believing the 'overwhelming' public health argument to outweigh any erosion of civil liberties.[60]

At a special conference in Aberdeen on 23 April 2004, meanwhile, John Swinney won a significant victory in modernising the SNP, winning backing for positive discrimination towards women in the selection of election candidates, a slimmed-down NEC and the appointment of a new business convener, in effect an unelected party chairman. A vote on the first, positive discrimination, had looked in doubt due to obvious hostility from the conference floor, but a rousing speech from Sturgeon turned the tide. 'We are not a minority,' she told delegates. 'We form the majority of the Scottish population. If we can't get it right for the majority, what chance do we have for getting it right for the minorities we want to see represented in our parliament?'[61]

In the course of the first Scottish Parliament and the year since the second election, Sturgeon had clearly matured and grown as a politician, even losing some of the hard edge associated with her public persona on first being elected. She was also much cooler under pressure. Ian Duncan, later a Conservative MEP but then a policy adviser to the Scottish Refugee Council, recalled seeing Sturgeon at a briefing in Glasgow City Chambers at some point in 2004, well attended by Labour politicians, local and national. 'No Labour MP spoke to Nicola or made any attempt to engage with her whatever,' recalled Duncan. 'They were more interested in grazing their way through the buffet lunch and talking amongst themselves.

Nicola retained her poise throughout; it was an impressively calm performance.'[62]

Speaking to this author in October 2003, Sturgeon had even entertained thoughts of taking a break from politics and returning to the law. 'It's always healthy I think to have an idea of what else you could and would want to do,' she said. 'I don't think any politician should get into the way of only having one possible option in their lives and I would never want to be in that position so I would never ever rule out going back to law.'[63]

Developments in Sturgeon's private life may have contributed to her more relaxed demeanour. As the *Sun* reported on 24 April 2004, she had 'found love' with SNP chief executive Peter Murrell, six years her senior. According to the report, romance had 'blossomed' at the previous autumn's party conference in Inverness. Still reluctant to speak about such things, all Sturgeon managed in terms of a response was curt and brief: 'Those things are private.'[64] 'Neither of us were keen to shout it from the rooftops too soon, until we had a better understanding of where it was going,' she explained later. 'There was a bit of awkwardness around that. But the longer it went on, the more people started guessing . . . a lot of people had put two and two together and guessed. So at that conference it became public.'[65]

By this point, elections to the European Parliament were less than two months away, and they had long become framed as a crucial, most likely the final, test for Swinney's leadership, a perception he fuelled by boldly predicting that the SNP would come ahead of Labour in terms of vote share. Few expected him to pass, and the journalist Iain Macwhirter judged Sturgeon 'the most likely successor if Swinney falls off his bike'. 'She is not a figure who inspires great public warmth but would do the job well enough,' he added. 'Nicola is quick on her feet, lacks any ideological baggage and has real determination – unlike the current deputy leader Roseanna Cunningham.' She, concluded Macwhirter, had once been 'the pin-up of social democratic nationalists' but had 'somehow lost her way, and her humour'.[66] *Holyrood* magazine had also tipped Sturgeon as likely to have 'the most positive impact on voters provided she had a sympathetic makeover'.[67]

Ahead of polling day Sturgeon reiterated her pro-European credentials in her *Evening Times* column, while deploying subtly Eurosceptic language, supporting the new European Constitution but rejecting further integrationist moves and advocating immediate withdrawal from the Common Fisheries Policy. From a justice perspective, she speculated, few Scots might be aware of 'the creeping EU influence in our civil and criminal legal systems' and 'immense' pressure for 'harmonisation of our criminal laws and legal systems' as was 'increasingly' the case when it came to health and education. 'When the EU passes a law in one of these areas,' she added, 'the Scottish Parliament has no choice but to implement it.' But, on balance, Sturgeon believed the EU to be 'a positive influence'. 'Even people who disagree', she concluded pragmatically, 'should recognise that ignoring it will not make it go away.'[68]

Ignoring speculation about Swinney's leadership would not make that go away either. On 15 June the SNP polled just 19.5 per cent of the Scottish vote in the European elections and, although it retained two MEPs, Labour finished well ahead and, therefore, the party leader looked increasingly vulnerable. On 22 June, following much public criticism from colleagues past and present, Swinney bowed to the inevitable and announced his resignation. Roseanna Cunningham, his deputy, announced her candidacy, as did Sturgeon two days later with Kenny MacAskill as her running mate. Alex Salmond, meanwhile, famously declared, 'If nominated, I would decline. If drafted, I will defer and, if elected, I will resign.' When asked, he said he wanted Sturgeon to win.

Interviewed in October 2003, Sturgeon said she got frustrated at questions about her leadership ambitions, though at the same time she was franker than most in refusing to deny they existed. 'Of course I wouldn't rule myself out,' she told this author. 'If there was a vacancy in a few years' time then no, of course I wouldn't rule myself out but equally, you know, I wouldn't rule myself in either because it is so hypothetical, I don't anticipate it happening in the foreseeable future so I would be pretty silly to spend a lot of time, any of my time in fact you know worrying about what might or might not happen.[69]

Within less than a year, however, events had turned such speculation from hypothetical into a political reality. But before announcing her candidacy there was the question of Sturgeon's friendship with Roseanna Cunningham. Although the two (despite a big age gap) had been extremely close from the mid to late 1990s their friendship had noticeably cooled in recent years, with Sturgeon unimpressed, like many others, with Cunningham's performance as deputy leader since 2000. Indeed, 'Republican Rose' was widely perceived as lazy (although she had also had to contend with the slow decline and death of her mother) and, given Sturgeon's Stakhanovite work rate, that was bound to leave a bad impression. The *Daily Record* reported that Sturgeon even attempted to reach a deal with Cunningham to clear her path for the leadership but the Perth MSP had refused, remaining loyal to Swinney and insisting there was no vacancy.[70]

Sturgeon's political proximity to Swinney's leadership, which made her de facto deputy leader, had also led to friction with Cunningham, as had Sturgeon's much higher profile over the past three years. 'Nicola had actually done the hard graft in terms of chairing the last few election campaigns,' recalled a colleague. 'In that sense, she was probably in a stronger position, although publicly the leadership was seen in terms of age.'[71] In other words, the 19-years-older Cunningham was naturally perceived as the senior candidate. Sturgeon's interest, however, worsened already cool relations. 'The 2004 leadership race did it with her and Roseanna,' observed one mutual friend bluntly,[72] while another recalled the split being 'really big'. 'Roseanna felt very betrayed,' she recalled. 'Nicola was very young, and sometimes you grow out of friendships, but they were still very close.'[73]

There was much, however, counting against Sturgeon's candidacy. Still seen by some as too young (although at 33 she was only two years younger than Salmond was in 1990), there was also an argument that, as director of most recent election campaigns, she carried a share of the blame for the SNP's poor performance, not to forget her failure (three times) to win Govan despite favourable circumstances. One journalist, meanwhile, questioned her intellectual credentials, observing (a tad unfairly) that she had shown 'little thought independent of Alex Salmond or John Swinney'.[74]

Initially Sturgeon had been coy ('I am talking to people and I will make a decision when I am ready') but appearing on STV's *Politics Now* on 24 June she confirmed her intention to run.[75] Under party rules, she needed 100 signatures to do so, two of which came from her mother Joan and Kay Ullrich, seated at the table in the Dreghorn house where she had first joined the party 18 years before. Sturgeon pledged to re-establish the SNP as 'a party of social democracy', 'combining a strategy for economic success with a much stronger commitment to tackling inequality and promoting social justice',[76] something that would dominate Nationalist strategy over the next decade, particularly during the independence referendum. And, batting aside predictable questions about her association with the leadership and successive failures in Govan, Sturgeon said simply, 'I have learnt what the SNP does well and what it needs to do differently or better.'[77] Her leadership slogan was 'Vision/Passion/Ideas'.

Sturgeon also claimed, less convincingly, that she and Cunningham were 'the best of mates' and hoped to remain so after the contest, although many interpreted Sturgeon's line about offering 'a new generation of leadership' as a dig at her much older rival.[78] For her part, Cunningham told *Scotland on Sunday* that she and Sturgeon were 'very different people'. 'We've been friends for a very long time,' she said and, although she was not saying Nicola would not be good in a leadership role, she reckoned the SNP needed a leader with 'perhaps a more sparky and outgoing personality; somebody with the kind of history and background; somebody that can speak right across the party'.[79] The obvious implication was that that someone was not called Nicola Sturgeon.

On 27 June *The Sunday Times* published a survey showing

that most constituency associations agreed, with 19 saying most of their members would support Cunningham, six Alex Neil (who would later withdraw), five Sturgeon and only one for Mike Russell, who despite no longer being an MSP was widely expected to stand. A majority of MSPs (at least those willing to say) also backed Cunningham. Sturgeon, meanwhile, had met Sir Sean Connery at Edinburgh's New Club, a courtesy he had not extended to any other candidate. The media, of course, played up the Sturgeon/Cunningham dimension, one newspaper even carrying the arguably sexist headline 'CATFIGHT'.

There was speculation that Sturgeon, initially perceived as the front-runner, was suffering a backlash after briefing against Swinney prior to his resignation. The outgoing leader told activists at a meeting in Stirling that he had always 'put the party's interests ahead' of his own, something that had 'not been the case with all of my colleagues', which again was interpreted as a dig at the woman who had been his leadership campaign manager in 2000.[80] The SNP also came under pressure to put its chief executive, Peter Murrell, on paid leave to avoid any potential conflict of interest, his relationship with Sturgeon by now being public knowledge.

In her *Evening Times* column, Sturgeon called the decision to stand the 'biggest' of her life, although she also noted that some had cautioned her *against* contesting the leadership, taking the view that 'now was not the best time to become leader of the SNP and that, with time on my side, I should wait until the party has recovered from the electoral difficulties it has experienced over the past few years'. But she believed the time had come for a 'different style of leadership' from the party, her goal being to 'inspire Scotland out of its disenchantment with politics'. She said, '[T]he SNP must stop acting in a way that only entrenches Scotland's political depression. That means we must stop sniping on the sidelines, talking all the time about what is wrong with Scotland. Much better to talk our country up, focus on its strengths and ask people to imagine how much better off we could all be if we have a bit more faith in ourselves . . . [it] is a positive, confident approach that I believe will enable us to turn the disappointment with devolution into a demand for change.'[81] This was prescient, for the SNP's decisive switch from (predominantly) negative campaigning to a more positive pitch would be a key part of the transformation in the party's electoral fortunes over the next few years.

In early July, meanwhile, Sturgeon unveiled her 12-strong campaign team, which included Dundee East MSP Shona Robison as campaign manager, MSP Richard Lochhead and MP Angus Robertson advising on policy and strategy, while Aberdeen councillor Kevin Stewart (later an MSP) was appointed her regional organiser for the north-east of Scotland. Stewart described Sturgeon as 'one of the best TV performers in Scottish politics' while Angus Robertson gushed that she had the 'commitment, drive, energy and political judgment' required of a party leader.[82] Sturgeon's campaign flyer said simply: 'Nicola Sturgeon for National Convener. A new generation of leadership.'

Sturgeon then made efforts to soften her image, talking up the prospect of her combining leadership with motherhood ('maybe it's what Scotland needs'[83]), and launching a manifesto positively brimming with policy ideas to combat criticism that she was an ideas-free zone: overhauling the benefits system, increasing pensions, reforming the curriculum and introducing more local decision-making into the Scottish NHS. She also signalled a change of tack on Europe, moving away from an emphasis on fishing and towards a more general debate about the wider implications of the recent EU constitution (which the SNP then opposed).

The pitch was essentially a Salmondite gradualist one, moving towards independence having secured power in the Scottish Parliament and then holding a referendum. Indeed, the resemblance was noted, particularly when Sturgeon hinted at a cut in business taxation to encourage enterprise (although she also said she favoured 'progressive taxation'). Discipline was also emphasised ('[I]t will be my job to bring cohesion and a sense of direction to the Scottish parliamentary group'), as was a stronger line on independence, including the impractical suggestion that SNP MSPs should spend a week each month concentrating on that issue in their constituencies.

'Unless there is a desire for independence,' explained Sturgeon, 'or at least a desire to move closer to independence as there was in the 1990s, the SNP will not move forward fast enough. Desire for change is the fuel in our engine. And for the last five years, the SNP has been running on empty in that regard.' She said a Sturgeon-led SNP would focus on the three 'big challenges' facing Scotland: inequality, economic under-performance and a lack of national confidence. Journalists at the Glasgow launch were impressed by her lighter style, joking that although her manifesto did not mention 'fish' the 'name Sturgeon' was 'every-where'. There was also a nod to her alter ego. Pointing reporters towards the refreshments, Sturgeon quipped, 'Help yourself to some sweeties. Like me, they're not nippy.'[84]

Then, on 15 July 2004, everything changed, changed utterly. After nearly four years of speculation, all the more intense in the past few weeks, Alex Salmond declared his intention to contest the SNP leadership for the second time in 14 years. In an impressive scoop for the *Herald* newspaper, it emerged that Nicola Sturgeon was to step aside and stand as his running mate. 'Champany Inn in Linlithgow will now be etched in the annals of SNP history', the newspaper observed, 'as the place where Alex Salmond persuaded Nicola Sturgeon to step aside and let the king return from across the water.'[85]

Sturgeon recalled the conversation thus: 'He [Salmond] told me straight what he was considering, why he was considering it, and what he thought we should do together as a team, but he said to me very very frankly that if I didn't want to do that and [if] I wanted to [continue] as [a candidate for] leader then that was fine, he would perfectly happily back me in doing that . . . he gave me a veto on it. I told him I wanted to take some time to think about it and I'm not sure he wasn't a bit surprised at that.' Surprised but also, as Salmond recalled later, full of respect: 'I think at the time she thought I was put out. I wasn't. I was impressed.'[86]

'I suppose what I felt most was I've put myself forward for

leader of the party,' Sturgeon recalled of the 24 hours she took to reflect on his proposition, 'What's it going to say about me and my seriousness in doing that if a few days later . . . I say no no this other person is far better able than me?' But, on taking a step back, she thought, 'Well, what do I think is best for the SNP? And there was no way that I could come to any conclusion other than Alex as leader with me if the party elects me as deputy leader I think is a pretty good thing.'

Obviously, as John Swinney recalled of the period, 'Nicola was the one having to make the biggest sacrifice in all of that'.[87] That she had, but on agreeing there had also been a calculation: if she had rejected Salmond's offer and lost, or even if she had won but failed to win the 2007 election, then her career within the SNP would have been if not over then severely damaged. Surely better to (virtually) guarantee election as deputy leader, serve as an old political master's apprentice and shore up her position within the party before standing again at some point in the future. 'My chances of succeeding Alex', she admitted with typical frankness, 'depend entirely on how I do as deputy leader.'[88] It was, as Sturgeon must have realised on reflection, a no brainer.

And losing to Cunningham was a very real prospect, not just because of the mood within the party but due to the general perception of Sturgeon – i.e. capable but a little aloof and probably not quite ready for leadership. Salmond certainly thought this was a realistic prospect, despite a recent fumbling performance from Cunningham on an edition of *Question Time*, and indeed it was almost certainly the decisive factor in his decision to stand. As he put it in 2009, '[T]hings weren't developing as I'd hoped.'[89] One MSP called it the 'ABR strategy – Anyone But Roseanna'.[90]

'What was he thinking in 2004?' reflected a source close to Salmond. 'That Nicola wasn't going to win, Mike Russell wasn't in a great place and I think Alex was genuinely reluctant. The party's finances were also in disarray. He was genuinely worried about what might happen, that the party might implode.'[91] Usefully, and although understandably bruised at having become a casualty of the Champany Inn agreement,

Kenny MacAskill bowed out of the deputy leadership race (having been asked to make way for Sturgeon) and backed what appeared to be the winning option. 'My ambition is for the future of the SNP and for the future of Scotland,' he explained. 'I believe that the Salmond/Sturgeon team is the best to unite the party and take the SNP forward.'[92] A joint ticket was a novelty for the SNP, but also a successful one.

Salmond, not always the most conciliatory figure, also did his best to build bridges with foes past, present and potentially future. 'If Nicola and I win then we are both agreed that everyone in the Scottish National Party starts from day one,' he said. 'There's no grudges, grievances, no prior record. Everybody starts with a clean slate and we will use all the talents available.'[93]

At the same time, and as agreed explicitly between Salmond and Sturgeon, the latter would undoubtedly be 'running the show' at Holyrood (to which the Scottish Parliament would soon move). 'I made it clear to him that if I'm going to lead in the Scottish parliament, I'm in charge there,' she explained. 'Alex and I will have a close working relationship, as we have had for some years, but I'm in charge.' Such an arrangement, she was clear, would 'fundamentally change the job' of being deputy SNP leader,[94] although it was perfectly possible that Salmond could win and she could lose.

Although Mike Russell and Cunningham realised the inevitability of defeat, their bruised egos injected an even more personal element into the campaign, with the former accusing Salmond of trying to run the party like an 'absentee laird',[95] and Christine Grahame, a candidate for the deputy leadership, claiming that Sturgeon would be taunted as 'Deputy Dawg' were she to take charge in her leader's absence.[96] Filling in for Salmond at one hustings meeting in Edinburgh, Sturgeon was unfazed, saying, 'let us see who comes out on top' in a contest between her and the First Minister. 'There is nothing about Jack McConnell that fazes me.'[97] Cunningham, meanwhile, claimed to be 'non-plussed' by her friend's decision. 'I think she has made a bad decision and I fear she will be the biggest loser – and that's said as a friend.'[98]

The campaign took many unconventional turns. After a few weeks of campaigning Alex Neil, who had withdrawn from the leadership race, surprised everyone by backing Salmond for leader but Christine Grahame for deputy. Meanwhile Ian Blackford, a former party treasurer and not exactly a bosom buddy of the former and future SNP leader, supported Sturgeon as deputy leader (he had served on her short-lived leadership campaign team) but refused to back Salmond for the top job. It underlined that, however warm the words, the new leader and his deputy faced a tough job in pulling together such a fractured party.

The result, when it came, was as unsurprising as it was decisive, with Salmond attracting 75.8 per cent of the 4,952 votes cast, more than 60 per cent of the party membership under the one-member-one-vote reform initiated by Swinney, while Sturgeon took 53 per cent of the vote in the deputy leadership contest, a more convincing victory than many had expected. 'My job in the Scottish Parliament is clear,' she said after the result. 'It is to shake up the SNP so that we can ship out Labour.'[99] That would be no easy task, with just 27 MSPs and a party leader who was not even a member of the Parliament he wished to lead.

The joint leadership at least served as proof that the SNP was not, as so often claimed, a one-man band called Alex Salmond, while Sturgeon's self-sacrifice in standing aside helped neutralise perceptions of her as ruthlessly ambitious. Inevitably, the leadership election later gave rise to what-if speculation. 'You'll read things that say Roseanna would have won; you'll read things that say I would have won' was Sturgeon's response when she was Health Secretary. 'Who knows? We'll never know now. I'm confident . . . if I had stayed in the race I would have triumphed.'[100]

The academic assessment in a 2012 study of the SNP's membership was less optimistic. 'It is impossible to determine whether Sturgeon would have defeated Cunningham and Russell had Salmond not intervened,' judged James Mitchell et al., 'though it can be assumed that she would not have won as much support as Salmond.' But importantly, as Mitchell added, based on his interviews with senior Nationalists, her standing was 'enhanced considerably during this period' and, as a consequence, in the view of many 'she became the clear favourite to succeed Salmond'.[101] Similarly, the journalist Colin Mackay later noted the irony that Swinney's leadership and its reforms had not only paved the way for Salmond's second stint as leader but also ensured that Sturgeon had 'emerged as his natural successor'.[102]

Chapter 6

'Project Nicola'

Towards the end of the campaign to succeed John Swinney as national convener of the SNP, Nicola Sturgeon had observed that a dual leadership would 'fundamentally change the job' of being deputy SNP leader.[1] It would also fundamentally change the deputy leader herself. Suddenly thrust into the spotlight as the de facto leader of the opposition at Holyrood, Sturgeon almost immediately demonstrated a growing willingness to play the political game and remove her rougher edges, politically, aesthetically and socially. One journalist referred to it as 'Project Nicola'.[2]

She faced Jack McConnell at First Minister's Question Time (FMQs) just days after her election, ripping into him over hospital closures. McConnell had called on MSPs to raise their game to match their gleaming new surroundings at the foot of the Royal Mile, and Sturgeon responded by telling him to raise his, saying health boards were taking decisions in a 'totally piecemeal manner' with local hospitals being downgraded or closed. She called for a moratorium while McConnell said he looked forward to convincing the new SNP deputy leader and her colleagues that Labour too had 'ambition for Scotland'.[3]

The Scottish Parliament's move from temporary accommodation on the Mound to Holyrood neatly underlined the change in SNP leadership and helped give the party a new lease of life. This exchange also indicated an important shift in tone, with Sturgeon making it clear she would not oppose for opposition's sake. As Magnus Linklater put it in *The Times*, the new deputy leader had made 'a useful point, while at the same time avoiding the strident point-scoring that has so frequently marked these exchanges in the past. At least as significant was the almost respectful silence with which her questions were greeted on the Labour benches.'[4]

As the journalist Colin Mackay later observed, Sturgeon 'continued to shine, turning in some of the best opposition performances at First Minister's Questions . . . the most consistent parliamentary performer since the start of devolution'. And although FMQs was not important in terms of public perceptions, it was when it came to media judgments formed within the Holyrood bubble so, by performing consistently well in that context, she demonstrated 'just how much she had grown as a politician'.[5] Jousting with McConnell helped cement Sturgeon's reputation as a formidable operator, a reputation that remained with her.

Sturgeon also moved swiftly to try to restore discipline. Everyone in the party, she later reflected, was 'thoroughly sick of the infighting' and realised the SNP 'would only go in one direction' if it persisted.[6] She made a point of meeting each of her 25 MSPs face-to-face and emphasised that while she would be inclusive (not an adjective many had used about her in the past) she expected loyalty and co-operation in return. 'We have a lot of sparky individuals in the SNP and my job is to make sure we add up to more than the sum of our parts,' she explained. 'I think the leadership election has given us the opportunity to make a fresh start.' Sturgeon insisted, meanwhile, that she remained on good terms with Roseanna Cunningham who had a 'big part to play' in the party.[7] Such was the trauma of the last few years, however, that Sturgeon did not find it difficult to restore order. 'All of us realised we had to pull together,' recalled one frontbencher, 'otherwise we were screwed.'[8]

On the policy front, meanwhile, Sturgeon acknowledged that almost everything was under review; indeed the journalist Hamish Macdonell later wrote that the 'speed with which [she and Salmond] buried the Swinney years was breathtaking'.[9] In her first conference speech as deputy leader, Sturgeon announced the creation of four new committees (entitled Economic Policy, Social Democracy, Active Citizenship and Scotland in the World) to feed into the manifesto for a general election expected the following year. 'Our policies will be geared towards meeting the three big challenges facing Scotland,' she said, revisiting themes from her original leadership pitch, 'inequality, economic under-performance and the lack of national confidence.' She continued, 'I believe in progressive government. In government that creates the conditions of economic success, tackles inequalities, frees people from the bonds of poverty, provides quality public services and protects the vulnerable. It is these social democratic principles that must underpin SNP policy.' Strikingly, Sturgeon also urged the SNP to abandon consensus politics and pursue a more 'radical' approach in order to achieve power. She said, 'We have had a cosy consensus in Scotland for the last five years and all it has delivered is disappointment and frustration. It is a consensus that has stifled our nation's ambition, held us back from our aspirations and sapped our country's morale. People are crying out for politicians to be bold and for leadership that offers an alternative. That is exactly what I want the SNP to deliver. I will not stand silent as I see my country told it can't do any better than the mediocrity of the last five years.'

She denounced the 'bland mediocrity of Labour and the Lib-Dems' and, referencing her own youthful idealism, said the SNP had to 'offer the same sense of radical change that attracted me to the SNP and independence when I was 17 years old (*sic*). It was in support of radical change that makes a radical difference in peoples' lives that I came into politics.'[10]

But the response to Sturgeon's confident maiden speech, as journalists noted, was low key. Although 'she got a standing ovation, both at the beginning and end of her speech', wrote Brian Currie of the *Evening Times*, 'it was not wholehearted and didn't appear to galvanise the activists'.[11] Project Nicola, clearly, had only just begun.

In addition to adopting Salmondite economics (to which Sturgeon added more convincing social-democratic rhetoric), the new deputy leader also learned to keep other long-standing political instincts in check. Having refused to swear her oath of allegiance to the Queen in 1999 and boycotted Her Majesty's visit four years later, when the monarch visited Edinburgh in October 2004 to formally open the new Scottish Parliament building, Sturgeon had little choice but to attend although, during her speech in Parliament House (fittingly, the custom-built premises of the *old* Scots Parliament), she told the Queen and other assembled guests that 'a devolved parliament is not the summit of our ambition. We desire independence for our country.'[12]

But the most noticeable part of Project Nicola was her personal transformation. While Alex Salmond exuded man-of-the-people bonhomie, critics had long argued that Sturgeon succeeded only in projecting the chilly, antagonistic side of her character. Although widely seen within the party as talented, what she lacked was the common touch, her 'seriousness and spikiness', as one commentator put it, being 'seen as disad-vantages in a political age where style so often triumphs over substance'.[13]

Sturgeon became more upfront, and even light-hearted, about her relationship with SNP chief executive Peter Murrell ('If you believe some things that have been written,' she told one newspaper, 'our relationship is like something from Dallas.'[14]), while the Nicola who had once declared, 'I don't enjoy clothes shopping and I only go when I need to,' was completely jetti-soned. A smart white trouser suit had certainly been noticed at Holyrood during her first week as deputy leader, while in an extensive interview with the *Herald* Sturgeon appeared unable to talk about much beyond all the things she once made a point of not talking about.

The piece opened with a scene-setter in her new Glasgow city-centre flat (only the second property she had owned), not least a 'built-in mirrored wardrobe' full of shoes, 'high-heeled, strappy little numbers . . . in every colour of the rainbow, with labels such as FCUK, Dune and Kurt Geiger'.[15] Again, the turnaround was striking. 'There is no way I can wear 6in[ch] heels I have to be able to walk about in them,' she had said in 2001, claiming she went 'for High Street shops and d[id]n't buy designer labels'.[16]

Now, in November 2004, Sturgeon professed to 'a weakness for shoes, especially high-heeled ones' (but not Thatcher-style handbags). There was, she argued, a practical as well as an aesthetic motivation, elevating her 5ft 4in frame in order to go into battle with her political opponents. At the same time Sturgeon admitted her new job meant she had 'to think' about her appearance, although she was careful to add a feminist perspective. 'One of the features of being a woman in politics is that, unlike a man, people focus on what you wear,' she explained. 'If I turned up with the same suit two days running, they'd notice. Yet my male colleagues can get away with it – they only have to change their shirt and tie.' Her trouser suits, meanwhile, were divided between Glasgow ('her small wardrobe is jam packed') and Murrell's house in Livingston.

Sturgeon said her aim was to look modern but not too trendy. Her hair was now longer and coloured, the dark grey-flecked bob a thing of the past. 'Because I'm young, there's the danger that I end up wearing stuff that makes me look older than I am,' she said. 'I have to be careful about my make-up too, and try to keep it subtle. If it's too heavy, you can put on years.' This led to prolonged chat about her weight, something else off limits before Project Nicola got under way. ('I'm not in politics to talk about my weight,'[17] she had protested two years earlier.) 'It was brutal,' recalled Sturgeon of her Carol Vorderman diet, continuing, 'Basically you stop eating and drinking. No alcohol, no caffeine, no wheat, just fruit, salads and seeds for a month. You couldn't stick to it for more than four weeks, but the great thing about it is that it helps you get out of all your old habits. It makes you aware of what's not good. For instance, I've stopped eating sandwiches at lunchtime because the wheat in the bread makes you lethargic and I can't afford to feel or look tired when

I'm doing first minister's questions. Now if I've been overdoing it I just do a quick detox.' A well-thumbed copy of the TV presenter's recipe book was, added Sturgeon, her 'bible' (her attendance at the gym was sporadic), and one of several things which had 'changed [her] life' along with GHD (Good Hair Day) straighteners. But beyond a 'groaning' wine rack and supply of ground coffee the *Herald* noted that her kitchen was 'bereft of any sign of food'.

The two-bedroomed Merchant City flat, which she had bought around the time of the 2003 election, appeared to be the bricks-and-mortar manifestation of Project Nicola. Her old home, a Victorian tenement in the West End of Glasgow, had been serious and traditional, whereas the new pad was unashamedly contemporary and close to city-centre bars and restaurants. 'This is a young person's place,' observed the 34-year-old Sturgeon, 'and for now it suits me perfectly.'

The flat was also close to Queen Street Station (Sturgeon did not drive), making it convenient for commuting to Holyrood and constituency work on Mondays and Fridays. It was clear that, like much of the last 15 years, Sturgeon's life revolved around politics, although she rarely made any attempt to claim otherwise, admitting she had little time for cooking or social-ising, saying she liked 'nothing better' than to spend nights in 'with a takeaway, a glass of wine and the telly'.[18] The US series *Sex and the City* was a particular favourite ('I love Sam because she's just so outrageous . . . she just does what she wants to do and I admire her for that'), but Sturgeon had held only one party since moving in. 'I still have two friends from university and we hang out and things,' she later told another profiler. 'I enjoy going out for lunch and drinks with them when I can and I also have friends in politics that are great fun to be with.'[19] Otherwise she tried to spend as much time as possible with her family, particularly her nephew Ethan, while a niece called Harriet would appear in July 2006.

Interviewers searched in vain for material insights into Sturgeon's character, although beyond a couple of small framed prints and a middle-of-the-road CD collection ('I like easy listening') all that stood out were several IKEA bookcases holding a sizeable collection of books, ranging from the Scottish crime fiction of Christopher Brookmyre and Ian Rankin to biographies of Margaret Thatcher, Hillary and Bill Clinton, Tony Blair et al. 'Reading is one way', she explained, 'to switch off.'

Sturgeon was typically frank in admitting that all this was a work in progress: 'I'm serious by nature and have to work hard at my lighter side.'[20] Advice had come from, among others, Sir Sean Connery, who had told her to stand up straight so she would appear taller on television, and also guidance on using her voice, which over time became less hectoring and more rounded, more conversational in tenor. Naturally, her recognition factor, never particularly high for most politicians, increased. 'I still find it a bit of a novelty when I am recognised,' she admitted to BBC Radio Scotland's Edi Stark. 'There are occasions when I am out and people will come up and say, "Is that you off the telly?" And I say, "Yeah, I am Victoria Beckham, pleased to meet you." It is funny to watch them looking at me knowing this is not Victoria Beckham.'

An irreverent, often risqué, sense of humour had long been a feature of Sturgeon's personality although until now it had largely been hidden from public view. This must have helped when it came to combating a persistent rumour that she had earned the nickname 'Gnasher' after allegedly taking revenge on an unfaithful lover during an intimate act. 'He was not unfaithful to me – there was no third party involved,' Sturgeon told Stark, most likely through gritted teeth.[21] The *Mirror* journalist Siobhan McFadyen revisited this story a few months later as part of another 'lifestyle' feature on the SNP's deputy leader, and Sturgeon admitted the hardest part had been explaining it to her mother. She said, 'The Sunday that story appeared, they didn't really go into detail but they made reference to the name "Gnasher" and my mum phoned me up and asked what did they mean. I just didn't know what to say to her – I mean – how do you explain to your mum what that story is about? There is absolutely no basis of fact in the story. My ex [presumably

Stuart Morrison] had every single newspaper in the land on his doorstep asking him if it was true. It's painful enough for me to go through having to ignore these rumours but there is so many other people dragged in and it can be very difficult, especially because I am in the public eye, not them.' Sturgeon said the rumour, which had circulated in the Scottish Parliament a few years before it made it into the press, was 'the most personal' and 'off the wall' thing to have happened to her but was 'also completely false'. Although discussing such things must have been difficult, confronting them in this way was also the best policy. After 2005 little more was heard about that particular moniker.

Was she still a feminist? The word 'feminism', replied Sturgeon, had been 'devalued'. She continued, 'What is wrong with saying women should have the same chances as men? Being a woman can be an advantage – but we should be judged on our own merit. I think it's great that I can put on a red suit and walk into Parliament and face Jack McConnell who only has the opportunity to wear a black, grey or blue suit. We should be celebrated as women and we need to be taken seriously.'

'People will comment on what you wear, how you look, who you are having a relationship with,' added Sturgeon, 'and they never do that with men.'[22] Although this was not quite true, several male politicians – Gordon Brown, Robin Cook and certainly Alex Salmond – had also received criticism over their personalities and dress sense, she clearly saw women as being subject to different criteria. 'She almost had to compromise her strong feminist principles', reflected a colleague of this period, 'in order to reach out to voters and counter media perceptions.'[23] As for her reputation for being surly, 'I have shaken it off a wee bit now but it hurt in the beginning when absolutely everyone made comment about the fact that I never smiled. There might have been a little bit of truth in it at the time – but people would never, ever say that about a guy.'[24]

Meanwhile, it took Sturgeon a while to completely master the most public, if little watched, aspect of her role as deputy leader – the weekly joust at First Minister's Question Time.

Although her initial exchanges with Jack McConnell had widely been judged a success, thereafter her performance was patchy; Presiding Officer George Reid was even caught on an open microphone describing one outing as 'poor'. He swiftly apologised and Sturgeon, who claimed to 'love' FMQs, accepted.[25] There remained grumbling from within. 'The whole concept of the two-leader SNP is failing,' one critic told the *Mirror* in February 2005. 'Morale is low and even Nicola is taking a bashing every step of the way.'[26]

Still, discipline had improved markedly; a year or two earlier such comments would have been openly attributed. It was true that some Salmond/Sturgeon initiatives had fallen flat, particularly the idea of MSPs calling up members of the public to evangelise about supporting independence, although the deputy leader had more success when it came to setting out the party's policy agenda ahead of the 2005 general election. Late the previous year, she had urged the First Minister to let local authorities use efficiency savings to freeze council tax, while at the SNP spring conference in March she renewed a previous pledge to introduce a weekly 'citizen's pension' of £110, a calculated pitch for the 'grey' vote. By March 2005, even unsympathetic media observers acknowledged that Sturgeon had 'wiped the parliamentary floor with Jack McConnell for three weeks running',[27] her spiky humour consistently bringing her out on top. And although at Holyrood the commentator Allan Massie still reckoned her 'a bit strident', in more relaxed settings she could be 'very much at ease', coming across 'attractively and convincingly'.[28]

There was no disguising, however, that the Salmond/ Sturgeon 'dream ticket' had not yielded an electoral return. As the 2005 general election approached, polling suggested the SNP was trailing behind Labour and the Liberal Democrats, in other words there had been no real improvement upon the Swinney years. Sturgeon had purposefully avoided talking up the party's chances at Westminster, cautiously suggesting that holding on to its current tally of five MPs (one of whom was, of course, Alex Salmond) would represent progress.

As a delayed reaction to the 1999 devolution settlement the number of Scottish MPs at this election was to be reduced from 72 to 59, meaning the SNP was notionally defending four seats. In the event its share of the Scottish vote declined slightly to 17.7 per cent and it won six seats, gaining one rural and one urban constituency from Labour, which returned its usual tally of several dozen MPs (41). The Conservatives, not far behind the SNP with 15.6 per cent of the vote, elected just one MP. But the point was that Sturgeon's expectation management had paid off, and the outcome was depicted as neither a triumph nor a disaster. She emerged from the campaign, meanwhile, with her reputation enhanced. Even the *Mirror* judged that Sturgeon 'came of age' during the election, having 'played a blinder in terms of attracting the young vote'.[29]

Nevertheless, it would have taken a committed optimist to look at less than a fifth of the popular vote and predict anything approaching a majority, or even minority, 'win' in 2007. To Sturgeon, Project Nicola was inseparable from Project SNP, seeing her personal ambitions as good for the SNP and there-fore a more electorally successful party as good for her career, and she was not reticent in admitting as much. 'Of course I would like to be First Minister,' she said a few weeks before the election. 'I think, for me, and everyone who is in politics and who is serious about it, you want to get to the top. It's when you get there, you can really change things.'[30] Later asked to pick three words to describe herself, Sturgeon said, 'Focused. Self-critical. Ambitious – not just personally, but for the party and for the country.'[31]

But progress in that respect remained modest. Although Labour held on in two by-elections in late September, there were modest swings to the SNP including in Livingston, where Angela Constance, a university contemporary of Sturgeon, came to within 2,680 votes of victory. Applying that swing nationally, Sturgeon said it would equate to 28 SNP seats in 2007, although that was not anywhere near what was required to pose any real threat to Labour.

There had been calls following the election for the SNP to

drop its policy of holding a referendum on independence after taking power at Holyrood, partly on the grounds that it would smooth the path for a coalition with the Liberal Democrats, with whom there was otherwise much common ground. But this, said Sturgeon, was 'non-negotiable',[32] and indeed she was often sensitive to criticism from some quarters that she and others were insufficiently left wing or even Nationalist. When the former senior Nationalist Isobel Lindsay, for example, wrongly suggested no SNP MPs had attended an anti-nuclear protest at Faslane, Sturgeon challenged her ('I was there') in a letter to the *Herald* to explain how her 'professed support for Scottish independence square[d] with her decision to join the anti-independence Labour Party'. 'Until Ms Lindsay sorts out the political confusion in her own head', added Sturgeon, 'perhaps she should desist from criticising those of us who campaign day and daily for the independence of our country.'[33]

Despite Sturgeon's protestations to the contrary, meanwhile, the SNP had actually begun to reflect more deeply on its constitutional *raison d'être*. The evening before Alex Salmond set out his 'road map' to independence, his deputy admitted at a *Sunday Times* conference that the case for independence was still some way short of commanding majority support. She also emphasised that independence, as she understood it, did not mean 'separatism', a charge regularly levelled at Nationalists by Labour opponents; rather devolution was 'a journey' (very New Labour) and she was prepared to co-operate with whoever was prepared to accompany the SNP.[34] During the 2004 leadership election, Sturgeon had spoken of forging an 'alliance' of pro-independence parties such as the SSP and Greens, an idea to which she would return during the referendum debate of 2012–14.

This fed into a broader ideological shift, reflected in the working title of the 2007 manifesto, 'A Culture of Independence'. 'Perhaps as Labour shifted and we tried to fill the ground they had vacated we maybe became a bit centralist and statist in our outlook,' Sturgeon conceded to Kenny Farquharson at the beginning of 2006. She continued, 'What we are trying to do is say we can get independence for our country – it is what we want and aspire to. But so too should we aspire to personal and individual independence in this country. I want all of our policies to be about enabling people to make the most of their lives and very much embrace that concept of individual aspiration and independence. That will be the strong theme that runs through our policy platform.' Naturally Sturgeon insisted this did not represent a New Labour-style shift to the right. 'I'm prepared for those accusations and I will refute them totally,' she said somewhat defensively, preferring to frame the change as in keeping with the SNP's long history. 'If you go back 20 or 30 years the SNP was very decentralist in its approach,' she explained. 'It talked more about individual aspiration. This is going back to what the SNP is all about. It's about independence in the fullest sense of the word.'[35]

Several months later, however, Sturgeon was selling the 'culture of independence' as 'a philosophy', one that was 'as much about individual liberation as it is about national liberation'. She denied being a libertarian but said she believed 'governments should not go around getting in people's way when they don't need to'. Getting rid of student debt, lightening the burden of local taxation and encouraging small businesses, argued Sturgeon, were all intended 'to give individuals a fair crack of the whip . . . aspirational policies about people progressing and making the most of themselves'. Furthermore, such an agenda would 'strike a chord with people in the middle classes'.[36] This was social democracy, but not as we know it, and drew criticism from the former SNP MSP Campbell Martin (he had been expelled in July 2004), who referred to the strategy, which he saw as emphasising the role of the individual over the nation or state, as being 'close to Thatcherism'.[37]

By this point, Sturgeon had already been selected (unopposed) to fight the Glasgow Govan constituency for the fourth time (or third in a devolved context), while strenuous efforts were being made to ensure she also topped the SNP's Glasgow list. Her Labour opponent Gordon Jackson, meanwhile, had only been allowed to stand again having promised to give up his legal work. There had also been developments in her private life, having bought a new-build house in Baillieston with her partner Peter Murrell. She did not rule out children. 'I'm in my thirties so it's something I don't have for ever to think about,' reflected Sturgeon. 'It's not something I have a burning desire to do right now . . . Let's just say I suppose I'm at the stage where it could go either way.' There was a sense, however, that talk of becoming a mother and taking time out from politics, which punctuated interviews during this period were – although they both may have contained elements of truth – predominantly contrived as part of Project Nicola, intended to humanise the SNP's deputy leader and impress upon voters that there was more to Sturgeon than a professional politician.

So the year 2006 was shaping up to be a significant one for both Sturgeon and the SNP. 'I'm a great believer in the fact that elections aren't won or lost in the three weeks or three months before polling day, but well in advance,' she explained. 'This is the year we've got to prove ourselves, and convince people we've got what it takes to lead the country forward.' And that included acknowledging where the party had gone wrong in the past. She explained, 'I think we probably underestimated that the Scottish people needed time to assess and judge the Scottish parliament before they would be ready to consider further change. If you think back to 1999 we effectively fought the first election to a devolved parliament arguing for independence. Now, with hindsight, that was never going to be a particularly easy thing to do. People naturally would think, "Hold on, we've got to wait and see what this is like before we decide if we want any more of it." ' Sturgeon reckoned that, in 2006, Scotland was in a 'very different position'. 'People have got a reasonable amount of experience of devolution and they can make a pretty informed judgment about whether it's good enough or whether we need more,' she continued, 'and I think that's why we see the arguments about fiscal autonomy and more powers really gathering momentum.'[38]

A Holyrood by-election in spring 2006 augured well, with the SNP holding Margaret Ewing's Moray constituency. As for the election, argued Sturgeon, it ought to be 'a battle of ideas'.[39] At the 2005 party conference she had spoken of scrapping the graduate endowment scheme (a 'back door tuition fee'[40]), replacing student loans with grants (a long-standing policy) as well as the additional, not to mention costly, proposal to cancel £1 billion of 'outstanding student loan debt',[41] although (unlike Nick Clegg) she was careful not to be photographed with potentially embarrassing 'dump the debt' banners. In advance of the SNP's 2006 spring conference, meanwhile, she also outlined proposals to replace council tax with a local income tax, grants for first-time homebuyers and reduced rates for small businesses. Otherwise her speech in Dundee was thin on policy but heavy on Labour and Lib Dem bashing, while it ended with Sturgeon imploring activists to go out and fight for an SNP victory the following May. 'It will have to be worked for, campaigned for, earned – in every constituency, the length and breadth of Scotland,' she said. 'For the next 390 days the things I have been talking about today need to be talked about by all of us.'[42]

By October 2006 Sturgeon was telling delegates at the last SNP conference before the election they had their best chance ever to realise their 'dream of independence',[43] something made easier by a convenient historical backdrop – the tercentenary of the Act of Union in January 2007. The party's deputy leader unveiled a poster highlighting the referendum commitment: '1707 – No right to choose, 2007 – The right to choose'. 'The case for independence is based on equality,' said Sturgeon, introducing another theme that would prove enduring, 'Scotland being on an equal footing with England and all the other nations of the world.'[44]

But the purpose of the referendum policy was actually to neutralise the independence question, long privately acknowledged as a millstone around the SNP's neck. By emphasising, as Sturgeon did repeatedly, that voting SNP in May would *not* lead to independence, but rather a plebiscite on the Scottish Question, she and the party were inviting Unionists to lend them their vote. Labour, naturally, tried to depict their

Nationalist opponents as a single-issue party, hell bent on separation at all costs, but this time the SNP was able to counter this with a detailed – and of course populist – manifesto with a handful of big-ticket pledges such as the abolition of the graduate endowment. Health, Sturgeon's old brief, was also central to this strategy, and she personally unveiled a dedicated manifesto promising to keep open Monklands and Ayr A&Es (then scheduled for closure), partially elected health boards, free school meals for P1 to P3 pupils and an end to prescription charges for those with chronic conditions.

Between 2004 and 2007, colleagues gave Sturgeon credit for having made the SNP appear 'sound' when it came to the NHS, which hitherto had been seen as 'synonymous' with the Labour Party, raising it again and again in Parliament and giving Health Minister Andy Kerr a hard time when it came to cancer treatment waiting times. Her strong performance as deputy leader also meant she had consolidated her position over those three years, not only as Salmond's number two, but increasingly as the next number one. 'Interestingly,' reflected a senior colleague, 'Alex came to rely more on her. Yes, she complemented his rougher edges, but sometimes she could be harder and him softer, although that usually got overlooked.'[45]

'People want to be reassured of two things,' said Sturgeon of the referendum policy, 'that the process of transition will be smooth, and second, that they'll be in control of it. The referendum reassures people on both counts.' Not everything, she added pragmatically, would be 'picked apart', with several governmental functions no doubt proceeding on 'a shared basis'. This, believed Sturgeon, would not take long, with 'mature, grown-up negotiations about a settlement that's in the interests of Scotland and the rest of the United Kingdom'. As a party of devolved government, meanwhile, the SNP did not intend to 'pick fights for the sake of it'.

This message – and its messenger – sounded eminently reasonable, but then such was the natural culmination of Project Nicola. 'I've learned a huge amount about myself, from the whole experience,' she reflected a few weeks before the election, 'of not simply having to worry about what I'm going to do, but about everybody else and what we're doing collectively.' That, she added, had been 'a discipline in itself'. 'I've learned a lot about my abilities to work as part of a team and to lead a team.'[46]

The previous year Sturgeon admitted to having 'lightened up hugely in the last few years', shedding her 'Nippy Sweetie' reputation and acquiring a more relaxed and wittier demeanour; one seasoned political commentator even found her 'sexy',[47] not an adjective anyone had used before 2004. It was, she explained, 'about getting older'. 'Particularly being a young woman in politics where you feel a pressure to be taken seriously,' she said. 'If I was honest I was probably a bit po-faced. But the older I get, the less like that I am.'[48]

Sturgeon also confessed to being happier courtesy of her stable relationship with Peter Murrell, 'a big, big factor'.[49] 'One of the things I value about him is that he's happy with me having the public role,' she wrote in a detailed piece about the relationship for *The Sunday Times*. 'He's not one of those guys who would feel threatened by it. He doesn't have that kind of ego, he's very self-assured. I've been in relationships where that was not the case, but Peter is totally laid-back and doesn't bother at all.' The feeling was mutual. 'Nicola's intellect continually challenges me,' wrote Murrell. 'She's very, very sharp and on top of whatever the issue of the day is. That spark is always there. We are constantly having conversations that I'm amazed by.' Sturgeon, he added, was 'also a very caring, loving person and very shy. Much shyer than anyone viewing from the other side would know.'[50]

Shy, perhaps, but also within the past few years the most confident that colleagues and voters had ever seen her. Once perceived as cold, severe and distant, Sturgeon was now perhaps the party's most fluent communicator. 'It's hard to believe that anyone who puts themselves forward for election – with their name and photo plastered over thousands of leaflets – could actually be shy, but that certainly was the case with Nicola when she was younger,' recalled one colleague. 'It was only when she was able to overcome her shyness that she really came into her own.'[51]

And although Sturgeon would later deny any 'sort of conscious restyling or revamp',[52] as the election approached she sought advice from the stylist Monica Loudon. 'I thought she looked fantastic,' said Loudon. 'I kitted her out with clothes that she would have not normally gone for but she was very pleased.'[53] This was aesthetically useful, for the branding of the 2007 election was ostentatiously Salmond and Sturgeon, with images of the duo appearing on most billboards and printed material. One voter even misinterpreted such images, berating Sturgeon during the campaign with the words 'and as for your husband, Alex Salmond . . .'[54]

Project Nicola would only be complete, however, when both she and her party triumphed at the polls. And so, on 3 May 2007, it proved: not only did Sturgeon capture Govan at her third attempt with a majority of 744 but the SNP – after a nail-bitingly close count in the Highlands and Islands region – became the largest party in the Scottish Parliament by a single seat. Alex Salmond was also back, properly back, and destined to become First Minister. It had taken a long time for a devolved Scotland to deliver benefits for the SNP, but it had now done so in politically dramatic fashion. In that context, Sturgeon's decision, less than three years earlier, to withdraw from the leadership race and instead run on a joint ticket with the King Over the Water now looked like one of the smartest moves she had ever made.

Chapter 7

Health Secretary

The Conservative politician Nigel Lawson once observed that the National Health Service was the closest thing the English had to a 'national religion'. A similar observation could easily have been applied to the Scottish wing of the NHS which, since its creation, had been administratively – if not politically – 'pretty much independent'[1] from that in the rest of the UK. And for more than five years Nicola Sturgeon, who skilfully exploited that autonomy to further the party's ideological and constitutional aims, was its high priestess.

The SNP, or more reverentially the 'National Movement', had always been based, at least in part, on faith and, on 4 May 2007, the belief of its followers that it was only a matter of time before Scots came round to their 'big idea' appeared to have been vindicated. Salvation, however, rested upon shaky foundations: while the party was now the biggest at Holyrood, its majority – actually a minority – rested upon a single seat. While Labour had 46 MSPs, the SNP emerged with 47.

There followed negotiations, of sorts, between Alex Salmond and the Scottish Liberal Democrats, then led by another north-east politician called Nicol Stephen, but these quickly foundered on the question of an independence referendum (the SNP wanted one, the Lib Dems did not). On 11 May a deal was instead struck with two Green MSPs, although this of course could not provide a majority. Opinion inside the SNP swung behind the formation of a minority administration (with Sturgeon's support) and on 16 May Salmond became First Minister by 49 votes to 46.

That day, Sturgeon recalled later, 'almost passed in a daze'. 'I had to force myself to savour the moment,' she said. 'I was very aware that it was a historic day and I really wanted to remember it.' Even a week or so after the election, hearing the phrase 'First Minister Alex Salmond' had the ability to prompt a 'double take'.[2] Sturgeon became both Deputy First Minister and Cabinet Secretary (rather than 'Minister') for Health and Wellbeing, supported by her friend Shona Robison, who became Minister for Public Health (strikingly, there was no room in the administration for long-standing SNP frontbenchers such as Alex Neil and Roseanna Cunningham). Sturgeon was just a few weeks shy of her 37th birthday.

On 6 June MSPs listened to the new health gospel according to Nicola Sturgeon. The NHS, she said, would follow a similar path as before, adhering to principles laid out in the Kerr Report, 'Building a health service fit for the future', which had been published back in 2005. 'We agree that it is important to shift, where possible, the balance of care into communities,' she said, 'to tackle inequalities by anticipating and preventing ill health; and to take account of demographic and workforce pressures in the planning of services.'

But the central point of Sturgeon's statement was to fulfil an important pre-election pledge, confirmation that the previous Scottish Executive's plans to close Accident & Emergency units at Ayr and Monklands hospitals were to be reversed. 'Reversing the decisions is the right thing for the public and patients,' Sturgeon told MSPs. 'The two boards did not give sufficient weight to the concerns expressed by local people.'[3] Later, the Health Secretary stated that, in future, there 'should be a clear policy presumption against centralisation'.[4]

This naturally delighted campaigners in both localities, but Andy Kerr, Sturgeon's predecessor and an articulate defender of his decision to close the units, said, 'The easiest thing for me to do would have been to reject all the health evidence, all the reviews and be popular. But I have to say that as a result of that, people will die.'[5] Professor David Kerr, the author of the report name-checked by Sturgeon, agreed, warning that the SNP's approach to hospital services was 'sentimental, emotional and irrational', while his plan was being 'unpicked and unravelled' for no logical reason beyond the 'purely political' need to satisfy 'an ill-thought through manifesto promise'. 'Reversing the decisions on Monklands and Ayr will come at a cost,' he added for good measure. 'Health boards have finite budgets and Sturgeon will have to rob Peter to pay Paul.' In response, the Health Secretary said her commitment to the principles of Professor Kerr's report did not 'mean every decision taken in the name of the Kerr report' was necessarily the right one.

It was, in essence, a balancing act between populism and clinical advice. As Sturgeon said, although she would 'take into account' how clinicians wanted services to be delivered, she would also give 'as much weight as possible to public opinion'. After all, it was the public that funded the health service, although Andy Kerr pointed out the obvious danger in such an approach. 'Whoever shouts loudest', he warned, 'will now determine how the service is run.'[6] There was also an important ideological shift. Within weeks of taking office Sturgeon declared that ministers rejected 'the very idea that markets in health care are the route to improvement',[7] thereby signalling opposition in principle to the contracting out of health service provision to private providers.

Sturgeon's debut performance as Health Secretary was widely judged a success. Confident, poised and clear in her delivery, she had asserted her authority over a notoriously difficult policy area, something all the more remarkable given that she – together with the rest of her colleagues – had no previous ministerial experience. As was usually the case with new ministers, Sturgeon had initially been suspicious of the Civil Service, although she quickly came to appreciate this was misplaced. At the same time, however, her arrival at St Andrew's House represented a culture shock. 'The officials didn't know what had hit them,' recalled a former member of staff. 'Under Andy

Kerr they had been used to bringing him up to speed on a briefing they'd written, but with Nicola not only had she read it she had questions about it, and it frustrated her that they hadn't anticipated her follow-up queries. That was the most noticeable thing – just how prepared she was, how on top of things she was.'[8] Before long Sturgeon (like John Swinney at finance) had won the respect of her officials.

The Director General in charge of health was Kevin Woods, with whom Sturgeon struck up an effective working relationship before his departure to run the health service in New Zealand. A key figure was also her special adviser Noel Dolan, a former television producer at Westminster (where he met his wife, a former head of press for the Liberal Democrats) who had started working for the SNP as a press officer shortly before the 1999 Scottish Parliament election. Lugubrious and loyal, Dolan was of London–Irish stock and had also worked for the housing charity Shelter, a provenance – with its social justice credentials – providing a common point of reference with his boss. Later Sturgeon would forge a similarly close relationship with Harry Burns, the Chief Medical Officer for Scotland, who like Dolan burned with indignation at inequalities – health and economic – that dominated parts of Scotland.

This mindset would inform much of what Sturgeon sought to do as Health Secretary over the next five years, and indeed before long she was presenting herself as the guardian of Nye Bevan's legacy, particularly as the 60th anniversary of the NHS approached, helpfully underlined by her commitment to abolishing prescription charges for those with chronic conditions. (Bevan had resigned from Attlee's government in protest at the introduction of charges for prescriptions, spectacles and dentures in 1950.) Sturgeon took to speaking of 'returning the NHS to its principles'.[9]

They were eventful days in other respects. On 30 June there was a terrorist attack at Glasgow Airport, near Sturgeon's adopted city, the first on Scottish soil and when she addressed an anti-terrorism rally just over a week later (strikingly, she refused to hide behind her governmental rank when it came to public protest), she acknowledged that, while Muslims in Scotland had 'grave concerns about what's happening in our world today', the 'way to effect change' was through 'peaceful democratic politics'.[10] Elsewhere she made a point of saying that Islam was 'a religion of peace'.[11]

On 24 August the SNP marked its 100th day in power by claiming 'significant progress' on its pre-election pledges including, of course, reversing the closure of two A&E departments. 'They have been the busiest three months of my life,' reflected Sturgeon. 'But it's also been the best time of my life . . . the biggest difference between being in opposition and being in government is the responsibility that comes with it. I used to work long hours before but this is a whole new experience. It's the sheer intensity and scale of it, the 24/7 nature of it. It would be difficult to say when my working day ends now . . . the past few weeks have been a whirlwind but in a good way.'[12]

Ten days earlier Alex Salmond had launched a white paper on independence, kicking off a 'National Conversation' on the SNP's long-cherished goal. It included the proposed wording of a referendum question, asking voters if they agreed or disagreed 'that the Scottish Government should negotiate a settlement with the Government of the United Kingdom so that Scotland becomes an independent state', its contrived nature reflecting the fact that ministers were still finding their way, legally and politically, through the most difficult element of the new Executive's agenda. Sturgeon's firm view, as she later told a Holyrood committee, was that a referendum was 'within the competence of the Scottish Parliament'.[13]

Here, too, Sturgeon was central, in terms of building support for the party (the journalist Gillian Bowditch later judged that Sturgeon's 'discipline, intellectual rigour and debating skills' had given the SNP 'much-needed credibility')[14] and governing competently when it came to the NHS, as a result of which she and her leader believed support for independence would grow. While Salmond utilised St Andrew's House as what Theodore Roosevelt called a 'bully pulpit' to advance his populist agenda, so too did Sturgeon, albeit more modestly, at the health department. And although opinion polls stubbornly refused to budge, in doing so they were aided by their opponents. In mid August Jack McConnell had quit as Scottish Labour leader to be succeeded by Wendy Alexander, a capable (if difficult) minister in previous administrations who never seemed to find her leadership groove.

The SNP pursued a policy of independence by stealth, looking and acting as if they already ran an independent country. On 3 September, with no prior announcement, the signs at six government buildings were changed from 'Scottish Executive' to 'Scottish Government', a provocative (and of course symbolic) move in addition to which Salmond set himself against the UK government at every opportunity, most notably on the sensitive issue of prisoner transfers and the Lockerbie bomber. 'I knew once Alex Salmond got his feet under the table', recorded Tony Blair in his memoirs, 'he could play off against the Westminster government and embed himself. It would be far harder to remove him than to stop him in the first place.'[15]

Sturgeon played a prominent part in an ongoing effort to differentiate Scottish from UK government in as many policy areas as possible. In October 2007 she announced that on prescription charges the SNP now intended to go even further, ending what she called a 'tax on ill health' for Scottish patients within four years (the Welsh Assembly Government had already done so a few months earlier), while the same month Sturgeon set out plans to scrap the Thatcher-era 'right to buy' for new council and housing association stock, of which her parents had taken advantage in the 1980s. A related target of increasing the number of public sector houses built per year from 25,000 to 35,000 (Sturgeon made much of the fact the previous administration had built just six) prompted comparisons between the Health Secretary and the pioneering housing minister John Wheatley. And like the first Labour government of which Wheatley had been a member, the SNP was engaged in making itself appear both radical and respectable.

The following month Sturgeon insisted the Scottish

Government would deliver on its plans to freeze the council tax (before replacing it with a Local Income Tax, or LIT) and increasing police numbers, although here matters were less straightforward: the freeze would be delivered (via the forthcoming budget) but not the LIT (Sturgeon described Treasury opposition as 'arrant nonsense, constitutionally confused and politically inept'[16]), while the police pledge was heavily contrived to disguise a U-turn. A promise to write off all student debt, with which Sturgeon had been heavily identified before the election, was also quietly shelved (although the graduate endowment would be scrapped, as promised, in February 2008). But such was her bravado in dealing with these setbacks, as the journalist Peter MacMahon observed, that opposition politicians found it incredibly difficult to land a blow. 'It is government by assertion,' he wrote. 'Even when things are not true, ministers convince themselves that they are. And the "facts" are asserted again, and again, and again in the hope that eventually they will be believed.'[17]

Often they – the voters – did, and none was more adept at this technique than Sturgeon, particularly when it came to presenting her party's all-things-to-all-men approach as authentic, and of course consistent, 'social democracy'. In certain areas this was an easy argument to make – i.e. opposition to private sector involvement in the NHS, opposition to nuclear weapons and the Iraq War and a general commitment to universality of benefit and service provision, but at the same time this involved unburdening largely middle-class voters while promising cuts in business taxation, Salmondite support for Laffer Curve economics (the belief that tax cuts produced growth and revenue increases) and approving noises about the Irish 'Celtic Tiger' model.

And while both Sturgeon and Salmond had a nice line in blistering anti-Tory rhetoric, this did not prevent them working closely with the Scottish Conservatives in order to secure Holyrood approval for its first budget in February 2008 (and indeed for the next few years). Although this was largely about presentation – even George Galloway was prepared to accept that in Scotland the SNP were 'the real Labour' (and where once Sturgeon 'was bitter', he added, 'now she is sweet and definitely ministerial calibre'[18]) – it became harder in the face of a growing economic storm that was to alter the axis of Scottish, UK and indeed global politics over the next few years.

In early 2008, Sturgeon was content to echo Salmondite lines about Scotland becoming as wealthy as its near neighbours in the 'Arc of Prosperity' (Ireland, Norway and Iceland), but by that autumn, when she dwelled on the impact of the crisis in an article for the *Sunday Express*, the intellectual contortions were all too obvious. It ought to be remembered, she wrote, that the crisis had 'happened on the Westminster Government's watch and, moreover, within the Union', as if somehow the 1707 Act of Union had led directly to financial meltdown. Gordon Brown, meanwhile, was guilty of 'hypocrisy' for having promised 'no return to boom and bust', which conveniently ignored the fact that her party, chiefly its leader Alex Salmond, had hardly demurred from that analysis.

But just as Gordon Brown had presided over an 'age of irresponsibility in the City of London', continued Sturgeon, the Scottish Government was, by contrast, determined to do everything it could 'to usher in a new era of responsibility', although she went on to imply that without PFI and illegal wars crisis might have somehow been averted.[19] She was on stronger ground in extolling the economic virtues of an oil fund (as in Norway), but undermined that by praising Ireland's response to the banking crisis, ignoring the obvious point that the hubris of the Celtic Tiger era (again, much praised by Salmond) had given rise to it in the first place. The weakness in this argument was not peculiar to Sturgeon, indeed the SNP's general response to the financial crisis (blaming London and the Union) demonstrated that the 'economic case' for independence was fine if the Scottish and UK economies were performing well, as they had been for the past decade, but not so convincing when they hit the buffers.

Sturgeon was at least conscious that championing 'prosperity' was not enough if it was 'enjoyed only by some, while

144

others suffer poverty and deprivation'. In a lengthy article for the *Daily Express*, she even set out the Scottish Government's aim that, by 2017, Scotland 'as a whole' would be 'richer' while the 'gap between the richest and poorest' would have narrowed. She was rightly wary of 'sticking plaster' solutions, preferring 'a more fundamental approach that sees the prevention and reduction of poverty as a priority across every part of government'.

The Health Secretary fully appreciated this would not be easy, although she argued that devolution had shown what could be achieved with 'control over many of the areas that can have an impact on poverty', although changes to the tax and benefit system, still controlled by Westminster, 'can blunt our efforts'. The 'central theme' of the Scottish Government's approach, she added, would be 'to make sure that as many people as are able are in quality employment', this being 'the most effective way to get at the root causes of poverty'.[20]

Launching a consultation on tackling poverty, Sturgeon said the fact that 880,000 Scots were living in relative poverty was 'a tragedy which we will not tolerate' before lapsing into the usual rhetoric about 'growing the economy and releasing Scotland's entrepreneurial and creative talents'.[21] All that, however, was about to become a lot more difficult in the face of huge debt, soaring deficits and stagnant growth rates, and although Sturgeon's concern was undoubtedly genuine, like Alex Salmond she would prove short on practical (as opposed to rhetorical) solutions and even a coherent response to what would fast become a global economic crisis.

Meanwhile, the good news continued to flow. Hospital car parking charges were to be abolished except in extreme circumstances, while Sturgeon appeared to get a grip on cancer treatment waiting times, which she had highlighted in opposition for several years. She scrapped so-called 'hidden' waiting lists and introduced a new system of monitoring, so by May 2008, as the SNP marked its first year in office, there was broad agreement that Sturgeon and Shona Robison had turned in a competent first year, although at the same time many observed that (major) structural reform for the Scottish NHS – and its massive budget – had been put on hold with no serious attempt to tackle the financial and demographic reality of ever-rising costs.

On its first anniversary in government, the SNP also reached 45 per cent of the Holyrood constituency vote in an opinion poll, its highest-ever rating and, as it turned out, precisely what it achieved at the 2011 Holyrood elections. 'A year after the historic elections,' enthused Sturgeon, 'and as Labour disintegrates, the growing SNP lead shows that the honeymoon continues on the back of solid policy delivery.'[22] The party's dual leadership, in government as in opposition, continued to work well, aided by the proximity of Sturgeon's office to that of Alex Salmond. 'He has a very firm grip on things, but does not try to micro-manage,' she said of her relationship with the First Minister. 'He does not interfere or get in the way of what you are doing.'[23] Indeed this, something that was not true of other ministers, indicated just how much Salmond rated – and importantly trusted – his deputy to do her own thing.

Early on in the 2007–11 Parliament, the Health Secretary had quickly emerged as one of a powerful triumvirate within the SNP, the other (in addition to Salmond) being Finance Secretary (and former leader) John Swinney. When, for example, academics asked senior Nationalists to rank the five most powerful SNP figures, 'Salmond was seen by all as the most powerful', while 'the only other figure mentioned by all interviewees' ('apart from herself') was Sturgeon, whose position as deputy leader was 'more than nominal, as it can be in other parties'.[24] It was Franklin Roosevelt's vice president John Nance Garner who famously described his office as not being 'worth a bucket of warm piss', but no such adage applied to Salmond's deputy. Far from being 'a bit-part player', Sturgeon was, as the academics Rob Johns and James Mitchell later observed, 'a close second in command' and one of the few Cabinet Secretaries 'who could successfully challenge Alex Salmond over matters beyond her formal ministerial responsibility'.[25]

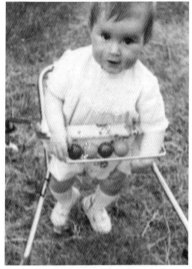

'A working-class girl from Ayrshire.' Sturgeon grew up in Dreghorn, a village not far from the New Town of Irvine. (Nicola Sturgeon)

Sturgeon at Greenwood Academy (left), where two teachers encouraged (in different ways) her interest in politics, and (right) sporting an SNP rosette. She joined the party aged only 16. (Nicola Sturgeon)

Above. Young Scottish Nationalists at the 1989 SNP conference in Dunoon. From left to right: Sturgeon, Lindsay Donaldson, Fiona Hyslop, Ricky Bell (Sturgeon's then boyfriend), Eilidh Whiteford and Angus Robertson. (© Scotsman Publications)

Right. Pat Kane's controversial leaflet urging Glasgow University students to vote for Sturgeon as SRC president. She lost, but had earlier helped Kane become Rector. (David Torrance)

A MESSAGE FROM
PAT KANE RECTOR

"You supported me to be a Working Rector committed to fighting for student's interests.
Today you have the chance to elect a strong Student Executive who will work with me in fighting against the Poll Tax,Student Loans and Campus Racism and for the provision of services such as a Student Creche.Use your Vote and make it count."

VOTE TODAY
NICOLA STURGEON	PRESIDENT
ALASDAIR ALLAN	V.P. UNI AFFAIRS
ANGELA CONSTANCE	V.P. SERVICES
SHIELA OLIVER	V.P. WELFARE

PAT
KANE **STRENGTH TO STRENGTH**

A rector for the Nineties

Sturgeon's first television appearance, on Grampian TV's *Crossfire* programme, in 1989. Watching was Peter Murrell, her future husband.

Sturgeon on an edition of BBC Scotland's *Left, Right and Centre* in early 1992. Even as an undergraduate she was a confident political communicator.

Dreaming of Home Rule as the SNP's candidate for Glasgow Shettleston at the 1992 general election. At 21, Sturgeon was the youngest Parliamentary candidate in the UK. (© Scotsman Publications)

Sturgeon and her grandmother following her graduation in law. Despite being heavily involved in politics, she narrowly missed getting a first-class degree. (Nicola Sturgeon)

On the march with SNP leader Alex Salmond. He spotted Sturgeon's potential early on and made sure she rose through the party ranks during the 1990s. (© Scottish Political Archive, University of Stirling)

Meeting future voters as the SNP's candidate for Glasgow Govan at the 1997 general election. Considered a winnable seat, Sturgeon ran an impressive campaign. (© Murdo Macleod)

Above left. Sturgeon following the Glasgow count in 1999, having failed to secure Govan. Instead she joined the first Scottish Parliament as a 'list' MSP. (© Scotsman Publications)

Above right. A flyer issued as part of Sturgeon's short-lived leadership campaign in the summer of 2004. Standing aside for Alex Salmond turned out to be a shrewd move. (© Kay Ullrich)

Right. Project Nicola: photographic evidence that after becoming the SNP's deputy leader, Sturgeon was prepared to revamp her image. (© Scotsman Publications)

Celebrating with Alex Salmond following the SNP's historic election win in 2007. Sturgeon would become Deputy First Minister and Health Secretary. (© Scotsman Publications)

Sturgeon's marriage to SNP chief executive Peter Murrell in July 2010. Colleagues considered him an important influence on his wife, politically and personally. (© Scotsman Publications)

Sturgeon's performance in the 2105 general election debates introduced her to a UK-wide audience. (Getty Images)

Sturgeon with the Scottish Cabinet following the 2016 Holyrood election. (Getty Images)

Civil Service briefing notes later released under the Freedom of Informatiom Act revealed that Sturgeon not only received a ministerial box each evening but also at the weekend, a testament to her Stakhanovite work rate. The document also revealed the Deputy First Minister's media awareness ('early consideration should be given to the publicity requirements and photo opportunities' of ministerial visits), punctilious-ness ('courtesy e-mails' were a must if the Health Secretary was to visit another MSP's constituency), speaking style ('Ms Sturgeon speaks at about 130 wpm . . . The Cabinet Secretary prefers short paragraphs and sentences . . . she often adds to the content off the cuff'), preferred manner of dealing with correspondence ('The bedrock is good written English . . . Ensure you empathise with the correspondent') and, impor-tantly, the 'constraints which a minority administration must operate within'.[26] Always a good team player, the Deputy First Minister had clearly taken to government like a duck to water, although official drafts of speeches tended to frustrate her, so used was she to preparing her own material.

Several interviewers noted that Sturgeon's fourth-floor Holyrood office was Spartan apart from photographs of her nephew Ethan and niece Harriet, and indeed without any children of her own ('[I]t's something that's a possibility,' she continued to say, 'but my hands are full at the moment'), she appeared to be a doting aunt. 'I love spending time with them,' said Sturgeon. 'The older I get, the more important family is to me. That is my sanity, that's what keeps me grounded.'[27] Her mother Joan was now working for her part time (having also been elected a councillor in Irvine East in 2007),[28] while cases from her move (with Peter Murrell) to Glasgow's East End remained unpacked several months later.

There simply were not enough hours in her days, although at least Sturgeon had the satisfaction of public recognition for her efforts. In late 2008, she was awarded the accolade of both 'Politician of the Year' and 'Donald Dewar Debater of the Year' (the latter for the second time) for her performances as both Health Secretary and deputy leader of the SNP, and for having handled both good news and bad with aplomb in a challenging brief.

On 4 May 2008 Wendy Alexander announced a remarkable change in the Scottish Labour Party's constitutional thinking. In a risky attempt to 'call Alex Salmond's bluff', she said she did not 'fear the verdict of the Scottish people' when it came to independence. As for a referendum, she added defiantly, 'bring it on'. This (essentially the approach adopted by David Cameron less than four years later) ought to have caused the SNP more problems than it did, compelling the Scottish Government to at least explain why it did not want a ballot sooner rather than later. But it was an indication of the SNP's strength and confidence after a year in power that it was simply shrugged off. The policy, responded Sturgeon, was for a 'National Conversation' followed by a vote in 2010 and, no matter what Alexander said, there was no intention of bringing it forward.[29]

In any case, the Scottish Labour line did not hold for very long, fatally undermined as it was by Gordon Brown's lukewarm support for Alexander's strategy. 'This has been a disastrous Grand Old Duke of York double act,' said Sturgeon. 'Wendy marches Labour to the top of the hill and Gordon Brown orders her down again.'[30] A subsequent poll found support for independence at just 31 per cent (and 26 per cent undecided), which she interpreted as meaning there 'was everything to play for' in the Battle for Scotland: 'The SNP will show credibility, competence and achievement in government over a number of years – not just the past year. As that process takes place, support for independence will continue to grow, particularly as the concept of Scotland becoming an equal and independent nation within a continuing social union across these islands, sharing a head of state with England, is further explained.'[31]

Significantly, in light of subsequent events, meanwhile, Sturgeon agreed with the First Minister that a referendum, when it came, would be 'a once-in-a-generation event'.[32] Two months after Alexander's unsuccessful intervention, there was further woe for Labour after it narrowly lost a Westminster by-election in Glasgow East, a result described by the Deputy First Minister as 'epic'.[33] Seven months later the Scottish Government would lose a parliamentary vote on its referendum plans, but again it did not seem to matter.

The Health Secretary had recently marked the 60th anniversary of the NHS by praising the 'unquestionable divergence' brought about by devolution in the UK.[34] It was indeed beyond dispute: as of 31 December 2008, car parking charges were to be abolished at Scottish hospitals (except at hospitals like Edinburgh's Royal Infirmary, where PFI arrangements made it impossible), while the Scottish Government planned to block a legal loophole that enabled private firms to bid to provide GP services. Sturgeon also thought in legacy terms with her proposal to introduce a 'minimum price' for alcohol. There was, she told the British Medical Association's annual conference, a 'battle of ideas' over the future of the NHS, 'a battle between the values of the market, of internal competition and contestability and the values of public service, of co-operation and collaboration'.[35]

Sturgeon's approach to the housing market, however, had been less ideologically clear-cut, with the interventionist and pro-ownership policy of giving first-time buyers a £2,000 grant not only appearing inconsistent with her hostility to the 'right to buy' but, in the event, proving undeliverable. Referring to 'the current climate', a polite way of acknowledging the growing economic crisis, she said encouraging shared equity schemes would, on reflection, provide 'more effective' help to buyers than direct grants.[36] Naturally, there were charges of breaking pledges (cutting class sizes to 18 had also fallen by the wayside), but from one perspective Sturgeon was simply being pragmatic in ditching policies that looked deliverable in opposition but were now impractical not only because of the economic situation but due to the Scottish Government's minority status. As the Health Secretary now understood, the realities of office acted as an inevitable check on the idealism of opposition.

Meanwhile, even the most competent politicians – and

Sturgeon was undeniably competent – could not avoid what Conservative Prime Minister Harold Macmillan had once laconically called 'events, dear boy, events'. This included an outbreak of the Clostridium difficile bacteria (or C. diff) at the Vale of Leven Hospital in Alexandria, Dunbartonshire, during 2008. A total of 18 deaths had been directly or indirectly linked to the hospital and not only were relatives planning legal action against NHS Greater Glasgow and Clyde but Sturgeon was accused of not acting quickly enough to tackle it. This was unfair, for as soon as she had been alerted to the incident she had ordered both a review of infection control procedures and an independent investigation. She also felt the criticism personally, for her grandmother had contracted the superbug during her final illness some years previously.

For the first time in office, Sturgeon felt, as one former aide put it, 'politically vulnerable', not least because she was the subject of sustained media criticism (a BBC Scotland documentary culminated with its presenter walking through a graveyard, prompting a rare complaint from the Health Secretary). 'But Nicola learned a lot from that,' recalled the aide, 'so when confronted with swine flu she was much more confident in dealing with both councils and health boards.'[37]

The swine flu epidemic came during Easter 2009 and generated much hysteria and hyperbole across the UK. Although it was certainly cause for concern – some patients were, after all, dying – throughout the crisis Sturgeon was at pains to strike a balance between, as she put it, 'taking this seriously and not behaving in a way that is unduly worrying to the public'.[38] By June, with 19 confirmed cases in Scotland, the Health Secretary announced plans to vaccinate the entire population against the virus at a cost of more than £100 million. Still she maintained there was 'no cause for undue concern',[39] and by the end of July she spoke of 'encouraging signs' that the number of cases was declining in the Glasgow area, although by October, when the mass immunisation programme finally got under way, 16 Scots had died.

'Everything was pushed aside in order to tackle that,' recalled a then aide. 'It wasn't that Nicola sidelined the First Minister, but after a couple of weeks he let her show what she was capable of. It was a huge political and logistical challenge.'[40] (When Salmond pushed officials a bit too far, Sturgeon told him, 'Look, it's not on. You know that it's not a priority,' firm advice that 'changed his reaction'.[41]) Nevertheless, throughout a potentially difficult health crisis Sturgeon had maintained a Zen-like calm, winning praise from friend and foe as a result. The journalist Kevin McKenna later put it well in saying that she 'seemed to possess those qualities that we Scots like to think we have on our best days: calmness, authority, reassurance and with a small dash of Presbyterian rectitude'.[42]

As she did in the face of a public spending squeeze: although in September 2009 Sturgeon announced a funding increase of 2.6 per cent for 2010–11, this – as opponents pointed out – was below inflation and also represented a slight reduction in the capital budget (£55 million had been earmarked to deal with the flu and vaccine programme). Thinking long term, the Health Secretary attempted to paint a more optimistic picture by pointing out that, as well as potentially reducing crime, a minimum alcohol price could save as much as £1 billion over a decade. Here she was willing to rank expert advice over popular opinion, although the proposal quickly ran up against political, commercial and legal opposition. At that year's SNP conference, meanwhile, Sturgeon found enough cash to bring the privately run regional treatment centre at Stracathro hospital back under NHS control. 'The language of priorities,' said Nye Bevan, 'is the religion of socialism', but in her New Year message for 2010 Sturgeon was clear where the blame lay for ongoing economic difficulties. 'As a country,' she said, 'we will face challenges and tough times ahead, as we all pay the price for Labour's recession.'[43]

A potentially career-ending row at the beginning of 2010 also demonstrated another Sturgeon quality: acute political judgement. It began when details emerged of a letter she had written to a judge on behalf of her constituent Abdul Rauf who, as it happened, had stolen money from dozens of people a decade and a half before, using his position at a local Post

Office to forge signatures on hundreds of benefit claims. He was subsequently found guilty of fraud worth £60,000 and sentenced to four years in prison; Sturgeon's letter asked that a convicted fraudster not be jailed despite having confessed to another £80,000 worth of benefit fraud.

Quite why his case warranted the support of an elected representative, let alone a Cabinet Secretary and a trained lawyer to boot, was the obvious question, and initially the SNP's spin operation, which rested upon an unconvincing interpretation of the ministerial code of conduct, arguably did more harm than good. Labour also overdid it by calling for the Deputy First Minister's resignation, a demand unsupported by the political mood (although that could easily have changed). Political trouble came in threes: not only had the First Minister and his deputy been rocked by a cash-for-access row dubbed 'lunch-gate' (they had auctioned lunches and tours at and of Holyrood), but Salmond had appealed for clemency on behalf of an illegal immigrant facing drug charges. In such a context, Sturgeon's recent authorisation of expenses improperly claimed by her special adviser Noel Dolan appeared to be small beer.

'I spent yesterday standing up for the victims of knife crime,' was Scottish Labour leader Iain Gray's carefully honed line of attack at First Minister's Questions. 'Nicola Sturgeon spent yesterday standing up for a criminal.' With his Health Secretary looking strained and tense beside him, Salmond said she had his '110 per cent' backing while claiming, weakly, that MSPs had an 'absolute obligation' to represent their constituents 'without fear or favour'.[44] The First Minister was himself under pressure for having admitted that he would miss his own preferred date for a plebiscite on independence, an announcement the Conservatives claimed had been deliberately contrived to divert attention from the scandal engulfing Sturgeon.

There was, recalled someone who spoke to her during the row, 'a real vulnerability' about Sturgeon at this time,[45] personally but of course also politically: everything she had worked for since the late 1980s could so easily have come crashing down, causing perhaps irreparable damage to a political life that, until then, had been sure footed almost to a fault. Such thoughts literally gave Sturgeon sleepless nights. 'It was a hugely personal and difficult time for her', recalled a former aide, 'in that it was about her constituency, nothing to do with the government; but she was Deputy First Minister and number two within that government, so it mattered.' If there had been a no-confidence motion then 'she would've walked'.[46]

Intuitively, Sturgeon realised she had to apologise to the Scottish Parliament and had resolved to do so by the weekend of 20/21 February. She also knew it had to be unequivocal, something that put her at odds with the First Minister, whose mantra was usually 'never explain, never apologise'. Although Salmond realised some sort of statement was probably necessary, he did not favour something he would have viewed as a potentially damaging display of political weakness. Sturgeon's reasoning, however, was largely selfless. Primarily, she realised she had made a mistake, and by failing to defuse the situation she would damage not only herself but more importantly the party and government of which she was a member.

When, on 24 February, Sturgeon addressed the Scottish Parliament she was under no obligation to do so, but it was good politics; as the *Herald* observed, public statements of 'contrition and apology are rare in the bear pit of politics, especially when expressed in the most simple terms'.[47] In a lengthy statement she defended sending the letter but having re-read it 'many times' believed that 'in certain respects it could, and should, have been written differently'. She continued: 'First, I regret the use of the word 'mistake' to describe Mr Rauf's offence. As I hope will be clear from other parts of the letter, I did not intend in any way to downplay the seriousness of the crime that had been committed. However, I accept that the use of the word 'mistake' was open to that interpretation. Also, having drawn the court's attention to Mr Rauf's personal circumstances, I should have left it there. I should not have gone on specifically to ask the court to consider alternatives to custody. On reflection, that was a request more suited to my former occupation as a solicitor than to my current job as an MSP, so I can and do understand why some people think that making such a request went too far.'

Although, added Sturgeon, she had 'assisted a constituent in good faith', in doing so she had 'got some things wrong' and for that she was 'sorry'. She went on to reflect more broadly on political culture: 'Of course, it is not easy for any of us to stand up and say that we should have done things differently or better than we did. Our political culture, particularly in a pre-election period, does not make that easy, but I think that it is right that I should do so. Indeed, my reflections over the past few days have made me wonder whether a more general willingness to allow each other space to reflect on honest mistakes, admit where we have got things wrong and learn lessons would not be much better for our politics than the instant judgment that we all, me included, so often rush to.'

Sturgeon was making a point of showing self-awareness, indeed she admitted the past couple of weeks had 'not been the easiest' of her time in the Scottish Parliament. But in keeping with her life-long commitment to self-improvement, she promised to 'learn the lessons of the past days' and 'make better decisions as a result of them'.[48]

The apology transformed Sturgeon in the eyes of the media, its dose of humility (she had made no attempt to blame her staff) softening her often intimidatingly superhuman competence as a minister. The Fourth Estate, however, had already begun warming to her. As one veteran political journalist recalled of a lunch with Sturgeon a year after she became Health Secretary: 'I was expecting an hour at the most. We ended up staying for three. She was really funny, droll and indiscreet. It was terrific fun. I told her that she seemed so much more relaxed. Her reply was: "I've just stopped giving a f★★★ about what my critics think, I've grown out of it".'[49]

Other journalists who fell ill or lost their jobs were also surprised to receive phone calls or emails from Sturgeon. But more importantly, her handling of the Rauf affair, and its implicit rejection of her mentor's way of doing things, also meant that in the space of a few minutes Sturgeon more fully became her own person, her own politician. 'Until that point,' recalled the journalist Euan McColm, 'she hadn't come out of Alex's shadow.'[50] None of this, of course, could have been planned, although Sturgeon must have realised than an apology, if deftly executed, could actually do her some good. After all, upon such unanticipated events, and the response of protagonists to those events, turned what Stanley Baldwin called the 'endless adventure of governing men' (and women).

The Abdul Rauf affair must have been all the more traumatic for having followed the relatively happy news of Sturgeon's engagement to Peter Murrell almost seven years after they had first begun seeing each other. 'We are very happy to be getting married,' said the couple in a short and rather bland statement, 'and are very much looking forward to celebrating the occasion with family and friends this summer.'[51] Murrell had proposed (on bended knee) at their Baillieston home on Hogmanay and a small civil ceremony was planned for July.

It was a good opportunity to soften the Deputy First Minister's image further and in an interview with the *Herald* Sturgeon discussed shopping for a wedding dress with her sister Gillian ('She's pushing me towards a white frilly meringue . . .We're not having a traditional wedding so I'm not having a traditional dress'), the after-party music ('swing band rather than a ceilidh') and the wedding cake (by Tunnock's; its company secretary was 'a neighbour and friend'). Sturgeon said Murrell was her 'constant reminder that while the SNP is important to us both, other things in life matter as well', while Murrell said, 'When it comes down to it, there is more to life than politics. Loving Nicola gives me a feeling of complete-ness.'[52] (Murrell – nicknamed 'Penfold' by journalists of a certain TV-viewing vintage – later demonstrated his sense of humour by paying £1,500 for a bizarre portrait by French artist Laetitia Guilbaud – entitled 'Naughty Nicola' – of his leather-clad and belly button-pierced fiancée brandishing a whip.) They wed on 16 July at Glasgow's Oran Mor (Sturgeon wore a dress from Dream Brides in Irvine), followed by an evening reception attended by, among others, the First Minister and several Cabinet colleagues.

By then the dust was settling on the May 2010 general election that, unusually for a UK ballot, had been dominated by a series of televised leaders' debates. The Health Secretary handled the logistics from a party perspective – there was even speculation she would take part in the Scottish debates rather than Salmond – and in an effort to maintain a Scottish dimension in a campaign otherwise dominated by the three main parties (and, latterly, an unlikely phenomenon called 'Cleggmania'), the SNP at first insisted on inclusion in the main network debates and, when that did not happen, pursued a judicial review of the BBC's decision.

The election itself, or rather its aftermath, was full of drama and constitutional uncertainty, the result of the first hung Parliament (the SNP preferred the word 'balanced') since February 1974. Salmond talked up the prospects of a broad, Labour-led coalition including the SNP's six MPs, but he well understood that the eventual outcome, a formal Conservative–Liberal Democrat coalition, offered the perfect electoral backdrop to not only the SNP's chances in Holyrood elections due in 2011, but its prospects of securing a 'yes' vote if a referendum on independence were to follow.

Post-crash 'austerity' had already made maintaining health-care in Scotland more challenging (shortly after the election Sturgeon announced health boards were to shed several thousand staff) and, given the Health Secretary's predilection for anti-Tory invective, the prospect of even more cuts delivered by the 'anti-Scottish' Conservatives (which emerged from the election with, as ever, a single MP), there would be much for Sturgeon et al. to rail against over the next few years, while the public spending context also meant the politics of differentiation could flourish. In October, for example, she confirmed that prescription charges would be abolished completely the following April.

Declining revenue did not, however, account for every setback. On 10 June opposition MSPs ignored Sturgeon's appeal to rise above party politics and rejected the central plank (minimum pricing) of the Scottish Government's Alcohol Bill (she promised not to 'shirk' from 'addressing this challenge' in future), while in pilot elections to two health boards the Health Secretary struggled to present a 14 per cent turnout in Fife and 22.4 per cent in Dumfries and Galloway as any other than a reality check for her vision of endowing local health management with a popular mandate. In retrospect it had been a bad idea in opposition, and proved expensive and difficult to implement in government (though, significantly, 16- and 17-year-olds had been able to take part).

Polls, however, suggested that the minority SNP government was heading for defeat the following year. Although Labour had lost the UK general election, its Scottish share of the vote had increased by 3 per cent and, with voters still in a Westminster frame of mind, most surveys between the end of 2010 and early 2011 suggested, however unlikely it appeared, Scottish Labour leader Iain Gray would become the next First Minister. Speaking before the autumn SNP conference Sturgeon teed up her party's narrative response, chiefly framing the Holyrood election as 'a choice' between Gray and the alternative vision of the 'statesman-like' Alex Salmond, as well as a verdict on the record of the SNP in devolved government and its team of ministers.[53] This, distilled into the simple triumvirate of 'team, record, vision', would be repeated ad nauseam during the campaign, and to good effect.

The record, Sturgeon argued, was a pretty good one, with 84 of the SNP's 94 headline manifesto commitments having been delivered. Writing after the Scottish Parliament endorsed the Scottish Government's fourth budget in February 2011, the Health Secretary maintained that, despite pressures on the health budget from 'an ageing population, increased drugs costs and improved technology', it would be 'totally wrong' for any government to cut the NHS budget.[54] Naturally, Sturgeon drew a contrast between her approach and that south of the Border (where reforms would 'end the NHS in England as we know it'), saying she was not 'a big fan of structural reform' beyond a planned integration of health and social care services.[55] During the election campaign, meanwhile, the Health Secretary spoke of Scotland heralding a new era of health care free at the point of need. Salmond praised Sturgeon for having 'reduced the rate of hospital-acquired infection dramatically, increased the number of doctors, nurses and medical staff, and cut cancer waiting times'.[56]

A manifesto to 're-elect' the Scottish Government, meanwhile, pledged to freeze the council tax for the duration of the next Parliament (which, due to a little-noticed change, would last five rather than four years), although there was no mention of progress towards the Local Income Tax mooted four years earlier. It also promised to protect spending on what Sturgeon called 'a national treasure', in other words the NHS, which she said would always 'be safe and secure in the hands of an SNP Government, unlike the wholesale dismantling of the NHS south of the Border, started by Labour and now continued by the Lib Dems and the Tories'.[57] Importantly, in the run-up to the election several big-ticket items – including minimum pricing and the abolition of prescription charges – had kept Sturgeon's media profile high.

In Glasgow Southside, which the Govan constituency became following boundary revisions, Sturgeon had the relatively easy task of overturning a notional Labour majority of 27. As ever, she worked phenomenally hard, taking nothing for granted; although her local campaign officially kicked off at the end of March, in reality it had been up and running for the past 12 months. Typically, Sturgeon was pessimistic and Alex Salmond later recalled that, on the Monday before election day, 'she was convinced that she had detected a big swing away from us'.[58]

By polling day, however, opinion polls had dramatically shifted to show a significant SNP lead and Sturgeon easily won the seat with a majority of more than 4,000, although even she must have been surprised to find the SNP overtaking Labour as the city's largest party. 'We have proved with this result, not only can we win in Glasgow, but we can hold seats in Glasgow as well,' she remarked at the SECC count. 'We are showing the SNP is a force to be reckoned with.'[59] Having fought safe Labour seats since 1992, it must have been quite something for Sturgeon to witness so many strongholds gained by her friends and colleagues.

In the minimal Cabinet changes that followed the election, Sturgeon remained as Health Secretary with the additional title of 'Cities Minister'. Over the last four years, there had been highs (her role in tackling the swine flu pandemic and getting cancer treatment waiting times under control) and lows (the Rauf affair and a failure to win support on minimum alcohol pricing), but so successful had she been in the role that it had become almost impossible to imagine anyone else doing it. More to the point, she now had a solid four years of ministerial experience behind her. 'I was surprised by how much you can do and how quickly you can do it,' she had reflected during the campaign, 'if you have a clear idea about what you want to do and have the determination to get it done.'[60]

In other words, the (British) Civil Service had offered her robust proof of its effectiveness and impartiality, both characteristics that Sturgeon and Salmond would deploy fully – and in places stretch – over the next few years, for the election, in which the SNP achieved the supposed electoral impossibility of winning an overall majority, had in an instant transformed the prospect of an independence referendum from an abstract debating point into constitutional reality.

To a degree this shift caught the SNP unawares, for even its most optimistic members had not anticipated dominating Holyrood to the extent it now did. Although the party had secured 45 per cent of the popular vote (albeit on a 50 per cent turnout), polls continued to show support for independence running at least ten points behind, so the task of negotiating a referendum and actually winning it remained formidable. Strategists wasted little time in attempting to present independence as something closer to 'Home Rule' (advisers even approved of the term 'independence-lite'), i.e. a less risky, and therefore less scary, version of the ultimate constitutional goal.

This involved some deft footwork, not least on the domestic front. Salmond, for example, finally determined that the NATO boil had to be lanced (the SNP remained opposed to member-ship, an unhelpful position in several respects), a process that culminated in a nail-bitingly close conference vote that autumn. Although Sturgeon came from a wing of the party that had little affinity with a nuclear-based military alliance (she did, however, praise its mission to 'protect the Libyan people from Gaddafi's regime'[61]), her pragmatism appreciated that such a move was politically necessary, even if justifying that lead to an uncharacteristically weak television performance when taken to task by *Newsnight*'s Jeremy Paxman. That Sturgeon was being given such high-profile interview opportunities, however, said a lot about her status within the Scottish Government, although it also ran the risk of exposing her political weaknesses, such as anything relating to economics.

This mattered, for when it came to the dismal science the vast majority of Scots, even those inclined to support independence, remained unconvinced that the SNP's *raison d'être* offered any sort of solution to both the current economic turbulence or Scotland's long-term financial prospects. Following the 2011 election Sturgeon attempted to tackle both, extolling the virtues of what she and others called, rather glibly, a 'Plan MacB', the Scottish Government's argument that bringing forward capital investment – which it had already been doing – rather than cutting public spending 'too quickly and too aggressively' was a better means by which to tackle the UK's deficit.[62]

In terms of the broader economic pitch, Sturgeon railed against 'myths [and] fantasy dressed up as fact' by the three Unionist parties in an article for the *Sunday Herald*, although many of these were arguably straw men. Scotland, she argued, accounted for 8.4 per cent of the UK population but in 2009–10 had contributed 9.4 per cent of overall tax revenue, '£1000 extra for every man, woman and child in Scotland' (the proposition that tax paid ought to correlate to population share was at least an interesting one), while (a hypothetically independent) Scotland's ratio of debt to GDP would be lower than the EU and G7 averages. North Sea oil, meanwhile, represented 'a trillion pound asset base' (she glided over the fact that much of that 'trillion' would end up nowhere near the Treasury) while the 'suggestion' that Scotland's oil wealth was 'fast dwindling, nearly depleted and not worth factoring into future economic assumptions' was 'another myth',[63] even though there was a broad industry consensus that it *was* dwindling and could not offer reliable guidance as to long-term economic performance.

All that would, during the referendum campaign as in late 2011, be dismissed as 'scaremongering'. Of course the real point Sturgeon intended to make was that, as she said at the SNP conference in October, 'with more powers' for the Scottish Parliament, she and others 'could do so much more' to stimulate a sluggish economy, although no one could have accused them of possessing a comprehensive vision as to how. 'With a majority SNP government,' she added, Scotland was taking its 'positive and confident . . . next steps in Scotland's journey.'[64]

Salmond and Sturgeon, meanwhile, remained a formidable political partnership, the strength of which was obvious from gentle ribbing at the First Minister's expense in his deputy's conference speeches, and the fact that she, perhaps alone among her ministerial colleagues, was able to give him what he called 'some pretty stern advice'. Sturgeon, said Salmond, was 'a very strong corrector' of his love for 'the cut and thrust'.[65] It also worked in gender terms, Salmond's worst alpha-male tendencies being tempered by his empathetic deputy.

Increasingly, Sturgeon took a leading role when it came to the referendum. When, in January 2012, Prime Minister David Cameron broke the constitutional impasse by offering to equip Holyrood with the (temporary) power to hold a 'fair, legal and decisive' plebiscite, she railed against it as a 'blatant attempt' to 'interfere' with a decision she claimed was for the Scottish Government to make.[66] This was disingenuous, for in fact she and other senior ministers privately realised a ballot would, in fact, be *ultra vires* under the terms of the 1998

Scotland Act, as was Sturgeon's later argument that including a 'second question' on 'an outcome short of independence' was a 'simple one of democracy',[67] when in reality she wanted a straight yes/no referendum. Finally, at around the same time, Sturgeon rewrote history in claiming that the SNP had 'always supported' the 1988 Claim of Right's reference to the 'sovereign right of the Scottish people to determine the form of government best suited to their needs',[68] when in fact every SNP MP (along with the devo-sceptic Labour veteran Tam Dalyell) had failed to put their names to that document. But the point, of course, was not to be consistent but to depict opponents (be they red, blue or yellow) as intransigent, inflexible and, above all, resistant to the onward march of the Scottish people.

Sturgeon pursued this strategy par excellence and often with a greater degree of credibility than her boss although, amid all this constitutional posturing, health appeared to drop off the agenda (along with much else) for the rest of 2012. The Health Secretary, however, had no choice but to reduce staffing in the Scottish NHS, although there was an emphasis on non-clinical posts so as to ensure 'an increasing proportion of the NHS budget is spent on point of care services'.[69] There was progress, meanwhile, on minimum alcohol pricing, the Conservatives and Liberal Democrats having decided to support the idea after a shift in UK Coalition thinking. Finally, in June 2012, Sturgeon had to handle an outbreak of Legionella in parts of Edinburgh, and while there were predictable criticisms from Labour even the Conservative health spokesman Jackson Carlaw recognised that she and chief medical officer Sir Harry Burns had a good track record of crisis management.

Meanwhile, in a thoughtful speech at the Glasgow University Law School, the first of many over the next two years, Sturgeon drew together her thinking on health, welfare and the constitution in order to make an argument about independence that would feature prominently in the debate ahead. She restated her confidence in Holyrood's 'competence to hold an advisory referendum', still clinging to the idea that Westminster need not be involved, while defending the autumn 2014 date (recently announced by the First Minister) as giving enough time for Scots to 'reach an informed decision'. The key point, however, was: 'In the past, the Union would have been seen as not just the creator but also the guarantor of the values and vision of the post-war welfare state. Today, many see that it is the Union that poses the biggest threat to these values and that vision. We have the power to protect our NHS but because benefits and pensions are reserved, we are powerless to protect the disabled from the worst aspects of welfare reforms. Independence would give us the power not only to protect Scotland from policies that *offend our sense of decency* and social cohesion, it would allow us to build a fairer Scotland.'[70]

Although this was historically confusing (What, therefore, had been the point of independence at the height of the post-war consensus?), it re-orientated the case for independence along utilitarian lines rather than being, as it had often appeared in the past, an existential end in itself.

Much more than other ministers, the Health Secretary often ranged beyond her portfolio, not only on the constitution but in terms of fire-fighting on behalf of the Scottish Government in general and the First Minister in particular. This often made her noticeably uncomfortable (and untypically irritable), especially when it clearly conflicted with her personal view. During a sustained barrage of criticism about Salmond's closeness to Rupert Murdoch, for example, she argued that the First Minister could not distance himself from the media mogul on the basis of 'who you like and who you don't like',[71] when of course that option *was* available and, indeed, applied in other cases, while Sturgeon was also deployed to defend Salmond's decision not to meet the Dalai Lama during a trip to Scotland, apparently under pressure from the Chinese government, something that cannot have sat well with her general approach to international issues (not to forget the principle of self-determination).

There were setbacks. Sturgeon's identification with the SNP's campaign to gain control of Glasgow City Council at local authority elections in May 2012 (the party, she claimed, would 'seize control of the city') proved unhelpful when Labour – despite a series of scandals and splits – actually increased its number of councillors, while her role in the unpleasant case of SNP MSP Bill Walker, who was suspended from the party when allegations surfaced of domestic abuse, again raised question marks over her judgement. It hinged on a February 2008 meeting between a member of her staff and Rob Armstrong, a former brother-in-law of the MSP's third wife; he claimed to have provided clear evidence of a violent past following Walker's election as a councillor, although it clearly had not alarmed the SNP enough to prevent his selection as a parliamentary candidate in Dunfermline a few years later. Of course Sturgeon had not been directly involved in either the meeting or Walker's political advancement, but it was nevertheless embarrassing.

Another non-health issue fronted by Sturgeon was that of same-sex marriage, which she had consistently championed over several years despite occasional foot-dragging from certain Cabinet colleagues, wary of upsetting Catholic and Asian opinion. When several quarters criticised it as a 'dangerous social experiment', Sturgeon stated unequivocally that it was 'the right thing to do', as she had regarding Section 28 more than a decade before.[72]

In all of this Sturgeon demonstrated great empathy with sections of Scottish society who felt marginalised, especially so when it came to those suffering from chronic health problems. In late 2014 Tommy Whitelaw, a dementia-awareness campaigner from Cardonald, told the journalist Peter Ross of a visit the Health Secretary made in August 2012 to his mother, whom he was nursing in her final weeks: 'My mum was very poorly. She couldn't walk, could hardly talk. But there was an absolutely incredible moment.' Sturgeon sat by the bed and held Mrs Whitelaw's hand; she told her how proud she was of Tommy's work and that her mother was called Joan, too. Mrs Whitelaw smiled at that and counted to five on Sturgeon's fingers. 'I had been desperate to hear my mum's voice again,' says Tommy. 'That was just magical. It was Nicola Sturgeon the daughter, not the politician, who knocked on our door that day.'[73]

This was not a one-off. As Sir Harry Burns recalled: 'I've seen her show real empathy, a really caring side, with people – in a meeting or visit – who might have been suffering a bit.'[74] After five years as Health Secretary, Sturgeon was not only popular with professionals ('Not only is she always well briefed. She is always very pleasant and extremely amicable,'[75] said the BMA spokesperson), but also journalists ('She made herself accessible from the start,'[76] said health journalist Helen Puttick) and civil servants ('I have never worked for a more competent minister,'[77] commented one former official). She had been accessible, direct and made a point of not hiding behind professional or political waffle. And in dealing with patients and members of the public Sturgeon had, as Puttick observed, 'stood out as different from the more cautious, remote, politicians who had gone before'.[78]

But wider changes were afoot. On 5 September the Health Secretary told BBC Radio Scotland that a deal between the UK and Scottish Governments on the referendum could be agreed 'in the next few weeks'. Again she said it was not for Westminster to 'dictate' terms, but for both sides to 'talk to each other to get these issues of process resolved'. She knew at that point that concluding those talks would fall to her as the new 'Yes Minister', a reference to her new role as lead minister on the constitution. This also involved Sturgeon stepping down as Health Secretary and instead becoming Infrastructure, Investment and Cities Secretary with a focus on economic recovery.

There were several aims in this change of roles, some personal and others strategic. Understandably, given she had spent more than five years in the role, Sturgeon wanted to move on from health ('She very much wanted out of health,' recalled an aide. 'Even without the referendum she'd have wanted to do something different'[79]), while in career terms she was acutely conscious of lacking any substantial experience of economics.

At health, she had decided how to spend an allocated budget rather than taking strategic decisions, something her new role was intended to address. It was also recognition that when it came to constitutional issues hers was without doubt the most articulate voice the Scottish Government possessed, thus putting her front and centre as the negotiations concluded – not to mention the need to win over more female voters – was a no brainer.

Speaking after the reshuffle, Sturgeon spoke of her pride in having tackled waiting times and hospital infections, providing safer patient care and of course her 'ground-breaking, world-leading legislation on minimum pricing', not to forget having protected both the budget and 'founding principles' of the NHS in Scotland. It could also have been argued, however, that Sturgeon's stewardship of the NHS (as the journalist Euan McColm put it) had been 'too managerial; that she preferred the calm of coasting to risking the potential political problems that might be thrown up by carrying through reform'.[80]

Indeed, during Sturgeon's last months in office, there had been indications that tighter health budgets, rising expenses and demand for services were beginning to take their toll. The College of Emergency Medicine had even written to her (although this only emerged later) warning that most A&E departments in Scotland were regularly unsafe, including those she had reprieved back in 2007 (high mortality rates at Monklands would later lead to an investigation). The Royal College of Physicians of Edinburgh and the Royal College of Nursing Scotland made similar noises, a sign that a relatively benign – and it appeared successful – period was coming to end, vindicating (at least in part) some of the warnings about growing demographic pressures made by Andy Kerr and others five years earlier. Sturgeon also departed at the height of a row involving manipulation of waiting lists by NHS Lothian, an incident that served to undermine all her apparent good work when it came to abolishing 'hidden' waiting lists and the reduction in cancer treatment waiting times. Some critics suggested a lucky Health Secretary had been reshuffled at exactly the right moment.

Sturgeon's new role would be even more challenging, not just the infrastructure brief but also the more pressing challenge of persuading a majority of Scots to support independence once a referendum was agreed. 'If we want a strong economy we must have access to all of Scotland's resources, not just the portion that the UK Government chooses to give us,' she said of the former role before alluding to the latter. 'If it is right, and it is right, for this Parliament to take decisions over health, education and justice, then how can it be anything other than right for this Parliament also to take decisions on the economy, welfare and defence?'[81] The high priestess of Scotland's NHS was about to take on an even bigger role, converting the masses to the one true faith: independence.

Chapter 8

'Yes Minister'

'I'm a huge fan of *Borgen*,' Nicola Sturgeon declared in early 2012. 'This is one of the most credible fictional accounts of the corridors of power and life in politics that I've seen on television, and it's from a woman's perspective too, which is rare.'[1] It was not hard to see why the Deputy First Minister identified so closely with the hit Danish TV series about a female Prime Minister, Birgitte Nyborg, of a small, social democratic nation in northern Europe. The actress Elaine C. Smith even referred to Sturgeon as 'our very own *Borgen* [sic]' during the referendum campaign.[2]

And although it was political drama, it also represented escapism for the Deputy First Minister: 'Looking for some *Borgen* relaxation,'[3] she once tweeted. Sturgeon was also a bit of a fan-girl. As emails released under Freedom of Information later revealed, when the star of the show, Sidse Babett Knudsen, visited Edinburgh for a screening at the Filmhouse cinema in February 2013, the Deputy First Minister's office swung into action in order to secure a meeting as if Knudson were actually Prime Minister of Denmark. Efforts were made to engineer a visit to Holyrood (which, in the judgement of special adviser Liz Lloyd, 'would go down incredibly well in the media, for all of us'), while other emails (some marked 'importance high') negotiated Sturgeon's role at the Filmhouse.

To Sturgeon's obvious delight, she ended up chairing a Q&A

with Knudsen. In short article for the *Sunday Mail* the Deputy First Minister said what she liked most about *Borgen* was that 'it remembers to show the passion people have for what politics can do, in the case of Birgitte, the fictional Prime Minister, for making the lives of Danish citizens better, in my case for helping to build a better Scotland. As a fictional politician elected because she spoke out, broke the rules and challenged the system Birgitte can be a good reminder that we should all, especially the women, remember to challenge the status quo and speak up for what we believe in. And of course, for those of us in Scotland, it shows a kind of modern politics in a northern European nation, making all their own decisions and I like that.'[4]

Sturgeon's appointment to lead for the Scottish Government on the referendum was a very Scandinavian move, although the 'Yes Minister' nickname was a nod to a much-loved British, rather than Danish, television series. Combining the infrastructure and constitutional briefs did not quite make Sturgeon's Scotland's answer to Birgitte Nyborg, but it was pretty close.

Sturgeon met the Scotland Office minister David Mundell in early September (she was amused when his mother called his mobile to check he was okay) and agreed further discussions between her and Scottish Secretary Michael Moore to pave the way for a final meeting between the Prime Minister and Alex Salmond in the next few weeks. Immediately, Westminster noticed a change in tone and style. While Bruce Crawford and Mundell had been able to sort out most of the non-contentious issues surrounding the referendum, it had always been clear to the UK Government that Crawford lacked sufficient authority to 'seal the deal'.

The main unresolved issue was that of how many questions ought to be on the ballot paper, and it was only on the appointment of Sturgeon, recalled someone involved in the negotiations, 'that things suddenly unblocked'. 'Something clearly happened behind the scenes in the SNP which led them to conclude, "Let's go for this referendum, let's make it happen",' he recalled. 'What that something was I doubt we will ever know, but there was a huge shift in attitude once Sturgeon was in post.'[5] At that initial meeting with Mundell, remembered another source, 'She [Sturgeon] made clear everything was on the table, particularly [when it came to] the single question; at one point Nicola talked as if there would be a single question and had to correct herself, saying, "Of course our preference is for two." '[6]

As Sturgeon herself later recalled, it was 'very clear they [the UK government] would not agree to a Section 30 order unless it was on a single question', and although she wished 'that hadn't been their red line',[7] the negotiations were now clearly headed towards a clear yes/no proposition. As one former Yes Scotland strategist recalled, 'Nicola came in [as Yes Minister] and decided within two days we'd go for a single question; she was very clear about that in her mind. At that point it took on a dynamic and momentum of its own.'[8]

Scottish Secretary Michael Moore met the Deputy First Minister towards the end of September and immediately struck up a rapport – and more importantly a feeling of mutual trust – with Sturgeon. 'There was no fun and games as before, she wasn't playing a status game,' recalled Moore, alluding to Alex Salmond's past refusal to meet him. He continued, 'I suggested five minutes to chat together privately and it became half an hour: we agreed we'd discuss pretty much anything without being tied. She wanted to be absolutely clear about the Scottish Parliament deciding key things [about the referendum] . . . we agreed to maintain radio silence, to have no running commentaries during the discussions. By the time we rejoined the meeting, which was full of nervous officials, my judgement was it's not going to be easy but there was a serious prospect of working our way through this. And the tone of that first half hour was then supported by Nicola's behaviour following each subsequent meeting: you could trust her and that was established early on.'[9] The feeling was mutual, Sturgeon later describing her relationship with Moore as 'very professional' and 'very good'. 'I've got a lot of respect for Michael Moore,' she said. 'We disagreed passionately, but I think he was good at his job.'[10]

A second meeting took place in Edinburgh, followed by two further conference calls while Moore was on holiday in Florida, but by 10 October everything was pretty much in place; Moore and Sturgeon even issued a joint statement saying 'substantial progress' had been made while anticipating a final meeting between David Cameron and Alex Salmond the following Monday. This took place on 15 October in Edinburgh, the pair shaking hands and posing for photographs alongside Moore and Sturgeon outside St Andrew's House.

The crucial element of what became known as the 'Edinburgh Agreement' was a Section 30 Order that would temporarily devolve to the Scottish Parliament the power to hold a single-question referendum on independence, conducted 'so as to command the confidence of parliaments, government and people; and deliver a fair test and decisive expression of the views of people in Scotland and a result that everyone would respect'. Thereafter it would fall to the Scottish Government, and Sturgeon as the responsible minister, to place a Referendum Bill before the Scottish Parliament, setting out the date of the referendum, the franchise, the wording of the question and regulations surrounding campaign finance.

Sturgeon and her colleagues believed they had negotiated a good settlement, for not only did it allow them to set the date of the referendum (provided it took place before the end of 2014) and extend the franchise to 16- and 17-year-olds (a long-standing Sturgeon aim), but also decide the wording of the question (subject to Electoral Commission approval). Although they had lost out when it came to the prospect of a second question on 'more powers', the Scottish Government regarded that as a price worth paying for everything else. A few days later Sturgeon addressed delegates at the SNP annual conference in Perth, saying that a Yes vote was 'there to be won, and I believe *will* be won in two years' time'.[11]

Meanwhile Sturgeon became, in the words of one adviser, the main 'interface between the party, government and the wider Yes movement'. Although instinctively a micro-manager, paradoxically on the most important issue of his career Alex

Salmond was content for his deputy to run the show. 'She very deliberately took that role and made it her own,' recalled the aide. 'She had his absolute confidence.'[12] Not only that, reflected an insider, but by this point the First Minister viewed Sturgeon 'as material to his own success'.[13]

The SNP leadership realised it could not run Yes Scotland itself, logistically or politically, but by making it nominally separate with Sturgeon co-ordinating relations between party, government and the campaign's advisory board, Salmond et al. achieved a workable solution. A theory did the rounds at the time that putting Sturgeon in charge also provided a scapegoat should Scotland vote No, but that completely misunderstood the real motivation. 'Nicola ran the show, and Alex was removed from it,' recalled another referendum strategist, 'but then as First Minister he was removed from most things in Scottish politics.'[14]

Although the 'broad church' nature of Yes Scotland did not necessarily sit well with Sturgeon's well-organised approach, she affected to be relaxed about the prospect that those under the Yes umbrella would 'not agree on everything'. 'That is healthy,' she added. 'Indeed, it is confirmation of the vibrant democracy that an independent Scotland would be.'[15] The left-wing 'Common Weal' agenda, for example, soon emerged as what Yes diplomatically called 'an interesting contribution to the debate'. Sturgeon was said to be 'broadly supportive' though 'wary of its tax implications',[16] which revealed a lot about her own ideological journey since the 1980s.

Common Weal, however, had a strong social justice core, and Sturgeon would prove a key figure in developing that aspect of the pro-independence narrative that the SNP hoped would deliver a Yes victory in the autumn of 2014 (the precise date was as yet unspecified), something that would strongly echo her commitment in 2004 to combine 'a strategy for economic success with a much stronger commitment to tackling inequality and promoting social justice'.[17]

This goal necessarily involved drawing points of contrast, not only with the 'austerity agenda' of the UK coalition government but also with the Scottish Labour Party, so when its leader Johann Lamont made a much-publicised speech suggesting her party would ditch policies such as the council tax freeze, free prescriptions and free tuition fees, with the memorable line that Scotland could not be 'the only something-for-nothing country in the world', Sturgeon was swift in attacking what she called Labour's 'cuts commission' (Lamont had announced a policy review group). 'What Johann Lamont fails to realise', she added, 'is that the social wage put in place by this SNP in Government delivers protection to households and families across Scotland from the impact of the UK Government's attack on living standards and economic growth.'[18]

Nuance and details inevitably got lost in the rhetorical mix. Lamont's 'something-for-nothing' line, for example, was intended to make the reasonable point that an economic model based on low tax and high spending was not sustainable, while many questioned how 'social democratic' or 'progressive' policies like freezing council tax (with a resulting squeeze on local authority budgets), free prescriptions (for the wealthy as well as the poor) and free university tuition (which had done little to improve access) actually were. The point Sturgeon was making was that independence would offer a choice between one approach (austerity) and the other (social democracy).

At First Minister's Questions Lamont tried to shore up her position by turning her fire on Sturgeon personally, pointing out that the Deputy First Minister lived 'in a household with an income of over £200,000 a year' (Sturgeon's salary together with that of SNP chief executive Peter Murrell). 'Is it fair that the Sturgeon household on £200,000 a year gets universal benefits,' asked Lamont, 'when families on average earnings pay more for childcare than they do for their mortgage?' In response Sturgeon drew attention to the 'dividing line in Scottish politics'. 'We will be proud to protect the council tax freeze,' she continued, 'we'll be proud to protect free education for working-class young people, we'll be proud to protect free personal care and bus travel for our pensioners.'[19]

Paradoxically, Sturgeon pursued her differentiation strategy just as her party was poised to bring an important element of its defence policy into line with political orthodoxy. The issue of NATO had been a long-running sore for Alex Salmond (it had been debated at an SNP conference in the late 1980s when the Young Scottish Nationalists, including Sturgeon, had been opposed to any change), but with the referendum looming he finally decided to lance the boil and commit the SNP to pursuing membership of the North Atlantic Treaty Organisation should Scotland become an independent country.

Given Sturgeon's CND background it was not surprising that she did not play a prominent role in the debate surrounding NATO (which was, after all, a nuclear alliance), nor did she contribute to a highly-charged debate at the 2012 SNP conference in Perth. In an attempt to pacify the SNP's left wing, Salmond also promised an 'explicit ban' on nuclear weapons in the written constitution of an independent Scotland, while defence spokesman Angus Robertson's statement that a future SNP government would only maintain NATO membership 'subject to an agreement that Scotland will not host nuclear weapons' was clearly intended to mollify doubters such as Sturgeon. The pro-NATO argument at conference, meanwhile, was framed entirely in tactical terms: without the change, the (implicit) argument ran, opponents would exploit the SNP's position and therefore weaken its chances of winning the referendum.

The main motion (in favour of NATO membership) was passed only narrowly, leaving the SNP split more or less right down the middle, with two Highlands and Islands MSPs, John Finnie and Jean Urquhart, later resigning in protest. For a party that had prided itself on unity and discipline since 2007, this was quite a blow, and indeed two branches in Sturgeon's constituency association had put their names to the defeated anti-NATO amendment. The Deputy First Minister, however, publicly, if unostentatiously, supported the move.

On 3 December 2012, meanwhile, Sturgeon made what the Scottish Government talked up as 'a significant speech' and a 'major address' to an audience of civic groups, business leaders and members of the international community at Glasgow's Strathclyde University.[20] The speech, which continued a series of thoughtful explorations of Nationalist thinking begun earlier that year, was a clear attempt by Sturgeon to give the differentiation strategy a philosophical basis. One key passage quoted what she called one of the Nationalist movement's 'great intellectuals', the late Professor Sir Neil MacCormick, who had distinguished between 'existentialist' (the belief in independence simply because Scotland was a nation) and 'utilitarian' (independence as 'a tool to deliver a better society') strands of Scottish Nationalism. Sturgeon continued: 'While I recognise the distinction Neil drew and realise that there are some in our national movement who base their political beliefs more on the fact of nationhood, I would suggest that today most SNP members are an amalgam of these two strands. For my part, and I believe for my generation, I have never doubted that Scotland is a nation. And while I might not go on about a thousand years of history and that sort of thing I take it for granted as a simple fact that Scotland is a nation with an inalienable right to self-determination. But for me the fact of nationhood or Scottish identity is not the motive force for independence. Nor do I believe that independence, however desirable, is essential for the preservation of our distinctive Scottish identity. And I don't agree at all that feeling British – with all of the shared social, family and cultural heritage that makes up such an identity – is in any way inconsistent with a pragmatic, utilitarian support for political independence. My conviction that Scotland should be independent stems from the principles, not of identity or nationality, but of democracy and social justice.'

Thus Sturgeon's 'central argument' was not just that independence was 'more than an end in itself' but that by 'bringing the powers home, by being independent', a Yes vote could enable Scots to 'build the better nation we all want'. She continued, 'So the debate we will have over these next two years must be a debate about the most effective political and economic unit to achieve the economic growth and the social justice that the Scottish people want. It is, in many ways, our version of the same question being asked across all mature western democracies: how to build a thriving but sustainable economy that benefits the many not the few. The Westminster system of government has had its chance – and failed. Today, independence is the pragmatic way forward.'

Sturgeon also reflected on the changing nature of the Union, suggesting that the creation of the Welfare State had played 'an overwhelming role in giving the union a new purpose' following the Second World War, while devolution to Scotland, Wales and Northern Ireland had also been 'an attempt to renew the UK state'. But 'the UK's ability to re-invent itself', she concluded, was 'spent'. 'The Westminster parties are at best sceptical [of] and at worst hostile to further substantial reform in Scotland's interests,' argued Sturgeon. 'The post-war economic decline has continued and now the very institutions which once made us distinct, the welfare state and – in England – the NHS, are under attack from the Westminster system of government.'

This touched upon another aspect of the SNP's developing narrative, the idea that only a Yes vote could protect what Nationalists saw as 'good' elements of the British Union, i.e. the NHS and Welfare State. And to those, continued Sturgeon, who said the answer was 'to change the occupant of number 10 and the colour of the UK government', she replied, '[W]e have been there and done that and the challenges we face remain undiminished.' This naturally supported her long-held view that the Labour Party, pre- and post-Blair, was 'not an alternative to Conservatism' but simply 'business as usual'.[21]

It was, in the opinion of the *Herald*'s Magnus Gardham, 'a measured, thoughtful and politically astute speech, aimed squarely at persuading Labour-minded voters that independence offers the best hope of delivering social justice in Scotland',[22] and indeed that was the first strand of the SNP's referendum strategy for 2013. The second, as articulated in Sturgeon's speech, was 'to lay out our ideas – and open up for wider debate – the ways in which the powers of independence can be used to address the deep seated challenges in our economy and society'.[23] Indeed, while 'existential' Nationalism could afford to gloss over the specifics of the independence proposition, the 'utilitarian' variety could not.

Much like putative membership of NATO, the details of an independent Scotland's relationship with the European Union (EU) fell to Sturgeon to explain in the closing weeks of 2012 and first few months of 2013. Back in 2007 Nicola Sturgeon had told MSPs that 'Scotland would automatically be a member of the European Union upon independence. There is legal opinion to back that up. I don't think the legal position is in any doubt.'[24]

It was not, however, that simple, not least the implicit claim that an independent Scotland's membership would be 'automatic', for the Member State was the United Kingdom (which included Scotland). More to the point, it seemed clear that, far from being a formality, independent Scottish membership would require unanimity among all 27 EU Member States (Croatia would become number 28 in July 2013), not to mention assent by the European Parliament and ratification by 27 legislatures. And although EU Treaties were opaque as to what might happen were part of a Member State's territory to secede, the SNP's position was also less than clear-cut. In March 2012 the BBC's Andrew Neil had asked Alex Salmond if he had 'sought advice' from his Scottish law officers, to which the First Minister said 'yes, in terms of the [debate]' while adding that he could not 'reveal the legal advice of law officers'.[25]

But when, in July 2012, the Scottish (Freedom of) Information Commissioner ruled that ministers had to publicly state if they had asked for advice on this point, the Scottish Government decided to challenge it in court. It seemed clear no serious work had been done on the SNP's European policy for quite some time and, instead, it fell back on rather tenuous debating points. Sturgeon, for example, cited a trio of 'eminent legal authorities' in support of the SNP's position[26] (Emile Noel, Lord Mackenzie-Stuart and Eamonn Gallagher), even though only one (Mackenzie-Stuart) had actually been a lawyer and all three had given their views between 1989 and 1992, prior to Maastricht, the single currency and a host of other major reforms, not least the Lisbon Treaty.

In October 2012, in her developing role as minister for damage limitation, Sturgeon informed the Scottish Parliament (to audible gasps from opposition MSPs) that, contrary to Salmond's March interview, there existed no such advice from the Scottish law officers, resulting in the First Minister's worst barrage of headlines since taking office in 2007 ('EU LIAR' screamed the front page of the hitherto friendly *Scottish Sun*). Sturgeon, with considerable understatement, told the BBC that creating the impression 'we had legal advice, that we were not prepared to reveal because somehow it didn't suit our purposes' had been 'unfortunate'.[27]

The EU issue warmed up again in February 2013 when the UK Government published the first of its 'Scotland Analysis' papers, the first of which asserted that, in the event of a Yes vote, the rest of the UK (rUK) would constitute the 'continuing state' and therefore an independent Scotland would have to apply for EU membership. Responding in a blog, Sturgeon described international law on state succession as 'ambiguous' (which it was) and said for 'the UK government to argue that the UK will be a "continuing state" and that an independent Scotland would have no rights betrays *a near colonial attitude* (author's italics) to Scotland's position as a nation and gives lie to any suggestion that they see Scotland as an equal partner in the UK. It also raises a very important question for the UK government – if they are prepared to lay claim to the assets of the UK are they also prepared to take on all of its liabilities, such as the UK national debt?'

Despite an uncharacteristic slip in the use of the word 'colonial', Sturgeon's latter point about national debt was a good one, for there were precedents under international law that only a recognised successor state could inherit debt liabilities. Furthermore, the legal opinion presented to the UK Government was, argued Sturgeon, 'just that – an opinion. It is not fact.' She quoted two authorities who believed independence would produce two equal successor states (although this seemed to be based upon the mistaken assumption that the UK comprised only Scotland and England), but was on strong ground in arguing that the status of Scotland and rUK following a Yes vote would be 'determined not by assertions of law, but by negotiation and agreement'.[28]

There had, for example, been the reunification of Germany in 1990, an example of realpolitik Sturgeon wielded as proof that the EU was, whatever the legal position, a 'flexible institution'. 'When the Berlin Wall fell in late 1989,' she wrote, 'few at that point would have expected a united Germany to be part of the then European Community within less than twelve months – but that is exactly what happened when German reunification took place on October 3, 1990.' Scotland's case, she added, was 'more straightforward' given its forty years of 'existing membership'. That much was also true, for Scots were already European 'citizens', a legal identity that could not easily be withdrawn.

The question of treaties and opt-outs was more difficult territory for the SNP, and Sturgeon instead resorted to assertion, arguing it was 'perfectly reasonable' to claim Scotland would 'jointly inherit' the existing UK opt-out of the single currency; that a new Member State could not 'be forced into euro membership' (untrue in theory, truer in practice), while Scotland's EU partners 'would understand' its desire to stay out of the Schengen borderless area and instead co-operate with Ireland, the rUK and Crown Dependencies via the Common Travel Area (Sturgeon later claimed, erroneously, that Croatia's membership of the EU would not compel it to join either the euro or Schengen).[29] None of this, of course, was by any means certain, not least an independent Scotland retaining a share of the UK's EU budget rebate.

The then European Commission president, José Manuel Barroso, had also made a series of statements that cast doubt on the SNP's confident position, prompting an interesting contrast in responses from the Finance Secretary and Deputy First Minister. While John Swinney rejected Barroso's statements as having 'no foundation', Sturgeon took a more constructive approach, saying his opinion was 'important' and ought 'to be respected'. She then embarked upon a European charm offensive, asking Barroso for a meeting (which he refused) and writing to the heads of the EU's other 27 Member States.

The prolonged EU debate also allowed Sturgeon to make another point of differentiation, particularly after David Cameron announced plans for a referendum on the UK's relationship with Brussels. As she and others pointed out, in that context it was more than a little ironic for the UK Government to warn that somehow independence posed the *only* risk to Scotland's continuing place in the EU. Speaking to the British–Irish Chamber of Commerce conference in Dublin, Sturgeon was careful to acknowledge (as she had in the past) that 'the EU needs reform', but said an independent Scotland would have the 'opportunity to build alliances and forge relationships with like-minded countries'. (Elsewhere, Sturgeon said she was 'not a huge enthusiast for ever more integration',[30] and that the EU's democratic deficit was 'not acceptable'.[31]) She also stated 'emphatically' that the Prime Minister's proposed 'journey' was not one the Scottish Government wished 'Scotland to be part of', for an in/out EU referendum would create 'uncertainty' and potentially 'deter foreign investors' and threaten jobs. Naturally, the SNP denied that the Scottish referendum would pose similar risks.[32]

Over time, however, the European issue became less of a problem for the SNP, with voters only marginally engaged with the minutiae of constitutional law and fishing rights, although Sturgeon's fire-fighting panache had also helped: slick and authoritative, she had defused the situation to a far greater extent than Alex Salmond might have done. As the *Daily Telegraph*'s Alan Cochrane observed, the First Minister was 'increasingly relying' on his deputy 'to get him out of holes he's dug for himself'.[33] And while the party's position was far from 'consistent', as Sturgeon claimed, the Scottish Government emerged in a stronger position as a result of her handiwork.

In January 2013 Sturgeon also attempted to neutralise

persistent Unionist questions as to what sort of diplomatic presence an independent Scotland would have, telling the House of Commons Foreign Affairs Committee that the Scottish Government was planning for around 100 embassies and consular offices compared with the UK's 270, as well as a new internal security service similar to MI5 (the prospect of an external MI6-type operation was merely 'an option').[34]

Issue by issue, Sturgeon was attempting to shore up the SNP's position while closing down opposition lines of attack, while in March 2013 she unveiled the Scottish Referendum (Franchise) Bill, which would lower the franchise allowing 16- and 17-year-olds to, as she put it, 'take responsibility for Scotland's future' by voting in the referendum – for Sturgeon the fulfilment of a long-standing policy wish.[35] (She was, however, uncompromisingly *against* giving prisoners the right to vote, despite that being a minority view among other European nations.)

At the SNP's spring conference in Inverness Sturgeon held the Referendum Bill aloft and told delegates: 'I joined this party when I was 16 years old. When I joined the SNP I of course imagined Scotland being independent, but I never ever imagined putting my signature on the Bill that will help make independence a reality. The Bill will set September 18 2014 as the date, Scotland's date with destiny.' Sturgeon said the SNP had 'shown beyond any doubt that Scotland can afford to be independent', while hitting out at what she called 'disgraceful welfare cuts being imposed on Scotland by a Tory government we didn't vote for'.[36] Indeed by March 2013 welfare had both become a central part of the Yes campaign, but also one of its policy weaknesses.

In one sense, the Conservative-led government at Westminster provided the perfect backdrop. In her conference speech, for example, Sturgeon claimed that by 2015 a 'cumulative cut' would take £4.5 billion 'from the purses and wallets of ordinary, hard-working people right across Scotland who can least afford it', the 'awful price' of 'Westminster control' and 'a dagger to the heart of the fairness and social justice that we hold so dear'.[37] This was hyperbole, for the actual figure was closer to £2 billion (lower than the UK Government's own estimate) while, despite Sturgeon's strong association with the social justice agenda, she was remarkably vague when it came to outlining policy alternatives rather than simply pledging to reverse aspects of UK reforms she did not approve of (for example, the so-called 'bedroom tax' and Universal Credit roll out).

A leaked Scottish Cabinet paper had talked of 'exploring the possibility of a combined tax and benefits service in the more medium term', while in the long term Sturgeon depicted it as a journey 'on the road to a separate Scottish welfare system that meets Scotland's needs'. Pushed for more detail, she described something that was 'fair and sustainable, protects the vulnerable and supports people into work', although that did not sound very different from the UK government's aim of making 'it fairer, more affordable and better able to tackle poverty, worklessness and welfare dependency'.

Sturgeon also announced another expert group (the first having done little more than describe the status quo) that would look at 'the medium- to longer-term options for reform of the welfare system and the delivery models that will best support that'. This included Jon Kvist of the University of Southern Denmark, a nod to the Deputy First Minister's respect for the Danish way of doing such things, although he and the rest of the group were told to bear in mind 'the economic and fiscal circumstances' and consider potential savings as well as the costs of any new policies. Even this report (due in early 2014), Sturgeon later conceded, would not actually firm up details of a new welfare system.

The mood music, however, was clear: independence would give Scotland the *opportunity* to chart a different path, even if it was not clear where that path would lead while, in the interim, Sturgeon announced initiatives like a £25-million fund for deprived areas to demonstrate that the Scottish Government was attempting to tackle inequality even without the 'full powers of independence'.

More broadly, Sturgeon's independence pitch – with occasional lapses – was markedly more realistic than many of her colleagues', not least the often-hyperbolic Alex Salmond. As Sturgeon reflected in a May 2013 speech, 'There isn't always an absolute objective truth to be found on issues where negotiation and the policy choices of governments yet to be elected will help shape Scotland. There are facts that will be set out, of course, but the referendum will not simply be a contest of competing "facts". Instead, when the Yes and No campaigns set out their stalls, people will be asked to make a qualitative judgment about which is more credible and compelling and about who they trust most with Scotland's future.'[38] This was true for, if the referendum resembled a trial, then each side was in the process of presenting their pro- or anti-independence evidence to the jury. In that context the legally-trained Sturgeon was the SNP's star counsel: cool, authoritative and persuasive, traits that proved helpful as she stepped up the more negative side of a campaign that had hitherto prided itself on being relentlessly 'positive'.

In that same speech, Sturgeon warned Scots that voting No to independence would represent a 'gamble' that would pave the way to a 'bleak' future of poorer children, longer working hours and a broken welfare state. This was part of the SNP's 'two futures' narrative, an attempt to regain the initiative amid Unionist questions about currency and pension arrangements in an independent Scotland, neither of which were the pro-independence side's strongest suit. Sturgeon also attracted a degree of media and opposition ridicule for her suggestion that there existed 'a natural majority' in Scotland for independence. 'I mean that people will vote yes', she explained, 'if we can persuade them that it opens the door to a wealthier and fairer country.'[39]

In another lecture, this time at Edinburgh University's Academy of Government, Sturgeon revisited her theme about independence amounting to a 'partnership' with the rest of the UK rather than 'separation' from it. 'Independence is not a departure from, but the logical continuation of the devolution journey that Scotland embarked upon in 1997,' she argued. 'Far from marking a separation from our friends and relations across these islands, independence opens the door to a renewed partnership between us.' She gave the example of Ireland, which the Prime Minister had visited the previous year: 'He and the Taoiseach produced a joint declaration which said: "The relationship between our two countries has never been stronger or more settled, as complex or as important as it is today." That statement could easily apply to an independent Scotland.'[40]

This was all about presenting independence as a perfectly normal – and generally risk-free – state of affairs for countries both small and large. In this context, the Scottish Government's White Paper or 'independence prospectus' was a significant development, and one in which Sturgeon was fully involved. 'She took ownership of the White Paper,' recalled a ministerial colleague. 'That was her baby . . . she was in charge of the whole thing.'[41] Pulling together material for the lengthy document was a huge logistical task, but one well suited to the methodical Deputy First Minister. The early stages were not without problems; at one stage the external affairs minister Humza Yousaf left his draft portion of the document inside a laptop case that was stolen from the back of a taxi. Although it was later returned, Sturgeon, recalled one aide, 'gave him [Humza] an absolute dressing down'.[42] As a former staffer observed, with Sturgeon the 'wrath' was 'certainly there', but manifested itself rarely and 'was neither as bad nor as personal' as that of Alex Salmond.[43]

The point of the White Paper was not only to set out how the 'powers of independence' might be used but also to have answers to voters' detailed questions once the electoral mindset switched more fully to the proposition early in 2014. Therefore it had to be voluminous but also accessible; 'the style of the White Paper,' observed a colleague, 'bore Nicola's imprint'.[44] A certain degree of hyperbole attached itself to the document, which in reality was not a White Paper at all, but a political manifesto. The First Minister said it would 'resonate down through the ages', while Sturgeon described it as 'a big moment in the referendum campaign, perhaps the biggest so far'.[45]

At its launch in Glasgow's Science Centre – an event well attended by domestic and international media – Sturgeon (sporting jacket cuffs made from Ayrshire lace) and Salmond stood side by side to unveil, and take questions about, *Scotland's Future: Your Guide to an Independent Scotland.* Sturgeon took the lion's share of work for the SNP before and after the press conference, media exposure that was significant, for it was the first time much of the London-based and international media had seen the Deputy First Minister in action.

Childcare, the major new policy at the heart of the White Paper, was testament to Sturgeon's influence. With independence, the Scottish Government pledged, 600 hours of free childcare would be made available to around half the country's two-year-olds, a very Scandinavian pitch. 'It would give parents, in particular women, the opportunities many of them are priced out of just now because of the prohibitive cost of childcare,' Sturgeon later told MSPs, 'the opportunity to participate in the workforce. It would grow the economy and increase revenues as well, allowing us to make that policy affordable and sustainable.'[46]

Later, under greater scrutiny, elements of the childcare proposal appeared less than robust; the Scottish Government even admitted it had not been tested via the usual economic modelling. But the point was to be aspirational, although that rather undermined Sturgeon's claim that *Scotland's Future* offered a 'comprehensive set of answers about the practicalities of independence', setting out both the 'vision and the detailed plan' for an independent Scotland.[47]

Tragic events in Glasgow a few days later, meanwhile, also kept Sturgeon in the media spotlight. When a police helicopter crashed into Glasgow's *Clutha* bar, she led the Scottish Government's response with typically good judgement and much-needed empathy. 'Our hearts go out to everyone who has been bereaved,' said Sturgeon at the scene. 'It is impossible to imagine the grief and loss they are experiencing, but they should know that the thoughts and prayers of everyone across this city, and across Scotland, are with them at this unimaginably difficult time.'[48]

Those unfortunate events aside, 2013 was not perceived by strategists as a good year for the Yes campaign, which had been beset with bad headlines and often pungent opposition attacks. Therefore Sturgeon, as a former aide recalled, was 'determined to go into the first few weeks of 2014 making a big impression'.[49] Speaking to the BBC, she predicted Yes would stage a comeback, saying she firmly believed that 'who wins the economic argument will win the referendum'.[50]

Whatever the broader campaign issues, Sturgeon personally was in a good place. Already widely perceived as the Yes side's standout performer, she had also seen off the new Secretary of State for Scotland, Alistair Carmichael, shortly after his appointment in an October 2013 reshuffle. Spun by the UK Government as someone who would take the fight to the SNP (unlike, by implication, Michael Moore), in their first televised head-to-head on STV's *Scotland Tonight*, Carmichael was reduced to appealing for the moderator to intervene. 'Oh come on,' Sturgeon told him in a killer blow, 'you can hold your own, surely.' Political commentator Fraser Nelson wrote that 'a genteel Liberal Democrat' had been 'disembowelled by a ferocious and merciless Nationalist', adding, 'She seemed to quite enjoy it.'[51] It was a useful reminder that, beneath Sturgeon's usually reasonable demeanour, there lurked a terrier-like instinct to go for the jugular.

Sturgeon was, if anything, even more prominent during the last nine months of the campaign than at any time since her appointment as Yes Minister in the autumn of 2012. She also continued to shape pro-independence strategy, telling another journalist that early 2014 would bring key 'strands' to the fore: a focus on the economic benefits of independence, a push on bread-and-butter issues such as pensions and (importantly) health rather than EU entry negotiations, and finally an attempt to put the No campaign under pressure as to the possible disadvantages of Scotland remaining part of the Union. 'If you say "Boo" once, you frighten somebody,' explained Sturgeon. 'You say it again, you don't frighten them quite as much.'

As ever, the Deputy First Minister rejected the contrary analysis, chiefly that the Yes side's 'evangelical optimism' might strike voters are unrealistic. 'As if on cue,' wrote her interviewer Tom Gordon, 'her serious face arrives.' 'I never have been the kind of Nationalist who says the streets are paved with gold,' said Sturgeon. 'Scotland, like every other country on the planet, will have its challenges.' She added, 'We face challenges – demography [a growing elderly population], constrained public finances – but the question is: does independence better equip us to face these challenges or not, and I think it does. I don't take a view that just by the snap of your fingers or waving a wand, becoming independent makes everything fine. But it does put you in charge of your own destiny, and that's always a better place to be.'

Sturgeon was also prepared to countenance referendum defeat, not a prospect Alex Salmond ever publicly contemplated. 'I'd be gutted,' she admitted. 'I'll be gutted. But will I stop believing in independence, will I stop arguing for independence? The SNP will still be in Government. We'll still have a country to govern. We'll fight the election in 2016.'[52] The use of the formulation 'we'll fight' was important, for of course it did reveal who Sturgeon believed would be in charge of both the SNP and the country in the event of a No vote.

The first event in Sturgeon's 2014 fightback was a speech at St Andrews University on 6 January, something that had been arranged in haste just before Christmas and then drafted by the special advisers Ewan Crawford and Noel Dolan, although with heavy input from the Deputy First Minister herself. Before an audience including academics and university staff, Sturgeon argued that the 'transformational potential of independence' was the 'over-riding' reason to vote Yes on September 18, not party loyalty. She continued, 'If you accept the principle that the best way of ensuring success is to give ourselves the powers that help determine it, then it doesn't matter whether or not you support the SNP or our specific plans for using those powers. Party loyalty should not be a decisive factor in this debate. Indeed, I would have thought that for most Tory voters the idea of a parliament that has the power not just to spend money but also responsibility to raise it and be accountable for how it does so, would be inherently appealing.' She also struggled to understand why 'a Labour politician would prefer to have a Tory prime minister in Downing Street than have a Labour prime minister in Edinburgh'. Then, pursuing one of her three 'strands', Sturgeon attempted to turn the tables on Unionists, saying they had 'asked – and had answered – a multitude of questions about what will happen if we vote yes'. 'But the many questions about what will happen in the event of a no vote', she added, 'go completely unanswered.'[53]

Sturgeon's St Andrews speech was significant for another reason. 'We were worried that no one would turn up,' recalled an aide, 'but actually it was packed, and I think Nicola got the idea at that point that public meetings could become a really important part of the campaign; at that moment I think she decided to commit more to it.'[54] Indeed, over the next eight months, perhaps no politician would have as much face-to-face contact with the voting public than the Deputy First Minister who, much more so than Alex Salmond, bore the burden of speaking at dozens of events with unfailing articulacy and good grace.

The *Guardian*, for example, was impressed with Sturgeon's performance at a packed community college in Livingston. 'She must have been exhausted but her focus never wavered,' wrote Libby Brooks. 'She was a passionate and charismatic advocate, bouncing from currency to the constitution with ease, but also human and good-humoured, reflecting the audience's anxieties and making obviously off-the-cuff – and properly funny – jokes.'[55] Similarly, this author watched a hitherto lukewarm (and predominantly English) audience at UCL warm to the Deputy First Minister in the course of an accomplished – and often very funny – Q&A session in February 2014.

Although undeniably effective, not all these appearances went to plan. A televised clash between Scottish Labour leader

Johann Lamont and Sturgeon on STV's *Scotland Tonight* could only loosely have been described as a 'debate', as the station's political editor later described it, more a 'stairheid rammy'. Characteristically, the Deputy First Minister made a point of being self-critical in retrospect. 'I think in our heart-of-hearts, Johann and I would both like to turn the clock back on that debate,' she said later. 'When you are in that situation, if you hold back, unless you know your opponent is going to behave, you just get steamrollered.' Sturgeon denied, however, being 'aggressive'. 'I think I was assertive. A woman is assertive in debate and is immediately described as aggressive.'[56]

It was also Sturgeon, rather than the First Minister, who led the Scottish Government's response to a major intervention from Chancellor George Osborne in February 2014. After months of speculation, in an Edinburgh speech the Treasury chief formally declared that in the event of a Yes vote the UK's three main parties would not agree to a 'currency union' between an independent Scotland and the rest of the UK. Several days before Salmond had responded at length in a rather inconsequential speech, Sturgeon warned that an attempt by the 'Westminster Establishment' to lay down the law to Scotland would backfire,[57] although that, of course, did not amount to a wholly credible rebuttal of the Chancellor's detailed case against currency union (although when Salmond wobbled on the idea of adopting a 'Plan B', Sturgeon and John Swinney cautioned against). 'Again she was left to do all the fire-fighting,' recalled a former staffer. 'The First Minister was nowhere to be seen.'[58] This, however, was deliberate. 'The agreement during the referendum', recalled one senior minister, 'was that Alex would play the role of the statesman, while Nicola would take the flak and get her hands dirty.'[59]

By the spring of 2014, momentum appeared to be back with Yes Scotland and the Scottish Government. At the SNP's spring conference in Aberdeen, Sturgeon delivered a bravura performance, urging Labour voters to back independence and 'get' their 'party back'. 'For everyone out there with Labour in your heart, the message is clear,' she said. 'Don't vote No to stop the SNP. Vote Yes to reclaim the Labour Party.' It was a clever message borne of her long-standing belief that Labour had begun abandoning its natural support base in the mid to late 1980s.

'After 80 years of campaigning,' continued Sturgeon, a reference to the SNP's recent anniversary, 'the last mile of our journey to independence is upon us. It may well be the hardest mile of all. So we will encourage each other, cheer each other and, yes, if needs be, we will carry each other over the finishing line. But, friends, we will not fall. I want you to hear this and believe it in your heart.'

The Deputy First Minister's 36-minute speech was greeted with a lengthy standing ovation from SNP delegates, her position within the party as Salmond's natural successor now irrevocably established. 'Her speech in Aberdeen was masterful,' observed a senior Nationalist. 'The content wasn't brilliant but her delivery was terrific – it was a real leader's speech. I thought to myself, she's now ready for this.'[60]

In Aberdeen the First Minister also announced that two junior ministers (and contemporaries of Sturgeon's), Angela Constance and Shona Robison, were to be promoted to the Cabinet, taking female representation to 40 per cent. Sturgeon boldly urged Salmond to increase it even further, while in June she chaired 'an all-women Cabinet' event in Edinburgh, bringing together representatives from 130 different organisations to discuss issues related to the referendum. Misogyny had long been a feature of Scottish politics and, on his 'Just Say Naw' speaking tour, the former Labour MP George Galloway disparagingly described Sturgeon as 'Thatcher in a kilt'. She had, he added, 'turned debate into something akin to domestic abuse', while attacking her 'empty dream of a Scandinavian Disneyland. Disnaeland more like.'[61]

The summer of 2014 and the last '100 days' of the referendum campaign were packed with key, and potentially beneficial, events for the Yes campaign. Ahead of elections to the European Parliament on 22 May, Sturgeon was prominent in framing it as a contest between the SNP's 'open and friendly view of Europe' and UKIP's 'anti-European agenda',[62] although this strategy backfired when UKIP's David Coburn ended up winning the 'third seat' earmarked by the SNP leadership for the former Conservative candidate and Glasgow Asian activist Tasmina Ahmed-Sheikh. Glasgow playing host to the Commonwealth Games in August, however, presented the Yes campaign with an ideal backdrop. 'I think it will inevitably leave a feel-good factor,' Sturgeon told the *Observer*. 'I think confidence not only in Glasgow but across the country is high. I think there is a very significant momentum behind the "yes" campaign and I feel it everywhere I go in the country. The momentum is with us and as we come out of the Commonwealth Games at the weekend that is us into the final straight of the campaign and that momentum will be visible.'[63]

By September 2014, even before a YouGov poll gave Yes its first lead, confidence among Nationalists was running very high, bolstered by internal analysis that gave them a four-point lead. 'I definitely sense a shift,' observed Sturgeon early that month. 'This is a referendum, it's not an election, but certainly I remember very well how that felt in 2011 when you just got the sense that something was moving in terms of opinion. And I feel that now.'[64]

When the three main Unionist parties responded to this perceived 'shift' (though voting intentions during this period were actually remarkably stable) with 'a Vow' to equip the Scottish Parliament with 'extensive new powers', Sturgeon dismissed it as a 'panicked scramble to try and bribe the people of Scotland with a last-minute flimsy offer',[65] while at the same time promising (during the 'Big, Big Debate' at Glasgow's Hydro) to help deliver it should a majority of Scots vote No.

More significant when it came to shifting undecided voters in the closing stages of the campaign was the SNP's claim that Scottish NHS funding and, indeed, its public sector status were threatened by remaining in the UK, an argument with a rather shaky factual basis (the Scottish Government already decided the NHS budget and whether or not it could be privatised) but which resonated, at least in part, because Sturgeon had been so successful as Health Secretary in presenting the SNP (rather than Labour) as the party of the NHS.

It was a very New Labour tactic ('24 hours to save our NHS,' said Tony Blair in 1997.) but an effective one. 'It was', Sturgeon recalled later, 'always an argument we intended to make . . . it was one of the arguments that I think started to shift opinion towards yes.'[66] As former policy chief Alex Bell recalled, Sturgeon had been the first minister 'to realise that the things that mattered in fighting the referendum were the areas that were already devolved'.[67] This had been her instinct since the start of the referendum campaign. 'In hindsight', a former Yes Scotland strategist later reflected, 'there should have been more campaigning on "devolved" issues from the outset.'[68]

On 4 September 2014, Alex Salmond and his deputy marked ten years as leader and deputy leader of the SNP with a remarkable walkabout in the centre of Glasgow, during which they were mobbed by hundreds of activists and members of the public. It had been, and remained, a highly successful partnership, and indeed one crucial to the growth and success of both the SNP and support for independence. The relationship, however, was not without tension, with internal differences over issues like restoring the 50p rate of income tax on which Salmond was a dove, and cutting Corporation Tax, on which he was more hawkish. His ill-disciplined freelancing in interviews, for example in *GQ* with former Blair spin doctor Alastair Campbell, must have infuriated his more meticulous and cautious deputy.

Although outwardly loyal, Sturgeon would often politely contradict or distance herself from something Salmond had said, while those who attended 'political' meetings of the Scottish Cabinet noticed that she was 'the only one who would and could challenge' the First Minister in front of colleagues.[69] The journalist Alan Cochrane even introduced a measurement called the 'Sturgeon Scale' to gauge her approval (or otherwise) of the man she described as her 'mentor'. 'A lot of noise from Ms Sturgeon in support of her party and leader' in the Holyrood Chamber, he wrote, 'would probably rate only about two on my new scale. Seven, eight or nine, on the other hand, would signify almost total silence from the lady and would suggest that she's not best pleased about the way things are currently going.'[70] Privately, according to former advisers, Sturgeon could be quite critical of her boss, comically rolling her eyes as she recounted his latest verbal.

When Salmond went head to head with Better Together's Alistair Darling at Glasgow's Royal Conservatoire in the first of two televised debates, one report said Sturgeon had been seen shaking her head at the First Minister's bizarre line of questioning about aliens and other 'scare stories'. Afterwards, there were rumours at Holyrood that Noel Dolan had briefed journalists to the effect that 'Nicola should have done the debate'. For the second joust Sturgeon was cleverly drafted in (via the unlikely route of having done the 'ice-bucket challenge' with the First Minister earlier that day) to ensure her boss was more robust. It indicated that, over time, the relationship had become less one of mentor/mentee and more one of parity. This time, Salmond was widely perceived the victor.

Inevitably, this success invited opposition attacks, often of a personal nature. With less than a week to go until polling day, the *Daily Mail* ran a 'story' that struck many observers, even those not normally sympathetic to the SNP, as scraping the pejorative barrel. At a pro-Union campaign event outside Murrayfield Stadium in Edinburgh, two Scottish rugby players claimed the SNP leader and his deputy did not have to worry about future generations of Scots as they were childless. 'The trouble with Alex Salmond and Nicola Sturgeon is they don't have kids so they don't understand parents' fears about the next generation,' said Steve Munro. 'The nationalists have established divisions in our country. If you walk down Ayr High Street wearing a No badge, things can get pretty aggressive.'[71]

Aggression, however, cut both ways. In 2013 Sturgeon had received what she described as 'death threats' on Twitter, a medium she admitted taking 'quite a lot of convincing' to join. Nevertheless, during the long referendum campaign she became one of its most prolific Tweeters (and was recognised as such at the 2014 Scottish Politician of the Year Awards), composing her own 140-word messages to an ever-increasing band of followers. About online abuse she was philosophical. 'The minority who will abuse folk on Twitter have always been there,' she said in August 2014, 'it's just that they've not had the platform before. We shouldn't get upset about it. I just ignore it and try not to read it.'[72] It was not just online. In October 2013 a man had even been charged with stalking the Deputy First Minister.

On 16 September Sturgeon made her last major intervention in the referendum debate, arguing that, if it voted Yes, Scotland would not be leaving the 'family of nations' known as the British Isles. 'Those ties are not about politics, those ties are about people,' she said. 'I'm the grand-daughter of an Englishwoman, I have family in England. We're going to continue to be part of the family of nations that make up the British Isles. We will work closely and co-operatively with our friends across these islands but we'll do so on the basis of equality, we'll do so knowing that we're responsible for the decisions that shape our future, that we're responsible for our own money as a country and we can decide the priorities for spending that money. That to me is the best of both worlds, being responsible and accountable and working with our neighbours where our mutual interests make that worth doing.'

She remained 'enormously optimistic' about the outcome of the vote. 'It's a joy to be part of this campaign. This country is alive, it's engaged, it's enthused, it's informed – everybody is talking about it, everyone is interested in it.'[73] Indeed, when Sturgeon found out that her university friend Claire Mitchell, now an advocate, was going to speak in support of the Union at a Better Together event, she sent Mitchell a message on Twitter (without a hint of sarcasm) to congratulate her on getting involved in politics. 'I was very touched when she sent that,' recalled Mitchell. 'That shows you the size of a person – she was pleased someone was engaging, even though it was with the other side of the debate.'[74]

Shortly after polls closed on the evening of Thursday, 18 September, it was clear the turnout across Scotland was unusually high, indeed almost 85 per cent (a year earlier Sturgeon had predicted 80 per cent). But although Sturgeon, Salmond and most other senior Nationalists awoke that morning genuinely confident of victory, when the first results came through it was immediately obvious that Yes was not where it needed to be. 'I thought until the close of polls that we would win,' she later told the journalist Tom Gordon. 'Mainly because I was campaigning in Glasgow.'[75] The Clackmannanshire result, a majority No, set alarm bells ringing, and soon it was clear the vast majority of local authority areas were voting No, although Glasgow, Scotland's largest city, said Yes, an outcome that must have given Sturgeon, an adopted Glaswegian since her undergraduate days, immense satisfaction as well as a political boost (the Yes vote in Salmond's Aberdeenshire patch, by contrast, had been much lower).

The Yes Minister left the Glasgow count at around 5 or 6 a.m. in order to meet the First Minister in Edinburgh, speaking to him en route and 'both pretty gutted at not having won'. Only when they met face to face in the Scottish capital, however, did Salmond make it clear he was intending to resign. 'There were a few tears – on my part I should say – and . . . I tried to persuade him not to do it,' she later recalled. 'I tried to persuade him at the very least not to do it that day, to take more time to think it through, to let the dust settle, to let the emotion of it all subside.' But even as she was doing so, reflected Sturgeon, 'I knew that I wasn't going to succeed'.[76]

Chapter 9

'No greater privilege'

During the long referendum campaign, there had been remarkably little speculation as to what might happen to the SNP leadership in the event of a No vote. In June 2014 Alex Salmond
had told the *Daily Record* he intended to contest the 2016
Holyrood elections 'whatever the political circumstances',[1]
although in reality an incumbent First Minister could not have
said anything else. In fact, he had informed Sturgeon during a
private meeting on 18 July that he would be 'minded to resign'
if they did not win the referendum.[2]

Nicola Sturgeon, meanwhile, had always been relatively
upfront as to her ambition to succeed Salmond. 'Anybody in
any walk of life – if they are ambitious – wants to get to the
pinnacle of their profession,' she told the *Daily Record* a few
months before the First Minister's statement of intent. 'So
hypothetically, of course that is something I would like to think
that one day I will get the chance to do.'[3] Later Sturgeon told
the same newspaper that she did not approve of politicians
'saying they have no ambition to be leader when you know
they're fibbing through their teeth'.[4] At the same time she was
cautious, telling this author in 2013 that she did not believe
there was 'any such thing as a natural successor' when it came
to the SNP leadership.[5]

Only occasionally did Sturgeon depart from this script, for
example the disingenuous claim to journalist Tom Gordon

shortly before polling day that she did not 'have a burning desire to be First Minister'.[6] In truth, however, ever since the Deputy First Minister had been put in charge of the referendum process an unintended but, as the columnist Euan McColm put it, 'far from unhelpful' consequence had been 'to showcase her credentials as a credible future First Minister'.

The 'triumvirate' at the top of the SNP for the past decade, Finance Secretary John Swinney, Sturgeon and Alex Salmond, had long operated on the understanding that, when the time was right, the Deputy First Minister was next in line, for Swinney had already been leader and Salmond was in his 20th year at the helm. This produced a remarkably harmonious dynamic that did not exist in most other political parties. And, as McColm observed, while success in the referendum might have been Sturgeon's 'primary objective', the experience of the campaign would also constitute 'another step' on what appeared to be 'her unstoppable rise to becoming Scotland's first female First Minister'.[7]

It had been a difficult balancing act, and not one that had gone unnoticed within both the SNP and wider Yes campaign. One insider even reached the conclusion that between 2012 and 2014 Sturgeon's 'priority was to become First Minister, whatever the result'. The source continued, 'I could understand that – she'd worked bloody hard. But things were done during the campaign, money was held back – no question about it – which could have been spent on the referendum, either because there wasn't confidence in how it would be spent or Nicola wanted it to fight the election in 2016, which was odd given the referendum ought to have been a priority. I always thought there was a part of her that would have been perfectly content running the [devolved] Scottish Parliament, perhaps with a few more powers.'

That, however, was hardly unreasonable, while even before Sturgeon had left the health brief in the autumn of 2012 only a politician completely free of ambition could have failed to view strategic decisions in the context of the succession. The source believed that in the Deputy First Minister's 'mind' a second referendum question would have led to Salmond staying on 'a bit longer' as leader, therefore depriving her of a chance to secure her own electoral mandate in 2016. Indeed, many involved at that time were struck by the alacrity with which Sturgeon moved to secure a more high-profile role. 'She was very forceful in her view of what she wanted,' recalled the source. 'There were no disagreements internally, but Nicola was absolutely clear about what she was going to get after Bruce [Crawford] left.'[8]

At the same time, however, Sturgeon's transition in 2012 simply highlighted how much she had consolidated her position as Salmond's heir apparent. Between 2004 and 2007 she had worked hard to cement her standing within the party and, after a few years as a highly competent Health Secretary and Deputy First Minister, it had become difficult to see anyone else emerging in competition. But even then it was not clear-cut. Within the party, there was talk, however improbable, that Education Secretary Mike Russell (who had also stood for leader in 2004) still harboured ambitions, but by 2014 even that prospect had disappeared. It had been the referendum, and Sturgeon's performance as its lead advocate, that had sealed her rise. 'Ten years ago there were those of us who just thought she couldn't be leader,' admitted one contemporary. 'She was too cautious, too introspective and lacked ideas, but later we saw the leadership she brings. She gets better every year.'[9]

On the morning of Friday 19 September, however, events took on an inescapable momentum. 'It was a very, very emotional moment,' Sturgeon recalled of the First Minister's decision, adding the important caveat that she did not think 'it was necessarily the right thing to do on that day'. Salmond, however, understood clearly the importance of timing. By resigning when he did, Better Together was deprived of victory headlines over the weekend and instead the story remained the SNP, his departure and, of course, who might succeed him. 'The transition in late 2014 was well planned,' observed one senior minister. 'I think Alex decided a long time ago that if the referendum was lost he'd go quickly and make way for Nicola.'[10] There were, however, ongoing discussions as to the choreography. 'The initial plan was for Alex to resign immediately,' recalled a former Salmond adviser. 'There was a chance he would change his mind, but we then agreed with Nicola that he'd carry on till the conference, which had already been delayed to November.'[11]

Even by the time Salmond declared his intention to stand aside in an elegant and movingly delivered speech at Bute House on Friday afternoon, the party had already rallied around Sturgeon. A poorly-worded statement from the Prime Minister that morning had also given Salmond and his successor the broad outline of a post-referendum narrative: that the UK Government would inevitably 'renege' on its pre-referendum 'Vow' and that the referendum outcome amounted to a verdict of 'not yet' rather than 'never'. Salmond had always been masterful in shaping the terms of debate, and he remained in control even as he prepared to exit the stage.

Sturgeon was fulsome in her praise. 'The personal debt of gratitude I owe Alex is immeasurable,' she said in a statement. 'He has been my friend, mentor and colleague for more than 20 years. Quite simply, I would not have been able to do what I have in politics without his constant advice, guidance and support through all these years. Alex's announcement today inevitably raises the question of whether I will be a candidate to succeed him as SNP leader. I can think of no greater privilege than to seek to lead the party I joined when I was just 16.' However 'that decision', added Sturgeon, was 'not for today'; her priority after a 'long and hard campaign' was to get some rest and spend time with her family. She also wanted 'the focus' over the next few days to 'be on the outstanding record and achievements of the finest First Minister Scotland has had'.[12]

A few days later Sturgeon maintained that such a 'big decision' was one she was 'considering carefully'[13] but, if there was any doubt about her candidacy, it existed only in the Deputy First Minister's mind. On the morning of Wednesday 24 September, Sturgeon officially launched her 'campaign' at the Royal Concert Hall, the backdrop of Buchanan Street underpinning Glasgow's position as not only her adopted city but also the apex of the 45 per cent Yes vote a few days before.

In doing so, Sturgeon also announced she would be standing down as the SNP's deputy leader at the forthcoming party conference, therefore allowing a contest for that post to take place 'in parallel' with that for leader. Introduced by her friend and colleague Shona Robison, Sturgeon was, despite the referendum result, upbeat in the face of rising SNP membership ('This is a party, and we are a nation, on the rise'), keen to send 'a strong message to every girl and young woman in Scotland' that there was 'no glass ceiling on ambition', and she also paid another tribute to Salmond, telling journalists she would be 'proud' to 'build on his remarkable legacy'.

But, in the manner of Antony, Sturgeon also intended to bury Salmond, not to praise him. 'At the risk of stating the obvious,' she continued, 'I am not Alex Salmond.' She continued, 'His are big boots to fill, but if given the opportunity to lead, I will wear my own shoes – and they will certainly have higher heels! I will be my own person and set my own course. We would not have come so far as a nation without Alex's vision, tenacity and statesmanship. But the challenges and opportunities of tomorrow require a different approach. They will demand the ability, not just to argue a case with determination and conviction, but also to reach out, to work with others and seek common cause on the issues that unite us.' The obvious implication was that the outgoing First Minister often had not reached out or sought common cause, indeed precisely the opposite. Sturgeon also closed down recent suggestions by Salmond that independence might occur by 'other routes', stating that it would 'happen only when the people of Scotland choose that course in the polling booth'.

If elected to lead, added Sturgeon, she pledged that the Scottish Government would be 'full, active, genuine and constructive participants' in any 'process of change', a clear indication that remaining aloof from the cross-party Smith Commission on more powers for Holyrood would not be an option, although she was 'equally clear' that it had to live up to pre-referendum promises of 'Home Rule' or 'something near to federalism'. From this moment on, the word 'constructive' would litter her public pronouncements.

Sturgeon then set out her political philosophy: 'My guiding ethos is a social democratic one and that will be the ethos of any government I lead. I believe that a strong, sustainable economy with a vibrant business community, and a fair society with strong public services are two sides of the same coin. We cannot succeed and flourish as a society without advancing both. My Scottish nationalism is one of aspiration and hope.'

Far from lurching to the left, as some opponents anticipated and some supporters earnestly hoped, Sturgeon promised to 'help Scottish business grow, to champion Scotland as a place to invest and to support well-paid sustainable employment as the central plank of our future prosperity'. Only with a strong economy, she reasoned, could Scotland 'tackle, effectively and for the long term, the deep-rooted social ills which drove me into politics in the first place'. Significantly, Sturgeon also said the Scottish Government 'must renew and recharge our efforts to tackle the poverty and inequality that blights the lives of too many of our people'.[14]

Even if the campaign launch was little more than a formality, it had been a typically slick and confident performance. Under questioning, Sturgeon was characteristically cautious, saying she would not be writing her party's 2016 manifesto on the hoof, although she would order a comprehensive policy review. When asked how she planned to tackle inequality and promote social justice, Sturgeon was vague, falling back on the argument (which contradicted her opening remarks) that the existing powers of the Scottish Parliament gave her limited options. Her (and indeed Salmond's) oft-repeated pledge that the referendum was a 'once-in-a-generation' opportunity, meanwhile, was quietly filed under 'things we didn't actually mean'; now 'circumstances in the future' and 'the demands of the Scottish public' would determine the date of any second referendum.[15]

Strikingly, when it came to engaging with the Smith

Commission, Sturgeon led for the Scottish Government as if she already *was* First Minister, a clear indication that the succession was already well under way. In her weekly *Evening Times* column, the Deputy First Minister asserted that two thirds of Scots wanted 'full devo-max, which is control of everything in Scotland except defence and foreign affairs'. Those, therefore, were the 'expectations' that must be met by the Smith process, anything less would lead, she predicted, to the Westminster parties paying 'a heavy electoral price'.[16] The framing, ahead of the May 2015 general election, was clear.

In her foreword to the Scottish Government's submission, *More Powers for the Scottish Parliament*, Sturgeon accepted that independence would 'not be the outcome' of the Smith Commission but again essentially set it up to fail, stating that, if its recommendations fell 'significantly short' of 'maximum self-government', then it would not live up 'to the expectations of the Scottish people'. Although the document essentially reiterated the definition of 'devo-max' first articulated as a result of the National Conversation a few years earlier, there was movement on, for example, Corporation Tax – rather than cutting the headline rate by 3p, 'tax incentives' would be deployed 'carefully'.[17]

Frequently mentioned during the leadership 'contest' was the so-called 'coronation curse', the notion that uncontested leadership elections often ended up hindering the 'winning' candidate – for example, in the cases of Wendy Alexander and Gordon Brown. Sturgeon said she would have 'relished' competition, but then the dynamic in Scotland was rather different, with the Salmond/Sturgeon duopoly having been nothing like the often-toxic Blair/Brown relationship. Sturgeon did, however, have to fend off claims she and her husband, SNP chief executive Peter Murrell, would wield too much power once she was confirmed as leader. One unnamed source told the *Sunday Herald* that, viewed from outside, it looked 'a bit incestuous'; but, in response, Sturgeon stressed that most administrative oversight resided with the party's business convener, Derek Mackay, appointed by whoever was leader rather than her husband.[18]

Nicola's mother Joan was also included in depictions of the Sturgeon clan, although as Provost of North Ayrshire she was hardly a Mafia-style matriarch. The SNP, she had told the *Irvine Times*, would go 'from strength to strength' under her daughter's leadership.[19] Nominations closed on 15 October and, at that point, it was confirmed Sturgeon was the only candidate. 'Thank you to @theSNP for choosing me as your new leader,' she tweeted, although of course there had been no 'choosing' involved. 'I now look forward', she added, 'to becoming FM for ALL of Scotland.'[20] Again, the emphasis on unity was clear.

The outgoing First Minister said he would be offering 'no words of advice' to his successor for she was, in his judgement, 'well capable of dealing with any events in the future'. Sturgeon would, added Salmond, be 'an outstanding leader of the Scottish National Party and an outstanding First Minister of Scotland'.[21] At Scottish Questions in the House of Commons the Scotland Office minister David Mundell mischievously congratulated Sturgeon on 'emulating' Margaret Thatcher in becoming the first female leader of her party, going on to praise her previously 'constructive approach to discussions with the UK Government'.[22]

SNP membership, meanwhile, had surged from around 25,000 before the referendum to more than 80,000 by the time Sturgeon emerged as the party's sole leadership nominee. In keeping with her promise to maintain levels of 'engagement' seen during the campaign, the leader-elect announced a tour of Scotland principally, but not exclusively, for new members. Sturgeon said the six events would set the 'template' for the kind of First Minister she wanted to be, 'open, accessible and determined to work with others across the political divide'. One gathering was to take place at the new SSE Hydro in Glasgow with a projected crowd of 12,000, making it, according to the SNP, 'the largest indoor political gathering held in Scotland – or indeed anywhere in the UK – in recent times'.[23]

Not only was it a skilful way of retaining momentum in the wake of the referendum, but a series of high-profile gatherings would enable Sturgeon to stamp her authority on the party and its phalanx of new members. A cynical old adage held that politics was merely show business for ugly people and, although clearly not ugly, Sturgeon on tour stood to attract concert-sized crowds. Thousands of (free) tickets were claimed within hours of becoming available.

The first 'gig' took place at Edinburgh's Corn Exchange towards the end of October. In a confident and frequently humorous performance, Sturgeon reflected on the 'best and most fulfilling experience' of her 'political life' while looking ahead to the UK general election due in May 2015, demanding a place for the SNP in any televised debates and pitching her party as the only alternative to the 'blue and red Tories'. Speculation was also growing that Alex Salmond was preparing for another Sinatra-style comeback, this time by contesting the Westminster constituency of Gordon. Sturgeon told activists she had 'no fear' of him remaining 'a big figure in Scottish politics', indeed she would 'love to have' him sitting behind her in the Scottish Parliament. True to recent form, the SNP leader-designate did not dwell on policy detail, but hinted she would back radical land reform proposals as well as making sure there was 'no hiding place' for those owing taxes. Again the intention was to hint at a modestly more left-wing agenda.

Sturgeon also demonstrated her authority by refusing to be led by party opinion. When invited to condemn the media she resisted in a way her predecessor would not, instead emphasising the importance of a 'free press' no matter how critical it was of independence, while another member's call for a unilateral declaration of independence following the general election was rejected out of hand. 'I don't believe a majority of seats at any election gives us a mandate for independence,' stated Sturgeon, going on to argue that a referendum was necessary for international 'legitimacy'.[24] Later, the timing of Sturgeon's appearance at the giant Glasgow Hydro on the same day as a gathering of the Radical Independence Campaign was also interpreted as an attempt by the incoming First Minister to show the broader Yes movement who was boss.

Sturgeon had never been the sort of politician to indulge the party faithful, and indeed a few weeks later when four SNP councillors posted a video of themselves on YouTube setting fire to a copy of the Smith Commission report, she moved swiftly, realising its potentially damaging effect on the SNP's hard-earned reputation for moderation. Sturgeon condemned the quartet and suspended their membership; '[I]n acting as she has,' judged Euan McColm, the First Minister had 'made life easier for herself' when it came to internal party discipline.[25]

The SNP gathered for its annual conference in Perth on 14–15 November, and it did so as the UK's third-largest political party in terms of members. On the Friday morning Sturgeon was confirmed as its new leader to rapturous applause from delegates, with Dundee MP Stewart Hosie the party's surprise choice as her deputy. She had been working on the assumption (shared by many in the party) that an MSP, Keith Brown, rather than an MP would be elected deputy, although that twist of fate later enabled Sturgeon to appoint as Deputy First Minister John Swinney, a solid performer with a trust-worthy 'bank manager' demeanour that nicely complemented the First Minister's more empathetic style. That afternoon Sturgeon was 'close to tears' as she introduced Alex Salmond's valedictory speech, having earlier told the *Today* programme that he was a 'colossus' in Scottish politics.[26]

The following day it fell to Sturgeon to deliver her maiden speech as SNP leader, and again it represented a deliberate departure from her predecessor's more bellicose style. She looked ahead to the general election, ruling out any deal with the Conservatives but talking up an accommodation with Labour as long as it reconsidered replacing the nuclear deterrent. 'With the UK hurtling headlong for the EU exit door,' she told delegates, 'with the Unionist parties watering down their vow of more powers, with deeper austerity cuts and new Trident weapons looming on the horizon, it may be that our opponents bring that day closer than we could ever have imagined on the morning of the 19 September.'[27]

Following conference, Sturgeon's succession as First

Nicola Sturgeon

Minister (rather than SNP leader) ran like clockwork; it was, in the view of one senior ally, 'mind-blowing'.[28] The following Tuesday Alex Salmond gave another valedictory speech, this time at Holyrood, and earlier the same day he chaired Cabinet for the last time (his colleagues gave him a golf bag as a goodbye gift). On Wednesday MSPs formally elected Sturgeon as the new First Minister, watched from the public gallery by Kay Ullrich, who had signed her up as a member of the SNP nearly 30 years before, and her family in the VIP section nearby. Sturgeon alluded to that younger self, 'a working-class girl from Ayrshire given the job of heading up the government of Scotland'.[29] It was a well-judged speech and ecumenical in tone, as was the following day's First Minister's Question Time, which she had resolved the previous evening 'to start off on a consensual tone'.[30]

Finally, on Friday 21 November, the new First Minister appointed her first Cabinet with its headline-grabbing 50/50 gender split. Although several veteran ministers departed, Sturgeon's new team did not radically differ from the old. Perhaps most surprising was the promotion of one-time confidante Roseanna Cunningham to the skills and training brief. There were suggestions that Sturgeon had 'long been troubled' by tension with the party's former deputy leader, thus the appointment, in the judgement of journalist Euan McColm, constituted a 'personal bridge'.[31]

SNP ministers enjoyed unusually close relations for two reasons: first, they were united strategically as never before in the party's 80-year history, while those sitting round the Bute House Cabinet table had known and worked with each other, in certain cases, since they had been teenagers. Not only did Sturgeon's friend Shona Robison become the new Health Secretary, but Angela Constance and Alasdair Allan, both contemporaries from Glasgow University, also took on senior posts. 'That means there's an excellent working relationship between us,' observed one senior Nationalist outside the Cabinet. 'There was no need to start afresh, which was massively useful.'[32]

When it came to Cabinet meetings, according to one

minister, Sturgeon's style was very different from Salmond's, 'very efficient, and very clear about the need to make decisions in an informed way that took account of the likely consequences'.[33] A former adviser also identified her 'main characteristic' as being that of 'a decision maker',[34] not a trait to which many politicians, or indeed ministers, could lay claim. This decisiveness applied to her team of special advisers, where there was also significant continuity. Long-term Sturgeon aide Noel Dolan had been planning to retire after the referendum, but now stayed on as the new First Minister's adviser on social justice, communities and pensioners' rights, while, underlining the emphasis on gender equality, Liz Lloyd was later confirmed as Sturgeon's chief of staff.

A few days after Sturgeon's triumphant, appearance before more than 10,000 SNP activists at Glasgow's Hydro (proof, judged the journalist Gillian Bowditch, that 'her transition from dour nippy sweetie to modern, post-ironic, Borgen-styled leader was complete'[35]), the new First Minister set out her first programme for government. Its 'clear focus', she told MSPs, would be on how the Scottish Parliament used its existing powers 'fully, creatively and constructively', aiming 'to build a sense of shared endeavour about how we create a wealthier and more equal society'. More specifically, Sturgeon announced a cross-party 'commission' to find a way forward on local government finance, while, to combat persistent charges the SNP was too centralist, she also reconvened the 'Island Areas Working Group' to oversee 'devolution of powers to our islands'.

Most press coverage subsequently focused on the First Minister's intention to 'embark on a radical programme of land reform', including ministerial power to 'intervene where the scale of land ownership or the conduct of a landlord is acting as a barrier to sustainable development'. In addition, there would be the removal of business rate exemptions for shooting and deerstalking estates. As well as being a useful way of presenting herself as more left wing than her predecessor, land reform, declared Sturgeon, remained 'unfinished business', as was the Community Charge Debt Bill, designed to 'finally end collection of debts from non-payment of the Poll Tax', which must have appealed to the Sturgeon of the late 1980s.

But the new First Minister's speech also included further indications that, if anything, pragmatism defined her ideological approach rather than lofty principle. She confirmed that the small business bonus would continue for the rest of that Parliament and, if re-elected, the next, while she intended to increase funding for the Scottish Government's Coalition-style Help to Buy scheme. But, at the same time, there would be more cash to 'mitigate' the impact of welfare cuts, while a new 'independent advisor' would hold ministers to account when it came to poverty and inequality. All private, public and third sector bodies would be urged (rather than compelled) 'to achieve gender balance on their boards by 2020', while, on the Scottish Government's flagship policy of free higher education, Sturgeon conceded more could be done to widen access for the most deprived fifth of the population and set 'a challenging long-term target to eradicate the inequality in access to higher education'.

Sturgeon ended by quoting one of her predecessors, Donald Dewar, who had said that devolution for Scotland was 'about more than our politics and our laws. This is about who we are and how we carry ourselves'. She hoped that, in her first major speech as First Minister, she had 'given an indication today of how the Government [she] lead[s] will carry itself – in a way that is open, listening, accessible and decentralising'.[36] Not everyone in the Yes camp, however, was convinced. Michael Gray of the Common Weal, for example, said Sturgeon's legislative plans did not 'go far enough' and that what was required was 'greater political will than in the last 15 years of managed devolution'.[37]

Naturally, political opponents also moved to frame the new First Minister in a way helpful to their own electoral chances. The Scottish Labour Party, which by the end of 2014 was engaged in yet another make-or-break leadership contest, tried to depict Sturgeon as being 'obsessed' with independence, while the Scottish Conservative leader Ruth Davidson said she would 'be the most left-wing First Minister Scotland has ever known', constantly trying to 'outflank' Labour in order 'to demonstrate a kind of socialist machismo, elbowing each other aside to lay claim to the collectivist crown'.[38]

This might have been clever positioning from a Tory perspective, but it was also a crude depiction of Sturgeon's point of view. Economics had never been a political strength, and nor did she navigate the business world as comfortably as her predecessor, thus she was conscious of the need to combat the impression that as First Minister she would be hostile to business. Sturgeon did so with typical alacrity, telling the *Financial Times* that companies had 'nothing to fear' from her administration, while her recent land reform proposals were 'not some kind of class warfare'. Later she would attend private events at the right-leaning Tuesday Club and the 'strategic communications consultancy' Charlotte Street Partners, co-founded by former SNP MSP Andrew Wilson, to cultivate the financial world further.

Sturgeon couched this approach, however, in ideological terms. 'I am a social democrat, I believe in pursuing greater equality and . . . social justice,' she said, 'but . . . you can't do that unless you have got a strong economy, unless you have got a vibrant business base earning the wealth that makes that possible.'[39] This was essentially orthodox Salmondism, and indeed Sturgeon ostentatiously rebutted as 'wide of the mark' the idea that she was 'suddenly going to shift' the SNP's ideological 'centre of gravity'.[40]

The First Minister fleshed out her thinking in a major speech at the Glasgow HQ of the energy company SSE on 1 December: 'Our drive as a government to tackle inequality in our society is also a key part of our support for business. We believe – in common with many economists across the world – that equality and cohesion are good for growth, as well as good for individuals . . . Creating greater prosperity and fairness isn't something any Government can do alone – it has to be a shared national endeavour and I am asking you to be part of it.' It was a deliberately inclusive approach, while Sturgeon also announced former chief medical officer Sir Harry Burns would be joining the Council of Economic Advisers to help it to 'align the objective of economic growth with the need to tackle inequality' better.

Beyond that broad and ambitious goal, Sturgeon buried her predecessor's attachment to reducing Corporation Tax by saying Scotland's challenge lay in determining how to compete with London's 'centrifugal pull on talent', not, she said, 'by engaging in a race to the bottom', but by creating 'long-term comparative advantage and genuine economic value'. There was also a nod to macroeconomics ('We all know that budgets need to be kept under control, and the deficit and debt reduced'), with the observation that 'badly-targeted austerity' had failed to 'bring down the deficit in the way the UK Government predicted', which rather implied there was such a thing as 'well-targeted' spending cuts.[41] Later, at UCL, Sturgeon condemned what she called 'morally unjustifiable and economically unsustainable' spending plans and set out an austerity-lite alternative, additional public spending amounting to £180 billion across the UK over the next four years.[42]

The SSE speech was a clear attempt to establish the new First Minister's economic credentials, although beyond vague talk of 'partnership' it did not represent a significant departure from the Salmond era. Sturgeon's aides made it known she had read and taken note of Joseph Stiglitz's book *The Price of Inequality*, although like Salmond it appeared she preferred its analysis (inequality acts as a drag on the economy) to its proposed remedy (tax rises and an 'assault' on vested corporate interests). Her aim of encouraging businesses to pay the living wage and employ more women, however, was ambitious, even though it was not clear how it would be achieved without legislative coercion.

Sturgeon also lacked her predecessor's deftness of touch when it came to tackling economic issues inconvenient to the Nationalist cause. Asked after the referendum about the SNP's stance on retaining sterling, she conceded it had not been 'an easy position to argue' but maintained that none of the 'alternative positions' would 'have been any easier',[43] which made it sound as if she considered monetary policy to be little more than a matter of positioning. In the face of a plunging oil price (less than half the $110-a-barrel predicted by the White Paper), meanwhile, the First Minister waved aside criticisms, arguing that it would have recovered before the March 2016 'independence day' planned by the SNP. 'We wouldn't have been independent right now,' she protested,[44] although that came nowhere near to dealing with Better Together's fundamental point about the resource's volatility. The previous summer Sturgeon had agreed with other Nationalists in predicting that Scotland was on the cusp of 'a second oil boom'.[45]

Similarly, Sturgeon's frequent claim, both during and after the referendum, that Norway's oil fund existed to 'help them through the period of [declining] oil prices' misunderstood that the Scandinavian country's two 'pension' funds existed to invest surplus oil wealth rather than plugging large year-to-year gaps in public spending.[46] Even among close supporters, there was frustration at the First Minister's sluggish response to the oil 'crisis' and resulting opposition attacks, her eventual response comprising a predictable attack on the UK Government for squandering oil resources, an industry 'summit' in Aberdeen and the call for a tax cut in order to stimulate activity.

More generally, Sturgeon took shelter behind the argument that not only did the Scottish Parliament lack fiscal levers but even if it did not (and under the Scotland Acts of 1999 and 2012 it clearly did) then only a 'whole panoply of powers' would suffice. 'You can't just look at these things in isolation,' she insisted, adding, 'Having power over tax and welfare does not automatically lead to higher taxes and a more generous welfare system. It allows you to do more to help people into work and if you have more people in work that generates more tax without having to put tax rates up ... If you were able, over time, to have a minimum wage that paid people something more akin to the living wage, you would reduce government expenditure on tax credits.'

Given the importance of economics to the ongoing campaign

211

for independence (and indeed its role in the referendum defeat), this constituted a major weakness in the otherwise impressive Sturgeon armoury. However, she did have that rare political commodity of genuine popularity. As an eventful year drew to a close, polling clearly indicated the new First Minister was the 'most trusted' of any political leader in Scotland or the UK, with more than half of Scots believing she would fight for their best interests, compared to less than a quarter who thought the same of David Cameron. Sturgeon had some surprising admirers, including the former Conservative Scottish Secretary Lord Forsyth, who said she had 'been brilliant' during the referendum campaign, her 'tone and her focus' both 'spot on'.[47]

Even the usually hostile *Daily Mail* gushed that while in 2001 Sturgeon had been 'a dead ringer for Angela Merkel – all elephantine linen trouser suits, death row haircut and M&S shoes – today she is as sleek as an otter'. The First Minister, judged journalist Liz Jones, had 'finally understood that in order for ordinary people to give you their trust, you cannot go to work every day looking like an overstuffed sofa'.[48] 'Project Nicola', begun in 2004, remained in play. She had lost weight during a gruelling referendum campaign, while her sartorial instincts remained sharp and stylish (although the comedian Rory Bremner dubbed her hairstyle the 'Barnett Formula').[49]

The SNP did not flinch from encouraging what the journalist Peter Ross termed an 'emerging Cult of Nicola', making available Sturgeon-branded merchandise during her speaking tour of Scotland. This appeared hubristic, although the copyright holder was keen to distance herself ('it wasn't my decision').[50] And as the journalist Mandy Rhodes observed, despite her reputation for frostiness (still present in 2014), Sturgeon was 'a quick wit' and laughed 'a lot more than she ever gets credit for'. 'In fact', added Rhodes, 'she is very much a woman's woman – depending on the woman – and can talk as eloquently about shoes and fashion as she can about macroeconomics and fighting inequality.'[51]

Sturgeon repeatedly responded to often-tragic events by emphasising her human side. When an out-of-control refuse truck killed six people near Glasgow's George Square, she described it as 'a broken-hearted city', [52] while after a meeting with former Better Together activist Gordon Aikman, who had been diagnosed with terminal Motor Neurone Disease, Sturgeon said it 'would be a very hard heart – *and I don't have one of those* – that would not be deeply moved' by Aikman's experience.[53] And asked if she had made a 'personal sacrifice' in not having children, Sturgeon said making such a conscious decision would have been '*a very clinical and very cold thing to do*, and that's not how it's happened'.[54]

The new First Minister had made a point upon her election of pursuing a more mature, less confrontational style of government than Alex Salmond. 'The referendum has changed things fundamentally,' she explained to the journalist Gillian Bowditch. 'People who have never been engaged in politics before have become engaged.' She continued, 'You also have people who are politicised and politically engaged but not in a party political, tribal way. I think that demands something different. It demands an ability to reach out beyond party divides. I want to be inclusive. It doesn't mean the Scottish Parliament is going to become cuddly but we have had a period of some years in Scotland, understandably and rightly, where we have been focused on what divides us. I think it is time to focus on what unites us.'[55]

But this political ecumenicalism proved difficult to sustain amid continuing constitutional flux and, in certain contexts, Sturgeon could be every bit as robust as her predecessor. Inevitably, neither could fully escape comparisons with one another. Asked if his successor was more left wing than he had been, Salmond replied that both he and Sturgeon belonged in the 'tradition' of social democracy, although the former SNP leader had always tended to define that tradition rather vaguely.[56]

Opponents, most notably Scottish Liberal Democrat leader Willie Rennie, were keen to depict the former First Minister as a 'backseat driver', and indeed in her first few months as leader Sturgeon was frequently placed in the uncomfortable position of being asked if she agreed with something Salmond had said or done. That she had to keep pointing out that she, rather than he, was 'leader of the SNP . . . and First Minister of Scotland', was revealing. [57] Shortly before her election, Sturgeon observed that, if she ever found herself 'feeling resentful of or precious about Alec giving me advice or Alec speaking out or saying things, I'll give myself a good shake because that would be a ridiculous position for me to be in. He is a colossus in Scottish politics; his experience, his ability, his understanding of the whole political scene in Scotland is such that I would be daft if I decided that was a well of experience I didn't want to draw on.'[58]

Inevitably, however, Salmond's lack of discipline (certainly when compared with Sturgeon), caused tension. 'She'd be the first to admit she's learned a lot from him,' reflected one former aide, 'but she's also learned a lot about how not to do things.'[59] The relationship, although long and highly successful, had always been more professional than it was friendly. Asked about Salmond's often-erratic behaviour in the wake of the referendum, Sturgeon simply concluded that he was 'enjoying himself'.[60]

In the relentless analysis that inevitably followed the referendum, Sturgeon usually agreed with Salmond's reading of the result that an 'onslaught of fear-mongering' following the second YouGov poll (which put Yes ahead) and the so-called 'Vow' had combined to convince 'enough people' there existed a 'safer option to give them a lot of what they wanted, but without the risks'.[61] There was actually little evidence to support this interpretation of the campaign's closing stages, but then it was necessary for Sturgeon to maintain political momentum among the self-styled '45' (the percentage of the electorate who had voted Yes) and all the new members flocking to join the party she now led, pursuing the twin-track strategy of both accepting the majority No vote while refusing to rule out another referendum.

Sturgeon even took to describing Better Together's ten-point margin of victory as 'narrow', and while she denied 'playing games' with her assertion that Scotland ought to exercise a 'veto' should a majority in the rest of the UK support withdrawal from the EU,[62] it was almost Salmond-like in its contortions. Under that logic then in a 'family of nations' such as the UK, England, Wales and Northern Ireland ought to have been able to veto a majority Scottish vote for independence, while the proposal had not previously featured in any Scottish Government statements on the constitution, not even Sturgeon's recent submission to the Smith Commission. It was, however, a clever piece of positioning ahead of three forthcoming electoral tests – the May 2015 UK general election, a Holyrood contest a year after that and another referendum, this time on the UK's membership of the European Union, on 23 June 2016.

Chapter 10

'Nicola-mania'

Writing on the first anniversary of her nomination as First Minister, Nicola Sturgeon remembered pledging that her government would be 'bold, imaginative and adventurous, a government with purpose'.[1] So when it comes to assessing her performance as SNP leader and head of the devolved Scottish Government since the first edition of this biography was published, it is worth doing so on Sturgeon's own terms. Indeed, only now, in the wake of the 2016 Holyrood election and the European referendum, is it really possible to take a step back and do so, unencumbered by the almost continuous campaigning that has characterised Scottish politics for the past six years.

But, in doing so, one must also discriminate between the public and private faces of Nicola Sturgeon – between the First Minister's undeniable style and her political substance. Since the 2015 general election, the public persona has been an undisputed triumph, easily making her the most visible politician in the British Isles, but the private politician has often been underwhelming. Usefully, from Sturgeon's point of view, however, the former generally masks the latter and whether that continues to be the case – together with the possibility of another independence referendum – will largely determine her fortunes over the next few years.

In a way her predecessor never quite managed, Sturgeon

emerged as a truly UK political figure during the general election campaign of 2015. And, in helping secure 56 out of 59 MPs, she extended her party's appeal to parts of Scotland others (including Alex Salmond) had failed to reach, taking the SNP within a whisker of a popular majority. For once, everything had worked in the party's favour: a widespread (but misplaced) belief there would be another hung Parliament, the ongoing collapse of the Scottish Labour Party and, of course, the lingering salience of the Scottish Question. For the first time since the 1970s, the SNP appeared 'relevant' in a Westminster election, something aided by the BBC's decision to include Sturgeon in its network leader debates.

Not only had Salmond's post-referendum resignation enabled the SNP to take ownership of defeat but the political calendar (elections in 2015 and 2016) had also allowed Sturgeon to maintain political momentum during her first year and a half as party leader. Tactically, she rejected moves to allow pro-independence candidates to run under a 'Yes' banner and instead enabled non-party members to stand on behalf of the SNP, a compromise that successfully harnessed the post-referendum mood. Although this ultimately produced a talented and varied group of MPs, the vetting process later gave rise to criticism for having failed to prevent damaging incidents involving several new members between 2015–16.

All that, however, was in the future. In December 2014, the SNP had conducted focus groups to try to understand its phenomenal rise in the polls and the results were so positive that a typically cautious Sturgeon, 'worried that support might be transient or that the groups might just have been unusually pro-SNP, asked for them to be re-done'.[2] But the new focus groups in January 2015 were just as supportive and also strongly pro-Sturgeon, which meant the campaign majored on the party leader, who mingled openly with voters in a way few other politicians could ('I don't want to be sanitised behind a cordon,' she said, 'I want to be out there').[3] And, instead of targeting just a few winnable seats as in previous elections, the

SNP ran a truly national campaign for perhaps the first time in its long history.

Towards the end of February 2015, the SNP's focus group expert Mark Cuthbert presented his detailed findings to the First Minister and her inner circle, having identified a huge gulf between voter perceptions of the SNP vis-à-vis Labour. Those interviewed viewed Sturgeon and her party as 'empowering the country, on the side of the people, unafraid, open and honest'. Thus such sentiments rapidly became campaign messages, including the mantra about sending 'a strong group of SNP MPs' to stand up for Scotland.[4] The SNP's main election poster also featured a friendly-looking Sturgeon with the legend 'My vow is to make Scotland stronger at Westminster', something that deliberately played on Better Together rhetoric before the independence referendum.

Such findings were not a complete surprise, for the SNP had been promoting itself in such terms for decades, but it showed voters were now on the same wavelength, particularly with Sturgeon as leader. 'She just seemed to get into a groove and into the conversation with the country,' was her husband (and SNP chief executive) Peter Murrell's take on her post-referendum success, 'and that's just continued from then until now.'[5] Focus groups backed up his impression. 'It's who you trust, and I trust Nicola Sturgeon more than any of the others,' said one voter interviewed during the campaign. 'She's direct, she speaks direct from the heart . . . She seems more like an honest politician, if there is such a thing. You can relate to her.' And asked who should play the First Minister in *Nicola Sturgeon: The Movie*, the starring role, by common consent, 'would go to Dame Helen Mirren, or, if the producers insisted on a Scot, Elaine C. Smith'.[6]

SNP HQ, meanwhile, personalised this 'conversation' through hitherto unseen levels of Sturgeon branding in what struck many as an almost presidential campaign. There are whistles, bongos and banners galore: 'Stronger for Scotland', 'YeSNP', 'Vote SNP Get Sexy' and, most popular of all, 'I'm with Nicola', which also became a hashtag accompanying thousands of selfies. 'It really deeply troubles me when I come across a phone I don't know how to work in selfie mode,' joked the SNP leader. 'At night, very, very often the sorest part of my body is my cheekbones.'[7] There was even a Sturgeon-liveried helicopter (inevitably dubbed the 'Sturgeon-copter') and later the Collins dictionary would consider adding 'Nicolabilia' to its ever-expanding lexicon. But asked how she felt about being a brand, the First Minister told journalist Tom Gordon she did not see herself in that way. 'I'm a party leader. I passed a hugely horrifyingly large lit-up [poster] last night on the way to STV', something she did not like 'very much at all'.[8]

At the SNP's manifesto launch, meanwhile, Sturgeon made a point of speaking to the whole of the UK rather than just Scotland, having made a series of speeches in England (particularly London) in the run-up to polling day. This pitch was repeated during televised debates, in which she came across as a fresh and articulate face, 'building on extensive experience in debates in the referendum, where she had routinely bested rival politicians'.[9] Sturgeon, therefore, gave the sort of assured performance familiar to Scottish voters but less so in the rest of the UK. To the comedy writer Armando Iannucci, the resulting 'Nicola-mania' (which surprised many long-standing SNP strategists) reminded him of the previous election's 'Cleggmania'. 'Whatever the phenomenon,' he wrote, 'Britain has become a land of Sturgeonettes, pining for the ability to be able to vote for her.'[10]

The critical phrase in the first debate came when Sturgeon called on Miliband to 'work with us to keep the Tories out of government', which played to the SNP's perceived strengths while making life difficult for Labour.[11] In January, the SNP had decided to base its campaign around three core themes – more powers for the Scottish Parliament, an end to austerity and opposition to Trident – the goal being to 'outflank Labour on the left and consolidate SNP support among Labour voters who had switched after the referendum'.[12] In policy terms, however, only opposition to nuclear weapons really separated the two parties. At the beginning of the campaign, Sturgeon had been cool on Labour's proposed tax rises but, by its manifesto launch, the SNP had adopted almost every one. In challenging her claim to be 'progressive', therefore, the BBC's Eddie Mair put it to the First Minister that she was 'about as brave and bold as Ed Miliband',[13] a comparison she naturally rejected.

At a UK level, however, there was not much scrutiny. In two Scottish TV debates, Sturgeon got a rougher ride over a second independence referendum as well as her party's performance since 2007. As the *Financial Times* put it, while the SNP might have a 'skilful leader . . . [what] it does not have is a spotless record in government'.[14] On everything from the NHS to the impact of 'free' university tuition, report after report highlighted a sizeable gap between rhetoric and reality. And, as the journalist Magnus Linklater observed of the 2015 SNP manifesto, it all added up to no more than a 'cornucopia of pledges, none of them embarrassed by anything as vulgar as a cost'.[15]

This was hardly anything new: election campaigns dealt in poetry rather than prose, mood music rather than discordant notes so, even when the Conservatives substituted Sturgeon for Alex Salmond in posters depicting them both with Miliband in their top pocket, it simply increased her standing and perceived influence among Scottish voters. Journalists might have been surprised to hear Chancellor George Osborne talk up Sturgeon after the first televised leaders' debate but his thinking was absolutely in keeping with Tory strategy – anything that helped the SNP also helped the so-called natural party of government by reducing the likely number of Labour MPs.

And, when the Scotland Office in Whitehall leaked a memo, a second-hand account of a meeting with the French Ambassador during which the First Minister appeared to suggest she wanted David Cameron (rather than Miliband) to become Prime Minister, Sturgeon's status in the election was assured. Under the #nikileaks hashtag, the document caused a memorable Twitter storm, although a swift rebuttal from Sturgeon helped neutralise the story (not all of which, significantly, she disputed). In the second UK leaders' debate, meanwhile, the SNP leader went from strength to strength, clashing with UKIP leader Nigel Farage (although, interestingly, she twice backed 'strong controls' on immigration) and warning Miliband that voters would never 'forgive' him if he failed to help the SNP 'lock' the Tories out of Downing Street.[16]

Media coverage, positive and negative, reinforced the message that the SNP and its leader were serious players, while newspaper subeditors struck gold: the First Minister was, *inter alia*, 'The Scotweiler' (*Sun*), 'The Sturgeonator' (*Sunday Herald*) or 'the most dangerous woman in Britain' (*Daily Mail*),[17] although Sturgeon thereafter wore the last as a badge of pride ('It's the nicest thing the *Daily Mail* has said about me.'[18]). The *Scottish Sun*, meanwhile, endorsed the SNP with the headline 'Stur Wars – A New Hope, May the 7th Be with You: Why it's Time to Vote SNP',[19] although an earlier edition of the English version had superimposed Sturgeon's face on that of Miley Cyrus atop a wrecking ball (something Sturgeon criticised as 'sexist').

But most newspapers reflected the reality. Sturgeon had become, as *The Times* put it, 'the defining figure of the election campaign', touring 'the country in her 6in heels and bright suits, posing for selfies with adoring fans'.[20] Her authenticity had triumphed, wrote the *Herald* columnist Ian Bell, doing 'ordinary to an extraordinary degree'[21]. A whole essay could have been written about Sturgeon's mastery of Twitter (which she joined shortly after the 2010 general election), the fact she clearly operated her own account (unlike other senior politicians) reinforcing the perception that she was not like other politicians. Twitter's European chief hailed the First Minister as the best public figure on the medium, while analysis later revealed her to have been the most popular during the general election, even more so than the Prime Minister. Journalists got used to being 'Sturgeoned' (taken to task online), while she was not beyond sending critics DMs (direct messages) with her own feedback. If necessary, it could also be useful for political deflection. Later, when the UK Supreme Court ruled against the Scottish Government's 'named person' legislation, the First Minister accused the *Press and Journal* of 'shocking' journalism when it focused on the judges' use of the word 'totalitarian' rather than the phrase 'legitimate and benign', helping create a partial distraction from a major setback for a flagship SNP policy.[22]

But, while during the election Sturgeon had avoided her predecessor's talk of Westminster being 'hung by a Scottish rope' ('we're different people,' she protested, 'we're different genders . . . that's not the kind of language I use'),[23] her own choice of words highlighted contradictions in the SNP's position. During the referendum, she had described the Westminster system as 'broken' (now it seemed fixable), the UK's ability to reform itself as 'spent' (now it had another chance) and that, after the referendum, Scotland would be put back in its box and ignored by Westminster (self-evidently untrue). There was also a sudden conversion to governmental legitimacy derived from majority control of the House of Commons (not something the SNP had recognised during the Thatcher era) and also the related hypocrisy of being prepared to help 'impose' a government upon England that its voters had not explicitly endorsed at the ballot box.

All this, however, proved academic come polling day, when the SNP won all but three of Scotland's 59 constituencies, a personal triumph for the First Minister even though a surprise Conservative majority deprived her party of much-anticipated 'influence', formal or otherwise. Sturgeon had remained cautious even on the day itself, Alex Salmond later recalling that she had phoned him, concerned that two voters in her Govan constituency had not looked her in the eye.[24] He had felt able to reassure his protégé that wider political forces were at work, as indeed they were, and, although subsequent analysis found it difficult to quantify the impact of the perceived SNP 'threat' on voters south of the border, Conservative and Labour strategists were united in believing this to have had a profound effect. UKIP leader Nigel Farage, for example, claimed to have detected 'indignation' from English voters about the prospect of the 'Ice Queen' (Sturgeon) 'controlling Ed Miliband'.[25]

This naturally left Sturgeon open to accusations of having helped produce an outcome she claimed to find unattractive

– i.e. another Conservative government – but even had Labour retained its grip on Scotland it would not have made much difference, and even that could not detract from the SNP having fought a typically slick campaign that chimed perfectly with the public mood. While Salmond (now the MP for Gordon) spoke of a 'Scottish lion' roaring 'across the country', Sturgeon played it cool, once again reassuring Unionist voters that the outcome did not mean another independence referendum.

Sturgeon also pledged to be constructive in her dealings with David Cameron, now unencumbered by the Liberal Democrats at Westminster. Her first meeting with the Prime Minister (usefully, he had travelled north to see her at Bute House) in Edinburgh was, in her own words, 'constructive and business-like',[26] although overshadowed by reports of her 'well-refreshed' predecessor telling journalists on the House of Commons terrace that the Scottish Government could now proceed with an 'indicative' ballot even without permission from the UK Government.[27]

There had long been a bond between the current and former First Ministers, one that neither would ever break by describing it, but it was one that increasingly required more from Sturgeon than the less disciplined Salmond. One journalist, observing the pair together shortly before Salmond formally resigned as First Minister, reckoned an anthropologist 'would have a field day with the status markers' in their 'primate group'[28] and, when the BBC's Eddie Mair asked if they had ever rowed, all he could elicit from Sturgeon was the coy response: 'We disagree on some things, not very often . . . we do it behind the scenes because we're on the same [side].'[29]

Nevertheless, Sturgeon had been in Salmond's company – if not his shadow – for so long that she found it difficult not only to completely escape his style of politics but also some of his personal characteristics. The journalist Chris Deerin identified what he called the Salmond 'head-butt', the manner in which she 'repeatedly thrusts her head forward while talking, as if subconsciously landing one on them',[30] while the parallels were most apparent when Sturgeon came under pressure at First Minister's Questions. Confronted with falling oil prices, for example, Tom Gordon wrote of her facing a choice 'between accepting reality and overhauling party strategy or snapping on the blinkers and bawling down all comers'.[31] On that and other occasions, Sturgeon did not hesitate in resorting to the Salmond playbook, giving the impression of regarding certain questions as impertinent or illegitimate, particularly if they emanated from the Labour opposition, who were frequently reminded of their electoral unpopularity as rhetorical payback.

But there remained more differences than similarities. 'Where Salmond offered a famously robust and almost mercurial style,' judged the *Scotsman*'s Tom Peterkin, 'Sturgeon's leadership appears to be characterised by a calm and clinical efficiency.'[32] Where Salmond could be robust in private meetings with stakeholders, his successor was usually charm personified and, where he had often winged it, she was usually meticulously prepared. After the general election, meanwhile, their relationship required even more careful management, with Salmond's appointment as foreign affairs spokesman contrived to give him a senior position while also keeping him out of a leadership role.[33]

Even so, there were often two concurrent commentaries on Scottish politics in the media, one emanating from Salmond and the other from Sturgeon, with that of the former periodically undermining that of the latter. Fundamentally, however, as James Mitchell and Rob Johns concluded in their study of the SNP's electoral rise, 'the change of leader brought no change of direction', the two having 'worked too closely together to suggest anything but continuity after the succession. Sturgeon was a leader-in-waiting but not one awaiting the opportunity to radically overhaul strategy or to lurch to the left.'[34]

In retrospect, the 2015 general election represented the triumphant emergence of Nicola Sturgeon as leader of the SNP and First Minister in her own right. Nearly half the Scottish electorate – mostly but not all those who had supported independence the previous year – delighted in seeing her take on the (supposed) big beasts in London and also seemed content to share the First Minister with the rest of the UK. An unusually 'Scottish' Westminster election had allowed Sturgeon to exchange familiarity for that most valuable political currency – authenticity.

This was, as the *Guardian*'s Ian Jack observed, the 'implication that her personality, like ours, has not been bent out of shape by ambition or the needs of politics'.[35] It was Sturgeon's self-deprecatory way of talking, a Glaswegian twang ('kinna' for 'kind of', 'wanna' for 'one of', 'ye kin' and not 'you can') that sounded agreeable to Middle Scotland (she had received voice coaching from Sir Sean Connery), and an acute emotional intelligence. Another journalist, Mandy Rhodes, described her as 'a woman's woman; she likes a gossip and a laugh and is entertaining company basically because she is interested in others in a way that Salmond never really was. She doesn't need to be the centre of attention – even though she frequently is.'[36]

Several observers noted that this represented a continuation of 'Project Nicola' (as explored in Chapter 6 of this biography) or what *The Times'* Peter Ross referred to as 'Nicola: the Brand':

There has been an effort to increase her visibility beyond Scotland and the usual media. Game on Jon Stewart's *The Daily Show*, glossy in *Vogue*, chatty and open (within her usual boundaries) on *Desert Island Discs*, the strategy seems to be to emphasise the 'sweetie' while never quite forgetting the 'nippy' bit; softness and substance is what we are being sold.[37]

To the columnist Chris Deerin, of all Sturgeon's achievements perhaps the greatest was 'the remaking of herself'. 'Dominant, venerated, victorious at Westminster and, in a few months, Holyrood,' he wrote in early 2016, 'it's Sturgeon's Scotland – we just live in it.'[38]

Of course the branding necessarily disguised elements of the reality and Sturgeon's private manner could often be strikingly different. As one civil servant who had worked with her closely reflected:

> She's quite removed and quiet and introverted as a person. It's like a light switch goes on when she's in front of the cameras or stakeholders or the public, compared to how she is in meetings with officials talking about policy, when she's stony-faced. She chooses what she gives to people.

The same was true of her relationship with Peter Murrell, something generally kept closed to all but a few friends and family, while certain journalists also picked up on the First Minister's ability to switch between registers in a split second, although one could argue it was a necessary trait to endure the demands of modern political life. But even Sturgeon's younger sister Gillian spoke of her being 'a very closed person'. 'There's times when even I don't know what she's thinking,' she added. 'It's how she was as a child. It's just her nature.'[39]

But even what the pro-independence blogger Andrew Tickell identified as a 'residual touch of reserve . . . of native shyness overcome' was an asset, something 'many Scots recognise, recognise in themselves, and find attractive'.[40] Sturgeon, therefore, was not afraid of admitting weaknesses (something her predecessor rarely countenanced) and conceding when criticism was legitimate, although even that was part of what appeared an enormous effort to come across as an ordinary human being. As the columnist Ian Bell observed, her actual background was 'a life lived in the discipline of party',[41] but it seemed to make little difference in the eyes of voters.

Sturgeon saw this as simply closing the gap between the old 'persona of Nicola the politician' and the 'real' person underneath, a 'divide' that had disappeared as she got older and therefore more comfortable in her own skin. 'The more experience I have got in politics,' she remarked during the 2015 general election, 'the more I have allowed me to shine through.' In interviews she often stressed her superiority to other politicians, making it clear that, unlike them, she kept promises and was (in a favourite adjective) 'principled'.[42] 'I like to be a straight talker,' Sturgeon said in April 2015, adding the important qualification, 'when I can be.'[43]

When it came to her leadership style, Sturgeon professed to feeling 'quite comfortable with decision making', having managed to 'convince' herself she had 'what it takes to be a leader',[44] although the fact she needed to do so spoke to that earlier lack of confidence. 'The most important thing I've learned in the last 16 months,' she reflected in early 2016, 'is that you've got to have the confidence to trust your own instincts, and make your own decisions and if you get them wrong, try not to beat yourself up about it too much, but just learn from it.'[45]

To Mandy Rhodes, Sturgeon was 'potentially even more autocratic than Salmond',[46] and a conference resolution banning SNP MPs from publicly criticising 'a group decision, policy or another member of the group' certainly smacked of control freakery[47], as did her widely criticised decision to appoint parliamentary aides to the Holyrood committees designed to hold the Scottish Government to account. She was also less able than her predecessor to delegate. Unlike Salmond, she felt the need to be more hands on when it came to certain ministerial portfolios (particularly health and education), although according to one colleague there was also an awareness that 'she needs to be less involved in absolutely everything'.[48] 'Nicola,' complained one ally of Health Secretary Shona Robison, 'is every bit as brutal as Tony Blair was in grabbing eye-catching announcements.'[49]

As a result, the First Minister tended to micromanage (a trait shared by Mrs Thatcher early in her premiership), something that must have increased her stress levels; there were even suggestions Sturgeon had developed a Salmond-like tetchiness with officials, an irritable side hitherto unknown in her seven-year ministerial career. The journalist Peter Ross understood her to be 'driven more by horror of failure than the will to win'. 'She has her own internal Project Fear,' he observed. 'She takes setbacks personally and to heart.'[50]

'I am quite driven,' Sturgeon admitted to an ITV interviewer. 'I know what I think and I know what I want to achieve.'[51] This drive was obvious to voters and therefore Sturgeon was widely perceived as a strong leader, even becoming a benchmark for those seeking to succeed Ed Miliband in the summer of 2015 – candidates were asked what 'qualities' they shared with the First Minister that might make them 'as successful'.[52]

Sturgeon's appearance, of course, was important in all of this. To Peter Ross all those jackets and dresses in vivid colours not only suited the First Minister 'but also give her uniformity, continuity and increase her level of brand recognition'. Sturgeon, he added, hadn't 'weaponised her wardrobe as Thatcher did, but has armour-plated it'.[53] It had been the SNP staffer Ria Robertson who had introduced her boss to the Scottish designers Holly Mitchell and Lynsey Blackburn of Totty Rocks, who would provide fittings at Bute House. They, in turn, were close friends of the First Minister's hairdresser and make-up artist, Julie McGuire, who cut and coloured Sturgeon's hair every four to five weeks, while also working on shoots was the stylist Zoe Radcliffe of Vi Nouveau, an Edinburgh-based customised vintage clothing and accessories brand. A speed-dial call from Bute House was known by the team as 'an Urgent Sturgeon',[54] although these were reserved for special occasions, 'day to day, for better or worse' the First Minister looked after herself.[55]

A Salmond-era 'coach', Claire Howell, was also an occasional part of Team Sturgeon and was said to have guided the then Deputy First Minister's weight loss during the referendum campaign. 'I'm a 45-year-old woman,' Sturgeon told the *Guardian* matter-of-factly. 'I've been on many diets over the years.'[56] There was no time for the gym, although an exercise bike and cross trainer had been installed at her home, which very much reflected her personality – neat, orderly, functional, and looking like thousands of other Scottish homes, which was perhaps the point.

Interviews filmed there revealed lots of books, politics and fiction segregated on different sides of her study; a pile of White

Papers stacked on their side. Indeed, Sturgeon was not afraid to be seen as the most bookish First Minister since Donald Dewar. 'A life without books and reading would, for me, be a life not worth living,' she declared with obvious sincerity at the 2015 Edinburgh International Book Festival, during which Sturgeon ably interviewed the crime writer Val McDermid (later she would play herself in McDermid's radio adaptation of John Wyndham's science fiction novel *The Kraken Wakes*), a role she reprised in August 2016 with the Scottish 'makar' Jackie Kay.

When the writer William McIlvanney died in late 2015, the First Minister spoke of the 'huge influence' his work, particularly the novel *Docherty*, had had on her childhood in Ayrshire.[57] She also revealed a childhood ambition to become 'a children's writer like Enid Blyton',[58] while, by her own admission, any future as a diarist was doomed to failure. Sturgeon regretted not having kept a daily record, like Salmond, of the referendum campaign, having only managed to fill three pages of a 2014 journal bought for that purpose. 'It is the kind of thing I keep saying to myself I must do,' she reflected after becoming First Minister. 'There is usually a public record of what happens day to day, but what you tend to forget after the passage of time is how you feel about it.'[59]

'She's a voracious reader of briefs; she likes information,' observed one close colleague,[60] suggesting a Margaret Thatcher-like love of statistics and perhaps John Major's sensitivity when it came to media criticism. 'Any politician that tells you it doesn't bother them when they read really horrible things about themselves in the papers,' Sturgeon reflected at one point, 'is not telling you the truth.'[61] Initially she kept the printed press at arms length, only beginning monthly press conferences at Bute House after having been prompted to do so by Alan Roden of the *Scottish Daily Mail* (with whom she got on surprisingly well). Even then there were awkward moments, not least one impromptu Q&A in the ministerial lift at Holyrood, the First Minister having attempted to evade journalists in the wake of a sex scandal involving her deputy

Stewart Hosie (he fell on his sword soon after). Sturgeon was also reluctant to associate herself too closely with Rupert Murdoch but did meet him briefly during a visit to the *Wall Street Journal* in New York City, an encounter conspicuous by its absence from Sturgeon's newspaper diary of that US tour.

Instead the First Minister prioritised the broadcast media – less intrusive, less likely to criticise and more likely to showcase her presentational strengths. Sturgeon even took the unusual step of appearing on STV's 2015 Hogmanay programme alongside her mother and sister while, in her dealings with the BBC, she was more constructive and less threatening than Salmond, making it known she had dined privately with the network political editor Nick Robinson, a bogeyman for some Yes supporters since the referendum. But appearing on television was a double-edged sword, Sturgeon complaining that 'literally every time I'm on camera' people ended up discussing her appearance in an often 'hideous and quite cruel way'.[62]

Although negative commentary certainly existed (particularly on social media), there was also a raft of positive feedback. Even the *Mail on Sunday* hailed the First Minister as 'living proof women become sexier with age, income and office',[63] while it was also suggested that Sturgeon's decision to pose for a fashion spread in *Vogue* was at odds with her complaint 'about the focus on women politicians and what they wear and how they look', something she conceded being 'slightly conflicted' about, but simultaneously feeling it was justified in order to 'talk to a different audience than you would otherwise'.[64]

Gender politics had been an impressively consistent feature of Sturgeon's leadership of the SNP and Scotland since late 2014, the bold statement of her gender-balanced Cabinet ('one of only three in the developed world') underpinned by her challenge to private- and public-sector boards to do likewise. 'If I leave office . . . without having helped make a difference for other women,' she remarked, 'then that would be a failure.'[65] Leslie Evans also became the Scottish Government's first female permanent secretary in July 2015, although other less high-profile appointments were not so balanced. After taking over as First Minister, for example, Sturgeon appointed nine men and one woman as Parliamentary Liaison Officers, traditionally a training ground for future ministers.

Sturgeon proved fearless in calling out everyday sexism in the media, labelling a *New Statesman* cover (although not its leading article) as 'crass' for depicting her, Home Secretary Theresa May, then Labour frontbencher Liz Kendall and German Chancellor Angela Merkel looking into a crib containing a ballot box and the headline: 'Why are so many successful women childless?' Several times the First Minister was asked if this had been a 'conscious decision'. 'It hasn't been,' she responded during the 2015 general election campaign. 'Life takes certain directions and it doesn't take other directions and that's about as complicated as it gets.'[66]

The First Minister's rapport with children and families was evident from both the 2015 and 2016 election campaigns, something underlined in policy terms with a commitment to extending childcare provision and also free, universal 'baby boxes', a key pledge (which attracted a degree of cynicism) during the Holyrood election. Sturgeon also took a political risk by telling the *New York Times* that Hillary Clinton being inaugurated US president in early 2017 would be a 'very significant moment for women worldwide'[67] (she later revoked Donald Trump's status as a 'Global Scot' for his inflammatory comments on immigration) and railed against women-only golf clubs, branding Muirfield's initial decision to reject women members as 'indefensible'.[68]

Sturgeon was therefore central to an extraordinary feminisation of Scottish politics, for decades the preserve of West Coast alpha males, becoming one of three female party leaders following the election of Kezia Dugdale as Scottish Labour chief in August 2015. Even so, she was required to compromise on her feminist principles, particularly when her predecessor attracted criticism for instructing the Conservative MP Anna Soubry to 'behave' herself during a Commons exchange. 'The fundamental question [is], "does that language indicate that

Alex Salmond is sexist?"' was Sturgeon's diplomatic response. 'Absolutely not, there's no man I know who is less sexist.'[69]

The First Minister also took care to cement her already strong reputation among Scotland's LGBTI+ community. As a consistent advocate of equal marriage, she acted as a witness to one of Scotland's first same-sex weddings on Hogmanay 2014, helped another couple propose at a public meeting in Oban and also raised gay rights with the president of Ghana. During the 2016 Holyrood election campaign, meanwhile, Sturgeon said a priority on winning re-election would be a legal change recognising 'non-binary' individuals without medical diagnosis.

It was one area where the SNP leader was willing to push societal boundaries although she was more reticent when it came to funding LGBTI+ inclusive education, perhaps fearing a backlash from Catholic state schools. Sturgeon, meanwhile, was obviously not unique in being an obviously talented female leader. When Home Secretary Theresa May emerged as the favourite to succeed David Cameron as Prime Minister, the German newspaper *Die Welt* even viewed her, Angela Merkel and Sturgeon as part of a new 'femokratie', 'postmodern Elektras in trouser suits and rubber gloves' clearing up the mess caused by men across Europe.[70]

In a 2015 article for the *Spectator*, the author James Bartholomew coined the insightful term 'virtue signalling' – the means by which individuals (such as politicians) expressed opinions in a way designed to show or rather signal that they were a better person than those holding contrary views.[71] Between 2014 and 2016, it could be argued that Nicola Sturgeon was a virtue signaller par excellence.

The First Minister's response to the Glaswegian nurse infected with Ebola demonstrated this empathy, as did her handling of the Clutha helicopter crash in 2013 and the bin lorry accident almost exactly a year later (both in her political base of Glasgow). There was also a public apology for failures in the newly unified Police Scotland – in particular, an accident on the M9 that left two crash victims lying in a wrecked car for three days (a 'dreadful failure . . . as First Minister you do feel these thing very deeply'[72]). Sturgeon also used virtue signalling to flag up points of difference between the Scottish and UK Governments, particularly regarding humanitarian issues, although, when it came to the refugee crisis, the First Minister was careful to observe that a 'welcoming and tolerant tradition' was 'not unique to Scotland', Britain having also 'distinguished itself' in that regard.[73]

However, the moral high ground is a complicated place, especially for a politician, and a potentially troublesome one too (for example when the First Minister said she would be willing personally to house refugees from the Middle East).[74] There was a risk of Sturgeon becoming such an articulate teller of the story that the SNP was not 'like' other parties and that where Labour had failed it would succeed that she and others would actually believe it to be true. This was evident from the First Minister's frequently peremptory tone towards Kezia Dugdale ('just because she says something in a sincere way it doesn't mean it's true'[75]) and rather undermined by Kenny MacAskill's admission that the Scottish Government had granted votes to 16- and 17-year-olds but not prisoners to 'avoid any needless distractions in the run-up to the referendum' (a decision Sturgeon herself had defended). 'It was the wrong thing done,' explained the former Justice Secretary, 'albeit for the right reasons.'[76]

But enough of Sturgeon's style as First Minister, what of the substance? Underpinning it all was her self-identification as a 'social democrat' which, to the left-wing academic Gregor Gall, meant someone 'in both words and deeds' who was prepared 'to use the state to intervene in the economy to ameliorate the processes and outcomes of free market capitalism – and to do so in order to make them fairer for most citizens'. Under Sturgeon's premiership, there were certainly examples of state intervention ('saving', for example, Scotland's remaining steelworks and shipyards) but little by the way of redistribution or determined assaults on inequality, thus, to Gall, the SNP could best be characterised as 'social liberal' rather than social democratic.[77]

The authors of a sharply contrarian study of Scottish politics preferred the term 'social nationalist', typified by Sturgeon's consensualism, her claim to Labour's Scottish legacy and her focus on utilitarian rather than existential goals. They continued:

> Social nationalism has an enormously popular leader at the head of its very own movement, with a mission, a clear and widely unpopular enemy and even the tacit support of swathes of the labour movement and the radical left. It is the dominant ideology of governance in Scotland, and its roots are now deep enough that it might remain so for decades.[78]

To *The Economist*'s Bagehot, meanwhile, the Sturgeon style of government was more akin to Argentina's Peronists than reformist Scandinavian social democrats, the SNP's 'soft autocracy' holding together the party's 'distinctive tartan of universal handouts, leftist posturing, melodramatic flag-waving and structural conservatism'.[79] Many sympathetic commentators, however, were all too willing to laud the First Minister as 'unquestionably Britain's most trusted social democrat' (Lesley Riddoch),[80] 'one of the leading voices on the contemporary British left' (Iain Macwhirter)[81] or the leader of 'Scotland's natural party of social democracy' (Jamie Maxwell).[82]

Sturgeon herself tried to steer a middle way, saying that voters did not 'just see left or right' in the SNP but 'a party that always seeks to do the right thing for Scotland',[83] while rejecting characterisations of herself either 'as a Bolshevik leftie taking the country down all sorts of horrendous paths' or as 'conservative and timid and not doing anything'.[84] At the same time, there was a genuine (if questionable) belief in her and her party's ideological consistency, certainly vis-à-vis other parties, when the only consistency lay in the SNP's inconsistency over much of its eight decades in existence.

The muddle was by no means specific to Sturgeon or the SNP, a clear 'progressive dilemma' having confronted every party of the centre left for several decades – a choice between persuading voters to support a genuinely progressive programme or simply identifying what they found politically tolerable and packaging it in the language of 'radical' reform. The First Minister, in common with lots of others, had simply opted for the latter. Of course it could be argued that she lacked the devolved powers necessary to deliver the former but that became less true as Holyrood accrued more and more autonomy under her leadership.

And, while Sturgeon generally played down the 'existential' aspects of her nationalism, they were certainly present, if not to the same degree as her predecessor. There were repeated references to Scotland's 'ancient' provenance and the importance of history – 'it grounds us and gives us a story', she told a Plaid Cymru conference. 'It gives us something to build on.'[85] To cynics, therefore, the ostensibly 'civic nationalist' SNP simply instrumentalised progressive ideas to advance its core aim of independence. The former Labour adviser David Clark reckoned the party under Sturgeon 'resembled nothing as much as New Labour in its pomp, combining the worst reflexes of authoritarian statism and market liberalism with a superior, "we know best" attitude that brooks no opposition'.[86]

This impression was supported by the First Minister's instant dismissal of Jeremy Corbyn upon his election as UK Labour leader in September 2015. Having long argued that the Auld Enemy had suffered for becoming too right wing, Sturgeon switched seamlessly to chastising it for being too weak and unelectable. The SNP, meanwhile, only really suffered in narrative terms, its 56 MPs no longer the sole proponents of anti-Trident and anti-austerity rhetoric. The cry of 'red Tory' was also laid to rest, while the personal conduct of certain of those among 'the 56' betrayed a New Labour or even Tory-like attitude towards personal financial gain. As one, Tasmina Ahmed-Sheikh, even admitted to *Prospect* magazine, the SNP's pro-business stance would 'traditionally be thought of as centre or centre right'.[87]

It was social democracy but not as we know it. Sturgeon even claimed at one point that being a social democrat *and* a pragmatist were not 'a million miles apart'.[88] She repeatedly

stressed rationalism and evidence-based approaches to governance rather than dogma, although this was applied inconsist-
ently. Professor Paul Younger, for example, spoke of the
Scottish Government's 'brief flirtation with evidence-based
policymaking' being 'swiftly superseded by policy-based
evidence making', clearly irritated by its failure to take on board
its own expert group's findings in relation to fracking.[89]

Unconventional oil and gas extraction was one of many
policy dilemmas still sitting in Sturgeon's in-tray following
the 2016 Holyrood election, stuck, as it were, between a rock
(putting off investors) and a hard place (potentially splitting
the party, a section of which was vehemently anti-fracking). All
the more so given that the plunging oil price provided a difficult
backdrop to her first year and a half in Bute House. This was
tricky because Sturgeon had been complicit in referendum-era
predictions about a second oil boom; now, as First Minister,
she tried to distance herself, spreading the blame by saying that
'everybody's projections about oil were wrong'[90] and even that
'the case for Scotland [as] . . . a strong independent country
was never based on oil',[91] both of which struck critics as post-
hoc rationalisations.

This context also made the SNP's claim to be 'anti-austerity'
somewhat harder to sustain, not least when the annual
Government Expenditure and Revenue Scotland (GERS)
figures in March 2016 revealed a massive £15-billion budget
'deficit' just days before what would have been 'Independence
Day' had Scotland voted Yes in September 2014. In an
uncomfortable interview with the BBC's Andrew Neil – arguably Sturgeon's least accomplished as First Minister – all she
could offer by way of counterattack was the line that Scotland's
economy remained 'fundamentally strong' and that a hypothetically independent country would be dealing with such a
deficit 'in the same way' the UK had dealt with its in 2009–10
– i.e. through spending cuts.[92] It was a testament to Sturgeon's
popularity that this interview produced little reputational
damage.

But then, as James Bartholomew had observed, one of the

crucial aspects of virtue signalling was that 'it does not require actually doing anything virtuous'.[93] When it came to actually tackling austerity, Sturgeon was off the hook, it being predominantly a reserved matter, so it mattered not when the Institute for Fiscal Studies (IFS) concluded that the SNP's 'stated plans do not necessarily match their anti-austerity rhetoric',[94] for the party had successfully entrenched itself in the (Scottish) public eye as *the* anti-austerity party, a position inherited from the closing stages of the independence referendum.

And although Sturgeon's analysis of the impact of coalition economic policy (it had, she said, 'undermined our public services, lowered the living standards of working people, pushed more children into poverty and held back economic growth'[95]) was, by all accounts, spot on, that did not mean her alternative was as compelling or credible. Indeed, when it came to the economic fundamentals, it was clear the new First Minister represented more of a change of style than substance with regards to her predecessor.

Although in early 2015 Sturgeon appeared to have abandoned Salmond's flagship pledge to cut corporation tax and showed reluctance to restore the 50p rate of income tax, in fact she remained in thrall to what were euphemistically termed tax 'incentives'. The First Minister did, however, attempt to present her Fair Work Convention, Living Wage Accreditation and Scottish Business Pledge as 'essential features of what is becoming a distinctive Scottish approach to growth'[96] (in which the Ayrshire businesswoman Marie Macklin and Scottish Enterprise chief executive Lena Wilson were significant allies).

Later, on a high-profile trip to the United States, the First Minister even spoke approvingly of 'Rhine capitalism', based on a strong sense of partnership 'between workers, trade unions, businesses and the public sector', encouraging 'competitive markets' but combining them with 'strong social protections'.[97] This economic middle way was standard social democratic stuff, although hardly original. 'Fairness and prosperity can go hand in hand,' was a typical Sturgeon sound bite during a speech at UCL in February 2015. 'Indeed, I'd put it more strongly – they *must* go hand in hand.'[98] But what the First Minister proposed in concrete terms was either voluntary (the Business Pledge) or bungled (it emerged her own office had not signed up to the Living Wage). And, when it came to attracting inward investment, Sturgeon appeared reticent (certainly compared with Alex Salmond) – she made efforts to secure, for example, a £10-billion investment from China but did not officially announce it or even brief Cabinet colleagues, only publishing details when reports surfaced in the state-controlled Beijing media.

Sturgeon did not articulate economic jargon with the ease of her predecessor and was noticeably less technical in her approach to explaining economic issues, although she was clearly conscious that links with Scotland's business community required work. In January 2015, the PR firm Charlotte Street Partners (run by former MSP colleague Andrew Wilson) hosted a dinner enabling 50 of Scotland's business leaders to meet the First Minister, while she appealed to London-based companies to establish offices north of the Border. Sturgeon was ostentatiously positive about the UK capital ('a great world city and a global business hub'), again in marked contrast to her predecessor.[99]

So, when it came to engagement, few could fault Sturgeon – the Scottish Trades Union Congress (STUC) probably had greater access to ministers than any equivalent body in Europe, although the Scottish Government's handling of industrial disputes revealed a First Minister overly willing to please and, therefore, yield pre-emptively when it came to avoiding potentially politically sensitive disputes with Abellio train drivers, Calmac and further education lecturers. It betrayed a policy agenda more focused on buying off sectoral interests than the more nuanced 'social partnership' Sturgeon frequently invoked.

The same was true when it came to tackling inequality, the rhetorical leitmotif of Sturgeon's career, and particularly so since the independence referendum. This, however, was diluted after the 2016 Holyrood election to achieving 'equality of opportunity for all', with the word 'inequality' generally used imprecisely and conflated with poverty. There was little evidence of a deep intellectual analysis of inequality – its causes and potential solutions – or the role of government in combating it, while the First Minister's unshakeable belief in 'the philosophy of universal benefits'[100] arguably hindered progress. Even the Scottish Government's own Independent Advisor on Poverty and Inequality, Naomi Eisenstadt, questioned the wisdom of universal provision and, indeed, her moderate recommendations for action were initially resisted by ministers.[101] A proposal to rename 'benefits' in the summer of 2016 was, for example, typical of the general focus on presentation rather than genuinely innovative thinking.

There was, as under Salmond, more of an interest in attracting star names than actually following their expert advice. Professor Mariana Mazzucato was one of Sturgeon's high-profile additions to the Council of Economic Advisers, although it seemed unlikely her call for 'some hard choices and some myth-busting', given that many policies 'recently justified in the name of "innovation" have actually only increased inequality', would be heeded.[102] The 2016 SNP manifesto pledge to 'lead a national drive to improve productivity' was, for example, in conflict with another to expand the Small Business Bonus, which would actually lower productivity.[103]

The tensions were most evident when it came to fiscal policy. Embarrassingly, the Scottish Government was bounced into making its new Land and Buildings Transaction Tax *more* progressive by Chancellor George Osborne's changes to the equivalent Stamp Duty in England and Wales, while, in terms of Council Tax and Income Tax, caution was the order of the day. At the 2007 Holyrood election, posters featuring Salmond and Sturgeon had promised to scrap what the latter described as the 'hated' Council Tax while she had also warned that 'tinkering with bands' (as Scottish Labour then proposed) 'would not make the system any fairer'.[104] Yet, when the First Minister finally responded to the recommendations of a cross-party commission on local taxation (which had advised abolition), she unveiled little more than tinkering of her own, albeit cloaked in the usual 'progressive' and 'radical' rhetoric.[105] Setting a cap on Council Tax increases (although a long-standing freeze would finally come to an end) also evoked Thatcher-era controls, while proposals to cut Air Passenger Duty paid homage to both Art Laffer's Curve and the more neo-liberal Alex Salmond.

'We won't vote for Labour policies that we think are just carbon copies of Tory policies,'[106] Sturgeon had declared prior to the 2015 general election but, as Scottish Conservatives took delight in pointing out, her own taxation plans came to resemble theirs quite closely. That was true of Council Tax but also the Scottish Rate of Income Tax (SRIT), in place as of April 2016. When Scottish Labour leader Kezia Dugdale announced plans to increase it (and therefore every band) by 1p, the First Minister (inaccurately) said it would prove 'anything but progressive'. Later, she went further, accusing Labour of its own virtue signalling, indulging in 'some kind of political virility test' to prove it was more left wing than the SNP, but without any realistic chance of electoral success.[107]

Eventually, Sturgeon unveiled her own plans, yet another piece of triangulation placing her between Labour's (which she accurately depicted as hitting lower as well as higher earners) and the Conservatives' (no tax increases at all) proposals – what she called 'exactly the right place' – by foregoing George Osborne's increase in the upper rate threshold (to take effect in 2017 rather than 2016) and U-turning on plans to restore the additional 50p rate, the First Minister now being convinced that it might compel higher earners to flee south of the Border. The fact this was similar to the analysis deployed by a Conservative Chancellor and not based on any new research or economic modelling did not go unnoticed. A *Times* editorial referred sardonically to 'Nicola Osborne' and thereafter Sturgeon repeatedly flip-flopped, later protesting that she would support an increase in the additional rate only if she could be sure there would be no adverse impact on revenue.

Obviously ill at ease in selling a policy that was perhaps at odds with her own instincts, some detected the hand of Finance

Secretary John Swinney, the only minister with any real influence on Sturgeon and even more cautious on fiscal matters than his boss. In one sense both had fallen into a Unionist trap – in granting Holyrood more powers, the opposition aim had been to compel the SNP either to put its money where its mouth was by increasing taxes or to retain the status quo and look hypocritical. In the event, Sturgeon did a little bit of both and ended up pleasing no one on her own side while presenting the Scottish Conservatives with a pre-2016 election gift.

There was a wider point, chiefly that the First Minister's fiscal approach was not only timid but dishonest for, like her predecessor, she apparently found it impossible to even inch towards stating the obvious – that, if her aspirations in terms of 'social justice' and reducing inequality were to be realised, then Scotland's tax base would have to increase significantly. 'Over time,' she suggested during the 2016 Holyrood campaign, 'we may well see Scotland and the Scottish Parliament moving away from the structure of income tax that prevails in the UK.'[108] This, however, was merely a promise of fiscal *mañana* and even some of Sturgeon's own supporters were left wondering, 'If not now, when?'

All of this spoke to a policy agenda that was reactive and lacking in either coherence or depth. For the SNP, whose policy-making apparatus had long been neglected by Alex Salmond, this was little surprise but, for the SNP-run Scottish Government, more than seven years old by the time Nicola Sturgeon became First Minister, there were fewer excuses. But then she was a product of a party that valued campaigners rather than intellectuals, good television performers more than original policy thinkers.

During Sturgeon's first year in office there were several missteps, initiatives and legislation that antagonised certain sectors without any obvious political return. A ban on GM crops, for example, not only came from nowhere – and apparently without Cabinet discussion – but also sent a terrible message to the scientific community, while an attempt to reform higher education governance came up against sustained and vocal opposition from university principals (although that was, to be fair, largely an inherited mess).

Perhaps conscious of this, the respected civil servant Graeme Roy was moved from the Office of the Chief Economic Adviser to run Sturgeon's policy unit, although he did not last long, departing for the Fraser of Allander Institute in April 2016 (he was succeeded by Chris Birt). In late 2015, Kevin Pringle, who also left the Scottish Government after more than a quarter of a century working for his party, called for the party's policy forums to be 'reinvigorated', arguing it would 'boost our national democracy' if the SNP strengthened 'its internal democracy' further.

Pringle suggested an SNP-aligned (but not controlled) think tank to support this process, realising that the dominance of a single, highly disciplined party made for a 'relatively limited policy agenda'.[109] Indeed, the prospectus following the 2016 Holyrood election rested heavily upon education, improvements to which Nicola Sturgeon staked her personal reputation as First Minister. She focused on the widening 'attainment' gap, the phenomenon by which pupil performance in less affluent areas of Scotland proved stubbornly unchanged and had done so since the SNP entered government in 2007. The issue had actually been put on the agenda by Scottish Labour leader Kezia Dugdale but the First Minister made it her own, stressing at every turn that not only would it be 'a defining priority' for her administration but also 'a personal passion'.[110]

There was certainly a change of tone, although Angela Constance proved a marginal figure as Education Secretary, certainly in comparison with Mike Russell, not least because Sturgeon virtually took personal charge of the portfolio. She made it clear, meanwhile, she disagreed with 'extreme opinions' at both ends of the educational spectrum,[111] stressing she was not 'ideological about this . . . if something can be proven to work then we should try it'.[112] There were visits to schools in Brooklyn and London, a change of heart on the merits of the English 'Teach First' scheme and a commitment to granting schools 'more autonomy to drive the improvements themselves', although a decision on the conversion of St Joseph's primary school in Milngavie into a 'free' school (at its parents' request) was left hanging for more than a year.

Sturgeon also promised to be 'confrontational' if necessary,[113] a sign she anticipated opposition from teaching unions and local authorities. But the First Minister's big idea, when it finally emerged, was underwhelming – an initially vague plan for standardised testing in schools, something she had opposed as SNP education spokesperson back in 1999 and which was subsequently watered down in response to teacher union opposition, leaving considerable confusion as to exactly what new information the tests would provide. At the 2016 SNP manifesto launch, Sturgeon had said her next government would be about 'doing things that we didn't previously think we'd do' and, indeed, back in 1986, she and the rest of the SNP would have been resolutely opposed to undermining local councils in such a way.

In that manifesto, there were references to greater local discretion on the one hand and more regionalisation on the other, although what transformational forces such moves were expected to unleash was less clear. Did it also mean the Scottish Government would experiment with Tory-style academies (most likely under a different name)? Again, it was not spelled out, although John Swinney, appointed Education Secretary after the election, kept himself busy with the usual retinue of educational 'summits' and advice from 'international experts'.

There was also a change of tone when it came to higher education. Alex Salmond had ended his days as First Minister gazing admiringly at his 'rocks will melt with the sun' mantra emblazoned on a rock at Heriot-Watt University, but his successor asserted that 'the principle of free education' was necessary but it was not sufficient for tackling educational inequality. As with education generally, Sturgeon made it clear this was personal, deriving moral justification for 'free' tuition from her own backstory, although it was a necessarily selective account.

The SNP leader rarely made any mention of grants, cuts

to which she partially restored as First Minister, although the gradual shift towards loans produced a curious situation in which Sturgeon continually talked about debt putting working-class children off university while presiding over a system that put that very group heavily into debt. To govern is to choose and it looked very much like the Scottish Government was continuing to prioritise the requirements of middle-class students over their less affluent contemporaries. A Commission on Widening Access *was* established, although its first report was, revealingly, heavier on critique of the status quo than praise for the Scottish Government's record.

Health policy, meanwhile, was particularly important to Sturgeon's own reputation for competent administration, which explained why Health Secretary Shona Robison got little credit for a (rather panicky) NHS spending boost in the form of £200 million for treatment centres. There were missed targets, a highly critical Audit Scotland report and hit squads in relatively new hospitals while, during the 2015 general election, the First Minister had come under scrutiny about the fact health spending had increased by only 1 per cent in Scotland but six times that (in real terms) south of the Border. She protested that health spending was higher per head in Scotland (true but beside the point) while retreating into jargon about the Institute for Fiscal Studies' (IFS) analysis excluding 'non-profit distributing capital investment'.[114]

The SNP leader's attempt to explain her Westminster group's U-turn on abstaining on English-only legislation was also contrived and unconvincing. The nadir came ahead of a vote on fox hunting, a matter fully devolved and with no financial implications in Scotland. Citing pressure from animal rights groups in England, Sturgeon instructed her MPs to vote against at their monthly group meeting, despite qualms from 'some more seasoned party hands wary of breaking the already crumbling commitment to standing aside from English only votes'.[115] Although it worked (the UK Government shelved the vote), the whole incident smacked of Salmond at his opportunistic worst.

At least on foreign and defence policy the SNP was more consistent, although Sturgeon's 'listening' mode over the case for Syrian air strikes was both short lived and disingenuous. Beyond that, she told the United States Council on Foreign Relations in Washington not to believe the Scottish Government took 'a markedly different position from the UK government on the vast majority of international issues. We don't.'[116]

Presentationally, however, the First Minister generally impressed – her US tour in the summer of 2015 was a high point, while an offer to mediate during a Catalan–Madrid impasse during Spain's own constitutional debate was calculated to boost her international profile and make her appear bolder when it came to external affairs.

The First Minister's handling of the independence question, at least prior to the EU referendum in June 2016, was less sure-footed. To be fair, on this front, Sturgeon found herself in a much harder position than Alex Salmond had – under his leadership, the first referendum had flowed inescapably from the 2011 Holyrood election but his successor could not pull the trigger on a second plebiscite without being sure of winning it and, therefore, as Peter Ross observed, 'the longer she holds her fire, the more she risks her store of goodwill dwindling away'.[117]

It was also notable that Sturgeon became the first SNP leader in modern times to fight an election (2015) by making it perfectly clear that independence would *not* be the outcome, no matter how well the party did. Partly this was tactical, using words like 'humility' and 'respect' to reassure and keep hold of No-voting supporters, but it was also realistic, support for independence having lingered at around 45 per cent. (A goal of achieving 60 per cent would emerge during the October 2015 conference.) At the same time, the First Minister had to keep Yes voters on side. This necessitated riding two constitutional horses at once although, in the absence of a clear strategy, she tended to swing wildly between the two.

Even so, Sturgeon came under pressure during the general

election campaign for appearing to equivocate. In a second Scottish leaders' debate, therefore, she hardened her line, talking of a 'triple lock'. 'Before it is inserted in the [2016] manifesto, public opinion has to change,' she elaborated, 'and then people have to vote for the manifesto if it is in it, then people have to vote for independence.'[118] Other caveats were added – for example, the need for that manifesto commitment to be 'clear' and for another overall majority but Sturgeon repeatedly emphasised that, rather than her 'imposing' another referendum on voters, it would 'always be driven by the democratic wishes of the Scottish people'.[119]

Nor was Sturgeon's line on 'full fiscal autonomy', a Salmond-era constitutional 'horse', especially clear. She said her government now wanted to phase this in over an unspecified time period while retaining the Treasury block grant to protect public spending levels in the interim. Such caution implicitly recognised that Scotland was a net beneficiary in funding terms, particularly since the oil crash. As even the newly elected SNP MP George Kerevan acknowledged: 'For Scotland to accept fiscal autonomy without inbuilt UK-wide fiscal balancing would be tantamount to economic suicide.'[120] But that, of course, would *not* be *full* fiscal autonomy.

Only a few months after the general election did Sturgeon start talking up independence and the possibility of another referendum, telling the Press Association that she would 'set out what we consider are the circumstances and the timescale on which a second referendum might be appropriate'. As ever, she stressed the Scottish Government could 'only propose' – it would be for 'the people' to decide, be it 'in five years or 10 years or whenever'.[121]

There was an inconsistency there, for 'the people' could only really decide at election time and, even then, another referendum would just be one among many different issues being decided upon. Nevertheless, the mooted timescale was interesting, revealing the thinking of many (past and present) SNP strategists that the most likely window lay between the 2020 UK and 2021 Scottish elections, on the basis that, in

Kevin Pringle's words, another Tory win would 'significantly boost support for independence'.[122]

Others in the party were concerned that waiting until then might leave things too late and, indeed, it also fell to Sturgeon to navigate a modest revival of the gradualist–fundamentalist divide that had characterised the SNP in the 1980s and 1990s. Craig Murray (who had been rejected as a general election candidate, proving the party's much-criticised vetting procedure had worked to an extent) spoke for many in warning 'of missing the key moment, letting the window of opportunity slide by' by squandering the 'favourable conjunction' of further Tory austerity and current 'SNP political dominance'.[123]

Alex Salmond, who wasted little opportunity to talk up another referendum, formed part of what might be called the 'impatient' wing of the party, while Sturgeon was resolutely in charge of the 'cautious' group. But this was the tactics – what of the substance? Again, there was little obvious progress. At the beginning of 2016, the SNP leader spoke of leading 'a renewed debate' in 'a realistic and relevant way',[124] but at no point did compelling new arguments for independence emerge.

For critics like Alex Bell (a former head of policy at the Scottish Government), this was because the SNP's 'model' of independence was 'broken beyond repair', particularly given the plunging oil price. It had, he added in a vivid phrase, 'become the cocaine of the politically active, fun to join in but dulling the senses, jabbering on at a hundred words per minute while disconnected from self awareness'.[125]

To some degree, Sturgeon found herself trapped by her predecessor's addiction to portraying independence in economically beneficial terms. She denied ever having said an independent Scotland would be 'a land of milk and honey' without 'any obstacles along the way' (although she conceded the 'overall presentation maybe appeared more like that'),[126] but it seemed unlikely a more 'realistic' independence case would acknowledge that Scotland might be worse off than the Unionist status quo.

'The big challenge,' said one SNP strategist, 'would be

fixing this idea that independence represents a free pass.'[127] Sturgeon did, however, achieve a significant interim victory in fending off a Treasury attempt to reduce Scottish Government funding by £7 billion as a quid pro quo for greater control over income tax. Instead, Chancellor George Osborne accepted her preferred formula for reducing Scotland's block grant, agreeing to review the settlement following the 2021 Holyrood election. This was doubly important in that it mitigated any need to raise taxes, something likely to erode support for independence among 'Middle Scotland' voters.

At the 2016 SNP spring conference, meanwhile, Sturgeon felt compelled to reassure the troops that independence remained on the agenda by announcing a new summer 'initiative' to 'build support for independence', although it later emerged this was only inserted into her speech the night before as an 'applause point' rather than a considered strategy. Delegates in the hall responded rather more enthusiastically to the word 'independence' (their leader, on the other hand, looked rather taken aback) than the qualifications that followed – it would not be an attempt to 'browbeat' anyone, strong supporters of the Union had her 'respect' and, continuing her 'realistic' theme, a preparedness 'to challenge some of our own answers'.[128]

But it was a mistake to interpret the SNP leader's 'initiative' as anything other than a useful applause point in a speech actually intended to kick a second independence referendum into the long grass, which is where many on the 'impatient' wing of the party suspected Sturgeon – finally First Minister after a long wait – was happy for it to rest. Of course, driving this was her innate caution (indeed, it was ironic that one so risk averse supported independence at all) but the Holyrood election of 2016 once again required Sturgeon to ride both referendum horses, simultaneously talking it up (for the benefit of existing supporters) and down (in order to attract what the SNP MP Tommy Sheppard described as the 'i-curious'[129]).

In pursuit of her own 'personal' mandate for the first time, Sturgeon said again and again that she took nothing for granted when it come to securing another overall majority. This was reflected in the #BothVotesSNP hashtag and campaigning slogan, one that necessarily involved dismantling the 'Yes' coalition as tribally as Scottish Conservative leader Ruth Davidson did in her battle to out-Unionist her Labour and Liberal Democrat opponents.

A refrain during the referendum had been that independence 'was not about the SNP', now it was *all* about the SNP, with Sturgeon warning voters not to back other pro-independence parties on the list vote (like the Scottish Greens) lest Unionist MSPs sneak in by the back door. The manifesto, meanwhile, set out two criteria – 'clear and sustained evidence that independence has become the preferred option of a majority of the Scottish people' or 'a significant and material change in the circumstances that prevailed in 2014, such as Scotland being taken out of the EU against our will'.[130]

Questioned about the former, Sturgeon said there would have to be evidence 'over a period of time . . . more than one or two opinion polls . . . that independence had become the preferred option of the Scottish people',[131] which suggested pollsters would have rather more influence than voters, while, at this stage, the latter looked more likely than it had the previous year, with 'Remain' and 'Leave' neck and neck in European referendum opinion polls. Adding to the SNP leader's reticence was Scottish Tory leader Ruth Davidson's determination to exploit any hint of a second referendum in order to attract Unionist voters. So, when the *Sunday Herald* asked Sturgeon a week before polling day if she expected it to happen and she replied in the affirmative ('Do I think it's more likely than not? Yes.'), the Conservatives could not believe their pre-election luck.[132]

The constitutional question loomed large at that election because all the evidence suggested it had become, as at the 2015 general election, the main driver of Scottish electoral behaviour. Beyond that, as the journalist Alex Massie observed, Sturgeon could ask to be 'judged on her record because she knows she won't be'.[133] Not only was that record no better or worse than previous devolved administrations but the SNP leader pursued a new mandate on the basis of 'safety first'. Her manifesto was hardly brimful of original policy ideas ('social justice' was not mentioned once) while the main election leaflet asked, 'Who benefits most from our policies?' before giving the implausible but reassuring answer, 'We all do.' A sort of nationalist utilitarianism remained in the ascendancy, although prominent policy ideas were often both unoriginal and bereft of basic detail.

The 'team, record, vision' mantra of 2011, meanwhile, was abandoned and, instead, it all came down to Sturgeon. Tens of thousands of 'Nicola for First Minister' T-shirts, bags and balloons were printed; 48-sheet posters bearing her face appeared on hoardings across the country; and, on polling day, double-page spreads in the country's top-selling tabloids. The only bum note came when the SNP leader was photographed holding a copy of the *Scottish Sun*'s endorsement – 'back Nic and her SNP crew for a new five-year mission and in turn their duty is . . . TO BOLDLY GO'[134] – just days after the Hillsborough verdict.

As in 2015, it was all very presidential, particularly the manifesto launch two weeks before polling day. This began with 'Nicola: The Movie', continued with a leader's speech couched in very personal terms and concluded with everyone present holding aloft copies of the manifesto emblazoned with an image of the lady herself. As usual, significant time was set aside on the campaign trail for photographs, invariably tweeted under the hashtag #ImWithNicola. But, as *The Times*' Mike Wade later wrote, amid all this excitement 'policies were perceived a distraction'. He recalled attempting to ask the First Minister about her government's contentious 'named person' legislation (which she had erroneously described as 'optional') during a campaign visit to South Queensferry, to which she responded curtly: 'Too busy.'[135] As a result, there was widespread concern within the party that the focus on Sturgeon at the expense of almost everything else – including policies, other candidates and even senior ministerial colleagues – had overplayed a strong hand.

A generally boring campaign was followed by a fascinating election night and, while the SNP gained more votes than ever before (more than a million) and Sturgeon got a higher share of the vote than Salmond had in 2011, the unpredictable nature of the regional list vote gave her six fewer seats and thus no overall majority – a failure of expectation management made it look like a bitter defeat. Symbolically, the SNP leader declared victory – behind a Downing Street-style lectern – outside Bute House the following morning – her version of Salmond's Prestonfield House appearance following the 2007 Holyrood election.

Ruling out a 'formal arrangement' with another party, Sturgeon said she had received a 'personal mandate' to implement a 'bold and ambitious programme for government', including her priority of closing the attainment gap.[136] Thereafter she described her (reduced) mandate as 'unequivocal' and, on her nomination as First Minister ten days later, 'clear', asserting that she had been elected, 'for the first time, in [her] own right'. In that speech Sturgeon also referred to the 'new principal party of opposition' (the Scottish Conservatives) making 'the choice of the kind of country we want to be sharper than it has been before',[137] but the messages as to parliamentary arithmetic were decidedly mixed – on the one hand, Sturgeon spoke ecumenically of building cross-party alliances (although not with the Tories) and, on the other, warning that it was 'not for the party which finished a distant second – or any of those which came after that – to dictate terms or to try and turn this session into one of obstruction for obstruction's sake'.

Given the behaviour of the SNP group at Westminster (no longer 'the 56' after the whip was withdrawn from Michelle Thomson and Natalie McGarry), the First Minster's warning against 'political gamesmanship or needless politicking' was a bit rich,[138] not least because it contradicted her intention before the 2015 general election to 'lock out' the Tories had they emerged as the largest party in a Westminster Parliament 'hung' as Holyrood now was.

And, if Sturgeon's speech on being re-elected First Minister was an uninspiring retread of that in November 2014, her post-election programme for government also felt flat and predictable, taking the usual 'year zero' approach to elections in talking of 'a precious opportunity' over the next five years to 'make real and lasting improvements for the benefit of this and future generations',[139] as if somehow the SNP had just ousted some tired old administration and not been in office for nearly a decade.

The reshuffle that followed the Holyrood election was minimalist, its guiding principle – as in November 2014 – remaining gender balance. It appeared, meanwhile, that, by the First Minister's own criteria, the likelihood of another independence referendum had receded given the lack of a clear manifesto pledge and an overall majority. All that remained was the prospect of 'material change' in the form of the European referendum held on 23 June 2016 which, as argued in the intro-duction to this biography, had a transformative effect on the Scottish Government. In danger of becoming, as one insider put it, 'the best managers Scotland has ever had',[140] the SNP once again found itself surfing the post-referendum wave.

But, while Brexit gave the new government a much-needed sense of purpose, it also disguised obvious problems. For example, while Sturgeon, a hugely talented politician by any measurement, had grown in stature since late 2014, her strengths and weaknesses increasingly reflected those of the party she led – strong on style but weak on substance. Certainly a better singer than Alex Salmond, her playlist consisted of the same old songs – a sincere but often shallow belief in the transformative effect of independence and an ever-increasing gulf between 'radical' rhetoric and the more prosaic reality, particularly as the economic case for independence shifted to the right following the EU referendum.

But then third terms for any government were generally challenging periods, during which once-disciplined parties (for example, New Labour) developed tensions and inevitable splits. And, as the SNP became more like the party it had displaced in whole swathes of the country, particularly West Central Scotland, it also began to display a familiar malaise – accusations of control freakery and an HQ overwhelmed with complaints from members, often the consequence of thwarted ambition or personal rivalries. All those zealous new converts were proving both a blessing and a curse.

And, although Sturgeon could be impressively disciplined and slick on the surface, there were often hints that she was not entirely comfortable with her party or in complete control of it, seeming unsure of some activists, her MSPs, her MPs and even the electorate. She is 'a deeply cautious politician', as the commentator Hugo Rifkind put it, 'who has no greater headache than her own supporters who thirst for her to throw caution to the wind'.[141] Nevertheless, she resented implications that supporters were 'brainwashed' or 'blind to our imperfections' – rather, she saw them as 'weighing them against our strengths and achievements'.[142]

On fracking and land reform, for example, the grassroots rather than the leadership appeared to be in control. The First Minister's approval ratings remained sky high, of course, but with a slight downward trend and even SNP activists were startled to hear references to 'that woman' on once-friendly doorsteps – an indication that, for as long as the constitution drove voting intentions, her appeal could only extend so far. As a pollster for the market research company TNS explained, support for the SNP was largely driven by emotion and identity rather than dispassionate logic and, as voters explored notions of Scottishness, they tended to project their resulting hopes and aspirations on to the SNP leader, 'who they see as their mouthpiece'.[143]

But this faith was a double-edged sword – it was easy for someone in Sturgeon's exalted position to believe their own hype and grow complacent. As Peter Ross observed, when the First Minister was flying around in a personalised helicopter and indulging endless requests for selfies, 'the words vanity and hubris do not seem far away'.[144] 'She needs a person on her shoulder every day,' reflected one supporter, 'saying memento mori.'[145]

In that respect, the loss of an overall majority in May 2016 was useful in neutralising talk of a 'one-party state' and ensuring the First Minster could not take anything for granted.

Nevertheless, under her leadership, the SNP again looked like a one-person band (as it had under Salmond in the 1990s) and Sturgeon doubters believed the magic would eventually wear off. 'She works so incredibly hard and does such long hours there really is nothing else in her life,' observed one critic. 'Eventually people will see that.'[146]

The word 'timid', meanwhile, was never far away from analyses of Sturgeon's performance. 'In the year or so of her leadership she has taken almost no risks I can think of,' was the view of self-confessed Sturgeon 'fan' Chris Deerin. 'She has kicked so many awkward issues into the long grass that she could be done for fly-tipping.'[147] It was true the First Minister showed little inclination to push boundaries or break the rules of the game, as Salmond had often done, although, when it came to education, there was a hint of iconoclasm – an attempt to renew the architecture of Scottish government for the first time in 20 years, even if it meant a fight with teaching unions and local authorities.

But taking on vested interests had not been the SNP's style since 2007, nor was it Sturgeon's, and some in the party feared that on educational attainment she was setting herself up to fail, raising expectations by promising to 'substantially close the attainment gap in the next Parliament and to eliminate it within a decade',[148] when the problem was decades in the making and largely outside any devolved politician's control.

The fortunes of party and leader, meanwhile, were inextricably bound up with those of independence. The SNP was divided between those who wanted another referendum quickly and those who wanted to get it right – a split that remained even after the majority 'Leave' vote in June 2016. Sturgeon was in the latter camp, acutely aware that moving too soon could bring a premature end to her First Ministership, something she hoped to maintain 'for a considerable period of time to come'.[149] And even if her political capital did diminish and the stardust lost some of its twinkle, Tom Costley of pollsters TNS agreed it was difficult to 'see past Nicola Sturgeon being First Minister for as long as she wants to be First Minister'.[150] In November

2015, after all, YouGov had deemed her 'the most popular and widely appreciated living person among the Scottish public – four places ahead of the Queen',[151] although Her Majesty pushed the SNP leader into second place (in the UK) when Forbes published its list of the world's most powerful women seven months later.

Sturgeon also spoke of life after politics, about 'lots of things' she would 'love to do', including writing something 'other than speeches'[152] – perhaps the books (crime fiction? a memoir?) she had dreamed of producing as a child. But, for a teenager who had joined the SNP more than three decades before winning her first 'personal mandate' and had therefore devoted most of her adult life to politics, it was hard to picture her as anything other than First Minister, yet there was still work to be done in defining herself in that role, telling a more compelling story about who she was and, more importantly, what she wanted to do.

The curse of the 'progressive' politician is high, often quixotic, expectations but the question remained that, after nearly two years as First Minister, most of it with a majority, two loyal (and large) parliamentary groups, opposition parties rarely able to land a blow and vast reserves of political capital, what big, landmark legislative achievement could Sturgeon point to? Beyond 'protecting' or mitigating benefits and services from 'Tory austerity', what had she or anyone else done to improve the lives of the poorest in Scotland beyond lofty rhetoric? To many – both inside and outside the SNP, sympathetic and cynical – the most popular First Minister in 17 years of devolution often seemed paralysed rather than emboldened by power.

So there was, as James Mitchell and Rob Johns put it, increasing tension between the SNP's 'radical goal of inde-pendence and its more mainstream goal of retaining office in Scotland'[153] – a dynamic not only present within the party's leadership and grassroots but among voters more generally. If Sturgeon was too timid, then it was in part because her party and electorate were timid too, as one in considering themselves to be more 'radical' and 'progressive' than their deeper views on economics and social policy actually justified. Perhaps, under her leadership, the inevitable strain of being both a party of protest and power, simultaneously an insurgent and establishment force, was beginning to show. And, given that the 'material change' it needed most was increased public support for independence, this was not unimportant.

Since 2007, the SNP had, as Kevin Pringle observed, 'cornered the market in defining, articulating and promoting a Scottish national interest'.[154] Dominating the market, however, was one thing but, no matter how good the presentation – and Sturgeon was up there with the best – there came a point when the product, be it 'social democracy' or independence, had to become worthy of the hype. And while Brexit had undoubtedly transformed Sturgeon's into 'a government with purpose', arguably it still lacked the imagination and boldness in policy terms for which constitutional change had so long been an inadequate substitute.

Endnotes

Preface

1. http://www.heraldscotland.com/comment/letters/lack-of-inside-knowledge.25402446

Chapter 1

1. http://www.newstatesman.com/politics/uk/2016/06/can-nicola-sturgeon-keep-scotland-eu
2. http://news.scotland.gov.uk/Speeches-Briefings/First-Minister-EU-Referendum-result-25ae.aspx
3. *Daily Record*, 25 June 2016.
4. https://twitter.com/jk_rowling/status/746214995763953667
5. *Financial Times*, 2 July 2016.
6. https://inews.co.uk/opinion/comment/nicola-sturgeon-can-post-brexit-voice-reason/
7. https://www.thestar.com/opinion/editorials/2016/07/04/a-modest-proposal-to-end-political-anarchy-in-the-uk-editorial.html
8. *Herald*, 28 June 2016.
9. http://www.cityam.com/244356/farewell-london-hello-edinburgh-financial-services-find-new
10. https://corporate.sky.com/media-centre/media-packs/2015/murnaghan-interview-with-nicola-sturgeon,-snp-first-minister-of-scotland,-310515
11. http://news.scotland.gov.uk/Speeches-Briefings/First-Minister-speech-to-European-Policy-Centre-1977.aspx
12. http://news.scotland.gov.uk/Speeches-Briefings/Resolution-Foundation-2330.aspx
13. *Newsnight* (BBC2), 26 May 2016.
14. *Telegraph*, 11 June 2016.
15. *The Times*, 24 May 2016.
16. http://www.bbc.co.uk/news/uk-politics-eu-referendum-36575937

17. Official Report, 16 June 2016.
18. *Sunday Herald*, 19 June 2016.
19. http://www.bbc.com/news/election-2016-scotland-36124382
20. http://news.scotland.gov.uk/News/EU-Referendum-25b0.aspx
21. *Sunday Times* (Scotland), 26 June 2016.
22. When this author highlighted the shifting tone on Twitter, the First Minister accused him of playing 'games with random phrases' (https://twitter.com/nicolasturgeon/status/747552100259856385).
23. https://corporate.sky.com/media-centre/media-packs/2016/murnaghan-interview-with-nicola-sturgeon,-first-minister-of-scotland,-260616
24. *Sunday Politics Scotland* (BBC1), 26 June 2016.
25. *Murnaghan* (Sky News), 26 June 2016.
26. *Andrew Marr* (BBC1), 26 June 2016.
27. *Murnaghan* (Sky News), 26 June 2016.
28. http://www.dailyrecord.co.uk/news/politics/nicola-sturgeon-hold-second-independence-8313741#mx5G7U95ftAiRape.99
29. Official Report, 28 June 2016.
30. https://euobserver.com/uk-referendum/134120
31. Official Report, 30 June 2016.
32. http://www.bbc.com/news/uk-scotland-scotland-politics-36689425
33. http://news.scotland.gov.uk/News/First-Minister-Speech-for-the-Official-Opening-of-Scottish-Parliament-25e6.aspx
34. https://twitter.com/nicolasturgeon/status/753951282189201408
35. Commons Hansard, 20 July 2016.
36. http://news.scotland.gov.uk/News/Scotland-s-future-in-the-EU-276d.aspx
37. https://www.holyrood.com/articles/comment/idea-brexit-could-suddenly-push-scotland-towards-yes-vote-isn%E2%80%99t-supported-evidence
38. http://www.bbc.co.uk/news/uk-scotland-edinburgh-east-fife-37026212

Chapter 2

1. *Desert Island Discs* (BBC Radio 4), 15 November 2015
2. *New Statesman*, 7–13 November 2014.
3. I am indebted to family history researcher Sandra Underwood for these details.
4. http://www.bbc.co.uk/news/uk-england-tyne-32991705
5. Author's notes, Edinburgh International Book Festival, 18 August 2016.
6. *The Sunday Times*, 6 May 2007.
7. http://www.totalpolitics.com/print/3128/lady-in-waiting.thtml
8. *The Week in Politics* (STV), 30 October 2003.
9. *Sunday Mail*, 12 August 2007.
10. Interview with Shelley Jofre, 14 October 2014.
11. *Irvine Times*, 5 January 2014.

Endnotes

12. https://www.holyrood.com/articles/inside-track/inequality-scotland-qa-party-leaders
13. *The Week in Politics* (STV). In a 1999 interview, Sturgeon more clearly recalled 'a feeling of depression' in her home following the 1979 referendum (*Herald*, 6 April 1999).
14. *Holyrood*, 31 May 1999.
15. *Daily Record*, 20 July 2014.
16. *Daily Record*, 6 July 2014.
17. *Holyrood*, 31 May 1999.
18. *Herald*, 6 April 1999.
19. http://www.totalpolitics.com/print/3128/lady-in-waiting.thtml
20. https://www.youtube.com/watch?v=AWfomb99QKw
21. *Holyrood*, 31 May 1999.
22. http://www.scotland.gov.uk/News/Speeches/better-nation-031212
23. Interview with Shelley Jofre.
24. *Scotland 2014* (BBC2 Scotland), 19 November 2014.
25. *Evening Times*, 24 December 2002.
26. *Scotland on Sunday*, 9 November 2014.
27. *Guardian*, 2 May 2015.
28. *Scotland 2014.*
29. *The Rory Review* (BBC Radio Scotland), 23 December 2014.
30. *Herald*, 13 November 2004.
31. *The Sunday Times*, 8 January 2006.
32. *Scotland on Sunday*, 9 November 2014.
33. Ibid.
34. *Guardian*, 24 August 2013.
35. *Daily Record*, 6 July 2014.
36. *Desert Island Discs* (BBC Radio 4), 15 November 2015.
37. *Holyrood*, 31 May 1999.
38. http://www.snp.org/media-centre/news/2014/apr/sturgeon-now-or-never-banish-trident.
39. *Holyrood*, 31 May 1999.
40. *Panorama: The Most Dangerous Woman in Britain?* (BBC1), 1 June 2015.
41. *Profile: Nicola Sturgeon* (BBC Radio 4), 30 November 2013.
42. Interview with Kay Ullrich, 11 October 2014.
43. *Scotland on Sunday*, 9 November 2014.
44. *Profile: Nicola Sturgeon*, ibid.
45. *Irvine Times*, 5 June 1987.
46. Interview with Kay Ullrich.
47. *Daily Record*, 6 July 2014.
48. *Irvine Times*, 19 June 1987.
49. *Sunday Mail*, 6 July 2014.
50. *Scotland on Sunday*, 9 November 2014.
51. Interview with Shelley Jofre.

52. *Holyrood*, 19 November 2007.
53. *Sunday Mail*, 12 August 2007.
54. *The Sunday Times*, 7 January 2007.
55. Interview with Fiona Hyslop MSP, 15 January 2015.
56. *Scotland on Sunday*, 9 November 2014.

Chapter 3

1. *Scotland 2014* (BBC2 Scotland), 19 November 2014.
2. http://www.gla.ac.uk/news/headline_391257_en.html
3. See Glasgow University's list of political alumni: http://www.gla.ac.uk/alumni/ouralumni/lifeafterglasgow/notablealumni/
4. Stephen Harte to the author, 4 January 2015.
5. *Guardian,* 2 May 2015.
6. *The Week in Politics* (STV), 30 October 2003.
7. *Holyrood* 3, 31 May 1999.
8. Pat Kane, *Tinsel Show*, p. 141.
9. David McCrone, *Understanding Scotland*, p. 196.
10. Kane, ibid., pp. 160–62 and p. 187.
11. *Guardian*, 29 March 1989.
12. http://newsnet.scot/2015/01/yes-couldnt-cope-better-together-spin-campaign/
13. *The Sunday Times*, 7 January 2007.
14. *Holyrood*, 31 May 1999.
15. Glasgow University *Guardian*, 13 November 1989.
16. Interview with Dr John Boyle, 9 October 2014.
17. Stephen Harte to the author, 4 January 2015.
18. Niall Bradley to the author, 18 October 2014.
19. Interview with Dr John Boyle.
20. *Independent*, 17 October 2014.
21. Niall Bradley to the author.
22. Iain Martin to the author, 9 December 2014.
23. Niall Bradley to the author.
24. *The Sunday Times*, 20 October 2002.
25. *Glasgow University Magazine* (GUM), Winter 91–92.
26. Niall Bradley to the author.
27. Glasgow University SRC archives, DC157/6/34/2.
28. Interview with Craig Cathcart, 16 October 2014.
29. Glasgow University *Guardian*, 3 May 1990.
30. Private information.
31. Glasgow University SRC archives, DC157/4/1/34.
32. Anonymous interview, 17 October 2014.
33. Glasgow University *Guardian*, 17 May 1990.
34. Interview with Fiona Hyslop MSP, 15 January 2015.

35. *The Scotsman*, 2 August 1990.
36. *Alex Salmond – A Rebel's Journey* (BBC1 Scotland), 19 November 2014.
37. *Guardian*, 6 September 2014.
38. Interview with Cliff Williamson, 7 January 2015.
39. *Scotsman*, 2 August 1990.
40. *SNP News*, 1990 regional elections edition.
41. Interview with Fiona Hyslop MSP.
42. *Profile: Nicola Sturgeon* (BBC Radio 4), 30 November 2013.
43. Anonymous interview, 16 December 2014.
44. http://www.channel4.com/news/sturgeon-snp-scotland-independence-campaign
45. Interview with Cliff Williamson.
46. *Scotland on Sunday*, 9 November 2014.
47. Campbell Martin to the author, 14 and 15 January 2015.
48. *Herald*, 24 September 1992. Bell later became the SNP's housing spokesman.
49. Anonymous interview, 16 December 2014.
50. Interview with Cliff Williamson.
51. http://www.allbacktobowies.com/podcast/all-back-to-bowies-mon-4-aug-2014-in-the-eye-of-the-storm-nicola-sturgeon-interview/
52. *Left, Right and Centre* (BBC Scotland), January 1992.
53. Interview with Craig Harrow, 10 January 2015.
54. Interview with Kay Ullrich, 11 October 2014.
55. *Evening Times*, 23 September 2014.
56. *Sunday Mail*, 6 July 2014.
57. *Independent*, 26 March 1992.
58. Press Association, 26 March 1992.
59. *The Sunday Times*, 8 January 2006.
60. *Herald*, 23 April 1992.
61. Pat Kane, *Tinsel Show*, p130.
62. *Herald*, 13 April 1992.
63. STV archive tape B6975, 12 April 1992.
64. John McAllion to the author, 6 January 2015.
65. http://www.totalpolitics.com/print/3128/lady-in-waiting.thtml
66. Interview with Caroline Summers, 16 January 2015.
67. Interview with Claire Mitchell, 28 January 2015.
68. *Herald*, 13 November 2004.
69. http://www.scotsman.com/news/opinion/alistair-bonnington-one-party-state-is-an-enemy-of-democracy-1-4183472
70. Iain Martin to the author, 9 December 2014.
71. Interview with Caroline Summers.
72. *Guardian*, 2 May 2015.
73. Anonymous interview, 20 January 2015.
74. Anonymous interview, 14 January 2015.

75. *The Scotsman,* 19 March 1993.
76. *Scottish Affairs* No. 5, Autumn 1993, p. 40.
77. *The Scotsman,* 29 October 1993.
78. *Herald,* 18 November 1994.
79. *The Scotsman,* 22 September 1995.
80. *Herald,* 27 September 1995.
81. *Herald,* 18 March 1995.
82. Interview with Michael Moore MP, 30 October 2014.
83. Kay Ullrich to the author, 14 January 2015.
84. *Daily Record,* 1 March 1995.
85. Interview with Cliff Williamson.
86. Anonymous interview, 13 January 2015.
87. *Tonight* (STV/ITV), 23 April 2015.
88. http://news.scotland.gov.uk/Speeches-Briefings/First-Minister-speech-to-European-Policy-Centre-1977.aspx
89. *Herald,* 11 September 1996.
90. *The Scotsman,* 2 February 1994.
91. *The Scotsman,* 9 October 1995.
92. *The Scotsman,* 27 September 1996.
93. Press Association, 29 December 1996.
94. Tom Gordon's interview notes, 26 September 2014.

Chapter 4

1. *The Scotsman,* 15 November 1995.
2. *Sunday Times,* 20 April 1997.
3. *The Times,* 9 April 1997.
4. *Herald,* 29 July 1996.
5. *Herald,* 24 July 2013.
6. Interview with Gerry Hassan, 10 January 2015.
7. *Herald,* 29 July 1996.
8. *Herald,* 15 December 1995.
9. Press Association, 22 June 1996.
10. *The Scotsman,* 29 March 1997.
11. *Herald,* 11 April 1997.
12. *Herald,* 16 April 1997.
13. *Independent,* 28 April 1997.
14. Interview with Gerry Hassan.
15. *Sunday Times,* 11 May 1997.
16. *Herald,* 24 June 1997.
17. *Daily Record,* 18 December 1997.
18. *The Scotsman,* 26 December 1997.
19. *Herald,* 7 June 1997.
20. *The Observer,* 14 September 1997.
21. Interview with Gerry Hassan.

22. *Herald*, 19 November 1997.
23. *The Scotsman*, 20 November 1997.
24. *The Scotsman*, 17 December 1997.
25. *Herald*, 24 February 1998.
26. *Mirror*, 6 March 1998.
27. *Herald*, 10 March 1998.
28. *Daily Record*, 16 June 1998.
29. *Herald*, 7 May 1998.
30. Peter Lynch, *SNP*, p. 238.
31. *The Sunday Times*, 3 May 1998.
32. *The Sunday Times*, 10 May 1998.
33. *Herald*, 13 August 1998.
34. *Edinburgh Evening News*, 23 February 1999.
35. Anonymous interview, 19 November 2014.
36. *Sunday Herald*, 24 August 2014.
37. *The Scotsman*, 7 May 1998.
38. *Daily Mail*, 29 July 1998.
39. *The Scotsman*, 30 September 1998.
40. *Daily Mail*, 12 September 1998.
41. *Edinburgh Evening News*, 4 September 1998.
42. *Herald*, 21 November 1998.
43. *The Sunday Times*, 27 September 1998.
44. Glasgow University *Guardian*, 17 February 1999.
45. *Times Higher Education Supplement*, 18 December 1998.
46. *Herald*, 8 December 1998.
47. Murray Ritchie, *Scotland Reclaimed*, p. 38.
48. Anonymous interview, 28 October 2014.
49. Legal Services Agency, *Home loss and disturbance payments*, p. 1.
50. Interview with Jim Gray, 13 October 2014.
51. Interview with Mike Dailly, 8 October 2014.
52. *Herald*, 6 April 1999.
53. Anonymous interview, 28 October 2014.
54. *The Week in Politics* (STV), 30 October 2003.
55. Malcolm Chisholm MSP to the author, 13 January 2015.
56. *Herald*, 29 October 1997.
57. Ibid.
58. *Guardian*, 4 May 1999.
59. *Daily Record*, 17 June 1998.
60. *Herald*, 1 January 1999.
61. Ritchie, p. 38.
62. *Daily Mail*, 13 February 1999.
63. *Daily Record*, 19 April 1999.
64. *Scotland on Sunday*, 9 November 2014.
65. Anonymous interview, 13 January 2015.

66. *Herald*, 5 March 1999.
67. Wilson, *Scotland: The Battle for Independence*, 48.
68. *Herald*, 6 April 1999.
69. *The Scotsman*, 8 April 1999.
70. *Herald*, 6 April 1999.
71. *Scotland on Sunday*, 14 March 1999.
72. *Daily Mail*, 15 March 1999.
73. *Sunday Herald*, 11 April 1999.
74. *Daily Record*, 29 March 1999.
75. *The Sunday Times*, 25 April 1999.
76. Brian Taylor, *Scotland's Parliament: Triumph and Disaster*, p. 45.
77. *Sunday Herald*, 18 April 1999.
78. Taylor, p. 45.
79. *Sunday Herald*, 2 May 1999.
80. *Evening Standard*, 29 April 1999.
81. *Daily Record*, 7 May 1999.
82. *Mirror*, 7 May 1999.
83. Anonymous interview, 15 January 2015.
84. *The Scotsman*, 7 May 1999.

Chapter 5

1. *The Times*, 8 May 1999.
2. *Daily Record*, 26 May 1999.
3. *Scotland on Sunday*, 29 August 1999.
4. Scottish Parliament Official Report, 19 May 1999.
5. *Scotland on Sunday*, 3 October 1999.
6. *Sunday Herald*, 9 May 1999.
7. *Herald*, 29 February 2000.
8. *Sunday Mirror*, 24 December 2000.
9. Anonymous interview, 13 January 2015.
10. *Edinburgh Evening News*, 10 November 2000.
11. *Herald*, 11 November 2000.
12. *The Scotsman*, 15 December 2000.
13. *Scotland on Sunday*, 2 January 2000.
14. *Guardian*, 28 April 2000.
15. Michael Torrance to the author, 5 December 2014.
16. Anonymous interview, 15 January 2015.
17. *The Scotsman*, 5 July 2000.
18. *The Times Educational Supplement*, 30 June 2000.
19. *Sunday Post*, 19 October 2014.
20. Anonymous interview, 13 January 2013.
21. *Sunday Herald*, 30 April 2000.
22. *Herald*, 28 August 2000.
23. Anonymous interview, 15 January 2015.

24. *Edinburgh Evening News*, 29 January 2001.
25. *Edinburgh Evening News*, 8 June 2001.
26. *Scotland on Sunday*, 8 July 2001.
27. *Daily Record*, 26 September 2001.
28. Project 2003 Review Group paper, 17 August 2001.
29. *Sunday Express*, 24 March 2002.
30. *Daily Record*, 3 May 2002.
31. *Herald*, 13 May 2002.
32. *The Scotsman*, 8 July 2002.
33. *The Scotsman*, 12 July 2002.
34. *Mail on Sunday*, 21 July 2002.
35. *Daily Mail*, 12 August 2002.
36. *Daily Mail*, 14 March 2001.
37. Andy Bain, *Don't Vote for an Idiot Vote for a Clown*, p204.
38. Gerry Hassan and Douglas Fraser, *The Political Guide to Modern Scotland*, p. 399.
39. *Scotland on Sunday*, 22 September 2002.
40. *Guardian*, 2 January 2003.
41. *Sunday Mail*, 5 January 2003.
42. *Evening Times*, 21 January 2003.
43. *Evening Times*, 18 February 2003.
44. *Evening Times*, 11 March 2003.
45. *The Times*, 25 February 2003.
46. *Daily Record*, 18 March 2003.
47. *The Sunday Times*, 7 January 2007.
48. *Sunday Mail*, 27 April 2003.
49. *Herald*, 3 May 2003.
50. *The Week in Politics* (STV), 30 October 2003. 'What I would say is I don't think I'm a quitter,' said Sturgeon when asked if she would fight Govan for a fourth time. 'If I believe in what I'm doing then I'll keep doing it, I'll keep trying.'
51. *Scotland on Sunday*, 13 July 2003.
52. *Sunday Herald*, 3 August 2003.
53. *Evening Times*, 4 March 2003
54. *Evening Times*, 27 January 2004.
55. *The Scotsman*, 26 September 2003.
56. *Herald*, 4 November 2003.
57. *The Scotsman*, 13 February 2004.
58. *Herald*, 15 July 2003.
59. *Daily Mail*, 27 October 2003.
60. *Evening Times*, 13 January 2004.
61. *The Scotsman*, 24 April 2004.
62. Ian Duncan MEP to the author, 5 November 2014.
63. *The Week in Politics* (STV).

64. *Scottish Sun*, 24 April 2004.
65. *The Sunday Times*, 7 January 2007.
66. *Sunday Herald*, 25 April 2004.
67. *Holyrood*, 19 April 2004.
68. *Evening Times*, 4 May 2004
69. *The Week in Politics* (STV).
70. *Daily Record*, 23 June 2004.
71. Anonymous interview, 15 January 2015.
72. Anonymous interview, 19 November 2014.
73. Anonymous interview, 28 October 2014.
74. *Sunday Herald*, 20 June 2004.
75. *Daily Record*, 24 June 2004.
76. *Daily Record*, 25 June 2004.
77. *Evening Times*, 25 June 2004.
78. *Daily Record*, 25 June 2004.
79. *Scotland on Sunday*, 27 June 2004.
80. *The Sunday Times*, 27 June 2004.
81. *Evening Times*, 29 June 2004.
82. *Press and Journal*, 3 July 2004.
83. *Mirror*, 5 July 2004.
84. *The Scotsman*, 8 July 2004.
85. *Herald*, 16 July 2004.
86. *Alex Salmond – A Rebel's Journey* (BBC1 Scotland), 19 November 2014.
87. Ibid.
88. *Sunday Herald*, 18 July 2004.
89. *Guardian*, 31 January 2009.
90. Anonymous interview, 13 January 2015.
91. Private information.
92. http://news.bbc.co.uk/2/hi/uk_news/scotland/3895575.stm
93. *Scotland on Sunday*, 18 July 2004.
94. *Sunday Herald*, 18 July 2004.
95. *Herald*, 22 July 2004.
96. *Daily Record*, 23 July 2004.
97. *The Scotsman*, 29 July 2004.
98. *Sunday Herald*, 8 August 2004.
99. *Herald*, 4 September 2004.
100. http://www.totalpolitics.com/print/3128/lady-in-waiting.thtml
101. James Mitchell et al., *The Scottish National Party: Transition to Power*, p. 28.
102. Gerry Hassan, *The Modern SNP: From Protest to Power*, p. 91.

Chapter 6

1. *Sunday Herald*, 18 July 2004.
2. I am indebted to Euan McColm for this term and chapter heading.

3. Scottish Parliament Official Report, 8 September 2004.
4. *The Times*, 8 September 2004.
5. Gerry Hassan, *The Modern SNP: From Protest to Power*, p85.
6. *Profile: Nicola Sturgeon* (BBC Radio 4), 30 November 2013.
7. *Sunday Mail*, 12 September 2004.
8. Anonymous interview, 13 January 2015.
9. Hamish Macdonell, *Uncharted Territory*, p120.
10. http://news.bbc.co.uk/1/hi/scotland/3680980.stm
11. *Evening Times*, 23 September 2004.
12. *Herald*, 9 October 2004. Three years later Sturgeon made it clear at events that she favoured an elected head of state but did not consider it a priority.
13. *Scotland on Sunday*, 5 July 2009.
14. *Sunday Mail*, 12 September 2004.
15. *Herald*, 13 November 2004.
16. *Daily Mail*, 14 March 2001.
17. *Daily Mail*, 12 August 2002.
18. *Herald*, 13 November 2004.
19. *Mirror*, 5 April 2005.
20. *Herald*, 13 November 2004.
21. *Daily Star*, 19 November 2004.
22. *Mirror*, 5 April 2005.
23. Anonymous interview, 15 January 2015.
24. *Mirror*, 5 April 2005.
25. *Daily Record*, 10 December 2004.
26. *Mirror*, 28 February 2005.
27. *Mail on Sunday*, 27 March 2005.
28. *The Sunday Times*, 4 December 2005.
29. *Mirror*, 6 May 2005.
30. *Mirror*, 5 April 2005.
31. *The Sunday Times*, 8 January 2006.
32. *Scotland on Sunday*, 15 May 2005.
33. *Herald*, 7 July 2005.
34. *The Sunday Times*, 4 December 2005.
35. *The Sunday Times*, 8 January 2006.
36. *Holyrood*, 9 October 2006.
37. Campbell Martin to the author, 14 January 2015.
38. *The Sunday Times*, 8 January 2006.
39. *Press and Journal*, 21 December 2005.
40. *Herald*, 28 July 2006.
41. *Holyrood*, 26 September 2005.
42. *Sunday Mail*, 9 April 2006.
43. *Observer*, 15 October 2006.
44. *Press and Journal*, 17 January 2007.
45. Anonymous interview, 15 January 2015.

46. *Herald*, 16 March 2007.
47. *The Sunday Times*, 8 January 2006.
48. *The Scotsman*, 5 July 2009.
49. *Sunday Herald*, 16 April 2006.
50. *The Sunday Times*, 7 January 2007.
51. Anonymous interview, 14 January 2015.
52. http://www.totalpolitics.com/print/3128/lady-in-waiting.thtml
53. *The Scotsman*, 4 July 2009.
54. *Sunday Mail*, 12 August 2007.

Chapter 7

1. *Women's Hour* (BBC Radio 4), 18 December 2013.
2. *Sunday Mail*, 12 August 2007.
3. Scottish Parliament Official Report, 6 June 2007.
4. *Pharmaceutical Journal*, 15 June 2007.
5. Scottish Parliament Official Report, 6 June 2007.
6. *Herald*, 4 June 2007.
7. http://www.scotland.gov.uk/News/Releases/2007/06/21083635
8. Anonymous interview, 13 October 2014.
9. *Evening Times*, 30 January 2008.
10. *Evening Times*, 9 July 2007.
11. Tom Gallagher, *The Illusion of Freedom*, p. 190.
12. *Sunday Mail*, 12 August 2007.
13. *Herald*, 12 December 2007.
14. *The Sunday Times*, 7 December 2008.
15. Tony Blair, *A Journey*, p. 651.
16. *Herald*, 10 April 2008.
17. *The Scotsman*, 13 November 2007.
18. *Daily Record*, 3 March 2008.
19. *Sunday Express*, 19 October 2008.
20. *Daily Express*, 31 January 2008.
21. PA Newswire, 31 January 2008.
22. *Herald*, 3 May 2008.
23. *Sunday Mail*, 12 August 2007.
24. James Mitchell et al., *The Scottish National Party: Transition to Power*, p. 48.
25. Johns and Mitchell, *Takeover*, 206.
26. http://www.scotland.gov.uk/About/People/14944/ministerial-preferences
27. *Evening Times*, 30 January 2008.
28. Joan Sturgeon would become provost of North Ayrshire Council in May 2012, resigning in August 2016.
29. *The Scotsman*, 5 May 2008.
30. *Daily Record*, 12 May 2008.
31. *Express*, 16 May 2008.

32. *The Scotsman,* 29 May 2008.
33. *The Scotsman,* 25 July 2008.
34. *Herald,* 4 July 2008.
35. *Express,* 9 July 2008.
36. *Daily Record,* 26 June 2008.
37. Anonymous interview, 22 October 2014.
38. *Sunday Herald,* 3 May 2009.
39. *Express,* 5 June 2009.
40. Anonymous interview, 22 October 2014.
41. *Scotland on Sunday,* 9 November 2014.
42. *Observer,* 14 February 2010.
43. *The Scotsman,* 2 January 2010.
44. Scottish Parliament Official Report, 18 February 2010.
45. Interview with Euan McColm, 8 October 2014.
46. Anonymous interview, 13 October 2014.
47. *Herald,* 25 February 2010.
48. Scottish Parliament Official Report, 24 February 2010.
49. *The Scotsman,* 4 July 2009.
50. Interview with Euan McColm, 8 October 2014.
51. *The Scotsman,* 30 January 2010.
52. *Herald,* 29 March 2010.
53. *The Scotsman,* 14 October 2010.
54. *Evening Times,* 15 February 2011.
55. www.theguardian.com/healthcare-network/2011/mar/22/scottish-health-secretary-england-ending-nhs
56. *Scottish Express,* 10 April 2011.
57. *Sunday Express,* 17 April 2011.
58. Salmond, *The Dream Shall Never Die,* 14 September 2014.
59. *Evening Times,* 6 May 2011.
60. *Sunday Herald,* 10 April 2011.
61. *Sunday Herald,* 30 October 2011.
62. *Evening Times,* 16 August 2011.
63. *Sunday Herald,* 30 October 2011.
64. *Press and Journal,* 20 October 2011.
65. *The Scotsman,* 11 June 2011.
66. *Press and Journal,* 10 January 2012.
67. *Good Morning Scotland* (BBC Radio Scotland), 25 January 2012.
68. *Evening Times,* 26 January 2012.
69. *Sunday Mail,* 5 February 2012.
70. *The Scotsman,* 6 March 2012 (author's italics).
71. *Good Morning Scotland* (BBC Radio Scotland), 28 April 2012.
72. PA Newswire: Scotland, 25 July 2012.
73. *Scotland on Sunday,* 9 November 2014.
74. Interview with Sir Harry Burns, 30 October 2014.

75. *The Scotsman*, 4 July 2009.
76. *Herald*, 20 November 2014.
77. Anonymous interview, 22 October 2014.
78. *Herald*, 20 November 2014.
79. Anonymous interview, 15 October 2014.
80. *Scotland on Sunday*, 28 December 2014.
81. PA Newswire, 5 September 2012.

Chapter 8

1. *Sunday Mail*, 29 January 2012.
2. Author's notes, 17 September 2014.
3. *Profile: Nicola Sturgeon* (BBC Radio 4), 30 November 2013.
4. *Sunday Mail*, 29 January 2012.
5. Letter to the author, 8 July 2013.
6. Anonymous interview, 9 July 2013.
7. David Torrance, *The Battle for Britain*, p. 29.
8. Anonymous interview, 12 October 2014.
9. Interview with Michael Moore MP, 30 October 2014.
10. Tom Gordon's interview notes, December 2013.
11. *Independent*, 18 October 2012.
12. Anonymous interview, 15 October 2014.
13. Anonymous interview, 17 January 2015.
14. Anonymous interview, 21 October 2014.
15. http://www.snp.org/blog/post/2012/dec/building-better-nation
16. *Sunday Herald*, 23 June 2013.
17. *Daily Record*, 25 June 2004.
18. *Herald*, 26 September 2012.
19. Scottish Parliament Official Report, 27 September 2012.
20. www.scotland.gov.uk/News/Speeches/better-nation-031212
21. http://www.scotland.gov.uk/News/Speeches/better-nation-031212
22. *Herald*, 8 December 2012.
23. http://www.scotland.gov.uk/News/Speeches/better-nation-031212
24. Torrance, p128.
25. *Sunday Politics* (BBC1), 4 March 2012.
26. *Sunday Herald*, 4 November 2012.
27. *Daily Record*, 25 October 2012.
28. http://www.scotreferendum.com/2013/02/11/uk-governments-legal-opinion/
29. *Sunday Herald*, 16 December 2012.
30. Author's notes, 11 June 2014.
31. https://www.youtube.com/watch?v=RhVI8LDIpxs
32. PA Newswire, 25 January 2013.

33. *Daily Telegraph*, 28 December 2012.
34. *Scotland on Sunday*, 30 January 2013.
35. *The Scotsman*, 12 March 2013.
36. PA Newswire: Scotland, 23 March 2013.
37. http://www.snp.org/blog/post/2013/mar/snp-spring-conference-address-nicola-sturgeon
38. http://www.snp.org/blog/post/2013/may/benefits-and-possibilities-independence
39. *Scotland on Sunday*, 12 May 2013.
40. PA Newswire: Scotland, 6 June 2013.
41. Anonymous interview, 15 January 2015.
42. Anonymous interview, 9 October 2014.
43. Anonymous interview, 14 October 2014.
44. Anonymous interview, 15 January 2015.
45. *Evening Times*, 19 November 2013.
46. Scottish Parliament Official Report, 26 November 2013.
47. PA Newswire: Scotland, 26 November 2013.
48. PA Newswire: Scotland, 30 November 2013.
49. Anonymous interview, 10 January 2014.
50. *Daily Telegraph*, 3 January 2014.
51. *Daily Telegraph*, 29 November 2013.
52. *Sunday Herald*, 5 January 2014.
53. *Daily Telegraph*, 7 January 2014.
54. Anonymous interview, 10 January 2014.
55. *Guardian*, 6 September 2014.
56. *The Scotsman*, 19 April 2014.
57. PA Newswire: Scotland, 12 February 2014.
58. Anonymous interview, 13 October 2014.
59. Anonymous interview, 13 January 2015.
60. Anonymous interview, 28 September 2014.
61. *"Just Say Naw" with George Galloway MP: The Official Booklet* (Respect, 2014).
62. PA Newswire: Scotland, 14 May 2014.
63. *Observer*, 3 August 2014.
64. Press Association Mediapoint, 3 September 2014.
65. Press Association Mediapoint, 18 September 2014.
66. *Guardian*, 17 December 2014.
67. Interview with Alex Bell, 23 September 2014.
68. Email to the author, 13 October 2014.
69. Anonymous interview, 19 November 2014.
70. *Daily Telegraph*, 22 May 2014.
71. *Daily Mail*, 13 September 2014.
72. *The Scotsman*, 4 August 2014.
73. Press Association, 16 September 2014.
74. Interview with Claire Mitchell, 28 January 2015.

271

75. Tom Gordon's interview notes, 26 September 2014.
76. *Alex Salmond – A Rebel's Journey* (BBC1 Scotland), 19 November 2014.

Chapter 9

1. *Daily Record*, 10 June 2014.
2. Salmond, *The Dream Shall Never Die,* 18 July 2014.
3. *Daily Record*, 19 March 2014.
4. *Daily Record*, 6 July 2014.
5. https://www.youtube.com/watch?v=AWfomb99QKw
6. Tom Gordon's interview notes, 5 September 2014.
7. *Scotland on Sunday*, 29 December 2013.
8. Anonymous interview, 12 October 2014.
9. Anonymous interview, 17 January 2015.
10. Anonymous interview, 13 January 2015.
11. Anonymous interview, 29 May 2016.
12. http://www.dailyrecord.co.uk/news/politics/alex-salmond-resign-first-minister-4289287
13. *Evening Times*, 23 September 2014.
14. https://www.evernote.com/shard/s58/sh/5eb28c20-4c02-48ad-aeec-a5d1f7655481/0bd6e33a5e0b60f5be584d47c11354d8
15. *Herald*, 24 September 2014.
16. *Evening Times*, 7 October 2014.
17. http://www.scotland.gov.uk/Resource/0046/00460563.pdf
18. *Sunday Herald*, 12 October 2014.
19. *Irvine Times*, 1 October 2014.
20. https://twitter.com/NicolaSturgeon/status/522314574281056256
21. *The Scotsman*, 18 October 2014.
22. http://www.publications.parliament.uk/pa/cm201415/cmhansrd/cm141015/debtext/141015-0001.htm
23. http://www.snp.org/media-centre/news/2014/oct/strong-government-powerhouse-parliament
24. Author's notes, 29 October 2014.
25. *Scotland on Sunday*, 7 December 2014.
26. *Today* (BBC Radio 4), 14 November 2014.
27. http://www.glasgowsnp.org/MSPs/Nicola_Sturgeon_MSP/SNP_Annual_Conference_Address_by_SNP_Leader_and_Scottish_Deputy_First_Minister,_Nicola_Sturgeon/
28. Anonymous interview, 16 December 2014.
29. Official Report, 19 November 2014.
30. *Sunday Mail,* 23 November 2014.
31. *Scotland on Sunday*, 23 November 2014.
32. Anonymous interview, 16 December 2014.
33. Anonymous interview, 13 January 2015.

34. Anonymous interview, 10 January 2015.
35. *The Sunday Times*, 8 February 2015.
36. http://news.scotland.gov.uk/Speeches-Briefings/First-Minister-Programme-for-Government-12b1.aspx
37. *The National*, 27 November 2014.
38. http://www.bbc.co.uk/news/uk-scotland-scotland-politics-29428818
39. *Financial Times*, 1 December 2014.
40. http://www.theguardian.com/politics/2014/oct/19/nicola-sturgeon-snp-not-my-job-prove-how-different-alex-salmond?CMP=twt_gu
41. http://news.scotland.gov.uk/Speeches-Briefings/FM-first-major-speech-to-Scotland-s-business-sector-12ca.aspx
42. http://scottishgovernment.presscentre.com/Content/Detail.aspx?ReleaseID=5604&NewsAreaID=139&ClientID=1
43. *The Sunday Times*, 28 September 2014.
44. *Financial Times*, 1 December 2014.
45. http://www.bbc.co.uk/news/uk-scotland-scotland-politics-28956405
46. *Andrew Marr Show* (BBC1), 25 January 2015.
47. *The Sunday Times*, 28 September 2014.
48. http://www.dailymail.co.uk/femail/article-2795023/liz-jones-goodbye-death-row-hair-hello-super-sleek-soon-minister-nicola.html
49. *2014 – The Rory Review* (BBC Radio Scotland), 23 December 2014.
50. *Scotland on Sunday*, 9 November 2014.
51. *Holyrood*, 15 September 2014.
52. http://www.bbc.co.uk/news/uk-30585404
53. http://www.bbc.co.uk/news/uk-scotland-scotland-politics-30201528 (author's italics).
54. *Scotland on Sunday*, 9 November 2014 (author's italics).
55. *The Sunday Times*, 28 September 2014.
56. *Representing Border* (ITV Border), 18 November 2014.
57. *Daily Record*, 16 December 2014.
58. *Alex Salmond – A Rebel's Journey* (BBC1 Scotland), 19 November 2014.
59. Anonymous interview, 13 October 2014.
60. *The Sunday Times*, 28 September 2014.
61. http://www.theguardian.com/news/2014/dec/16/-sp-real-story-scottish-referendum-final-days-fight-for-independence
62. *Scotland 2014* (BBC2 Scotland), 29 October 2014.

Chapter 10

1. http://www.snp.org/one_year_on
2. Cowley & Kavanagh, *The British General Election of 2015*, 149.
3. *The Times*, 25 April 2015.
4. *Sunday Herald*, 10 May 2015.
5. *Tonight* (ITV), 23 April 2015.

6. Ashcroft & Culwick, *Pay Me Forty Quid and I'll Tell You*, 106, 111.

7. *Observer*, 20 December 2015.

8. Tom Gordon's interview notes, 29 April 2015.

9. Cowley & Kavanagh, 158.

10. *Independent*, 9 April 2015.

11. Cowley & Kavanagh, 147, 191 & 287–88.

12. http://www.newstatesman.com/politics/2015/05/snp-sweeping-scotland-westminster-prepared-what-will-happen-next

13. *PM* (BBC Radio 4), 27 April 2015.

14. *Financial Times*, 25 April 2015.

15. *The Times*, 21 April 2015.

16. http://www.politics.co.uk/comment-analysis/2015/04/17/tv-debate-verdict-sturgeon-spoke-up-for-scotland

17. *Daily Mail*, 4 April 2015.

18. *Observer*, 20 December 2015.

19. *Scottish Sun*, 30 April 2015.

20. *The Times*, 25 April 2015.

21. *Sunday Herald*, 26 April 2015.

22. https://www.pressandjournal.co.uk/fp/news/politics/holyrood/987238/named-person-scheme-twitter-row-erupts-sturgeon-outburst/

23. Tom Gordon's interview notes, 29 April 2015.

24. http://www.scotsman.com/lifestyle/books/politicians-brought-to-book-at-brainy-borders-book-festival-1-3802091

25. Ross, *Why the Tories Won*, 173.

26. http://www.bbc.com/news/uk-scotland-scotland-politics-32746049

27. http://www.theguardian.com/politics/2015/may/14/snp-prepared-overrule-cameron-second-independence-referendum-scotland

28. http://europe.newsweek.com/interview-alex-salmond-plots-his-next-moves-against-british-state-283751?rm=eu

29. *PM* (BBC Radio 4), 27 April 2015.

30. https://medium.com/@chrisdeerin/interview-nicola-sturgeon-39a403ca73f#.dyzrendcl

31. *Herald*, 11 March 2016.

32. *Scotsman*, 5 February 2015.

33. Salmond would later stand for election to the SNP's National Executive Committee in order to maintain a formal link with the party leadership.

34. Mitchell & Johns, *Takeover*, 246.

35. *Guardian*, 23 April 2015.

36. https://www.holyrood.com/articles/inside-politics/smiling-assassin-interview-first-minister-nicola-sturgeon

37. *The Times*, 31 December 2015.

38. https://medium.com/@chrisdeerin/venerated-victorious-and-revamped-what-now-nicola-b777585690d0#.aoloazx8x

39. *The Times*, 16 April 2016.

40. http://lallandspeatworrier.blogspot.co.uk/2016/05/spinning-plates.html
41. *Herald*, 26 April 2015.
42. http://www.itv.com/goodmorningbritain/news/nicola-sturgeon-scottish-national-party
43. *Representing Border* (ITV Border), 29 April 2015.
44. *Desert Island Discs* (BBC Radio 4), 15 November 2015.
45. https://medium.com/@chrisdeerin/interview-nicola-sturgeon-39a403ca73f#.sioklwqlr
46. https://www.holyrood.com/articles/inside-politics/smiling-assassin-interview-first-minister-nicola-sturgeon
47. *Daily Record*, 3 March 2015.
48. Pike, *Project Fear*, 289.
49. http://www.dailymail.co.uk/news/article-3277593/ANNE-McELVOY-Labour-MPs-secretly-fantasise-steely-Nicola-Sturgeon.html
50. *The Times*, 31 December 2015.
51. http://www.itv.com/goodmorningbritain/news/nicola-sturgeon-scottish-national-party
52. *Scotsman*, 18 June 2015.
53. *The Times*, 31 December 2015.
54. *The Times*, 10 May 2015.
55. http://lifestyle.one/grazia/news-real-life/opinion/election-exclusive-nicola-sturgeon-fear-found/
56. *Guardian*, 2 May 2015.
57. *Herald*, 5 December 2015.
58. *Dream Job* (BBC Radio Scotland), 15 October 2015.
59. *Sunday Mail*, 15 November 2015.
60. Pike, 289.
61. *Dream Job* (BBC Radio Scotland), 15 October 2015.
62. http://www.dailymail.co.uk/news/article-3225121/Sturgeon-attacks-hideous-cruel-focus-appearance-posing-glamorous-Vogue-photoshoot.html
63. *Mail on Sunday*, 5 April 2015.
64. *Observer*, 20 December 2015.
65. http://www.independent.co.uk/news/uk/politics/generalelection/nicola-sturgeon-i-want-to-help-women-10042980.html
66. http://www.itv.com/goodmorningbritain/news/nicola-sturgeon-scottish-national-party
67. http://www.nytimes.com/2015/06/09/world/europe/nicola-sturgeon-star-of-scottish-politics-vows-to-secure-more-power.html?_r=0
68. http://www.bbc.co.uk/news/uk-scotland-36333641
69. http://www.huffingtonpost.co.uk/2015/06/09/nicola-sturgeon-defends-alex-salmond-sexist-comments_n_7548840html?utm_hp_ref=uk&ncid=newsletter-uk
70. http://www.welt.de/debatte/kommentare/article156778285/In-den-Haenden-dieser-Frauen-liegt-Europas-Zukunft.html

71. http://www.spectator.co.uk/2015/04/hating-the-daily-mail-is-a-substitute-for-doing-good/
72. *Telegraph*, 19 April 2016.
73. https://audioboom.com/boos/3539376-first-minister-nicola-sturgeon-hosts-humanitarian-summit-september-4-2015
74. Interview with Dermot Murnaghan for Sky News, September 2015.
75. Official Report, 25 May 2015.
76. *National*, 27 May 2015.
77. http://www.scottishleftreview.org/wp-content/uploads/2015/05/SLR-June-20151.pdf
78. Gallagher *et al*, *Roch Winds*, 116.
79. http://www.economist.com/blogs/bagehot/2015/10/rudderless-hegemony
80. *Guardian*, 8 May 2015.
81. *Sunday Herald*, 3 May 2015.
82. http://www.newstatesman.com/politics/2015/05/snp-sweeping-scotland-westminster-prepared-what-will-happen-next
83. http://www.snp.org/_snp15_nicola_sturgeons_conference
84. https://medium.com/@chrisdeerin/interview-part-2-nicola-sturgeon-e770185946ff#.md9sj5s4r
85. http://www.snp.org/nicola_sturgeons_speech_at_plaid16
86. http://www.newstatesman.com/politics/2015/04/if-you-think-snp-are-left-wing-force-think-again
87. http://www.prospectmagazine.co.uk/opinions/interview-tasmina-ahmed-sheikh-the-snp-has-a-right-wing-and-here-she-is
88. *Newsnight* (BBC2), 14 October 2015.
89. *Herald*, 11 May 2016.
90. Official Report, 19 March 2015.
91. *Andrew Marr* (BBC1), 24 January 2016.
92. *Sunday Politics* (BBC1), 13 March 2016.
93. http://www.spectator.co.uk/2015/04/hating-the-daily-mail-is-a-substitute-for-doing-good/
94. http://www.ifs.org.uk/publications/7725
95. http://www.heraldscotland.com/news/13210531.In_Full__Nicola_Sturgeon_s_SNP_manifesto_launch_speech/
96. http://news.scotland.gov.uk/Speeches-Briefings/Launch-of-the-Scottish-Business-Pledge-192b.aspx
97. *Herald*, 11 June 2015.
98. http://news.scotland.gov.uk/Speeches-Briefings/First-Minister-Speech-to-University-College-London-15e4.aspx
99. *The Times*, 14 July 2015.
100. *Scotland 2015* (BBC2), 1 September 2015.
101. http://www.gov.scot/Publications/2016/01/1984
102. http://www.sussex.ac.uk/internal/bulletin/staff/2014-15/060315/mazzucatocea

103. http://www.snp.org/manifesto_plain_text_extended
104. *Herald*, 2 March 2016.
105. *Representing Border* (ITV Border), 2 March 2016.
106. http://www.economist.com/news/britain/21647993-scottish-national-partys-canny-leader-could-yet-break-up-united-kingdom-calling-tune?fsrc=scn/tw_ec/calling_the_tune
107. https://www.holyrood.com/articles/inside-politics/smiling-assassin-interview-first-minister-nicola-sturgeon
108. Author's notes, 11 April 2016.
109. *Sunday Times*, 27 December 2015.
110. http://news.scotland.gov.uk/Speeches-Briefings/First-Minister-David-Hume-Institute-166a.aspx
111. http://www.dailyrecord.co.uk/news/politics/nicola-sturgeon-tells-record-readers-5757414#8iLjVWwQ0wbRU5Mx.99
112. *BBC Scotland Investigates: Educating Sir Tom* (BBC2), 29 February 2016.
113. https://medium.com/@chrisdeerin/interview-part-2-nicola-sturgeon-e770185946ff#.net23oiyc
114. *Today* (BBC Radio 4), 27 April 2015.
115. http://blogs.channel4.com/gary-gibbon-on-politics/snp-foxhunting-move-raiding-party-english-lawmaking/31149#sthash.2VWyBYC6.dpuf
116. https://www.commonspace.scot/articles/1593/first-minister-talks-us-uk-foreign-policy-washington-raising-eyebrows-among-left-indy
117. *The Times*, 31 December 2015.
118. *Daily Record*, 9 April 2015.
119. http://www.euronews.com/2015/06/03/nicola-sturgeon-on-how-scotland-fits-into-the-eus-future/
120. *National*, 9 May 2015.
121. Press Association, 13 September 2015.
122. https://medium.com/@cstreetpartners/holyrood-2016-place-your-bets-74f65a1f8f7e#.oibu8xiji
123. https://www.craigmurray.org.uk/archives/2015/06/the-snp-membership-not-the-leadership-must-decide-on-the-second-referendum/
124. http://www.snp.org/nicola_sturgeon_launches_sp16_campaign
125. http://rattle.scot/snp-independence-is-dead-start-again-or-shut-up
126. https://medium.com/@chrisdeerin/interview-part-2-nicola-sturgeon-e770185946ff#.wgny8pd5y
127. Anonymous interview, 25 May 2016.
128. Nicola Sturgeon's conference address, 12 March 2016.
129. *National*, 30 May 2016.
130. http://www.snp.org/manifesto_plain_text_extended
131. *Face to Face* (STV), 28 April 2016.
132. *Sunday Herald*, 1 May 2016.
133. *Sunday Times*, 17 January 2016.

134. *Scottish Sun*, 30 April 2016.
135. *The Times*, 7 May 2016.
136. *Scotsman*, 7 May 2016.
137. Official Report, 17 May 2016.
138. *Sunday Herald*, 15 May 2016.
139. Official Report, 25 May 2016.
140. Anonymous interview, 29 May 2016.
141. *The Times*, 26 May 2016.
142. http://www.snp.org/nicola_sturgeon_launches_sp16_campaign
143. *Herald*, 2 May 2015.
144. *The Times*, 31 December 2015.
145. *Sunday Times*, 15 November 2015.
146. Pike, 289.
147. http://www.dailymail.co.uk/debate/article-3299687/CHRIS-DEERIN-Adored-winning-s-gone-wrong-Nicola-popularity-t-save-her.html#ixzz49OKopzfd
148. http://stv.tv/news/politics/1351400-education-will-be-my-number-one-priority-says-sturgeon/
149. *Sunday Mail*, 15 November 2015.
150. *Sunday Mail*, 3 January 2016.
151. https://yougov.co.uk/news/2015/11/01/nicola-sturgeon-scotlands-most-popular-person/.
152. *Sunday Mail*, 15 November 2015.
153. Mitchell & Johns, 221.
154. *Sunday Times*, 27 December 2015.

Bibliography

Secondary sources

Michael Ashcroft and Kevin Culwick, *Pay Me Forty Quid and I'll Tell You. The 2015 election campaign through the eyes and ears of the voters* (Biteback, 2015)

Andy Bain, *Don't Vote for an Idiot Vote for a Clown* (Argyll, 2003)

Tony Blair, *A Journey* (Hutchinson, 2010)

Esther Breitenbach and Fiona Mackay (eds.), *Women and Contemporary Scottish Politics: An Anthology* (Polygon, 2001)

Philip Cowley and Dennis Kavanagh (eds.), *The British General Election of 2015* (Palgrave Macmillan, 2015)

Sarah Craig, Simon Collins and Paul D. Brown, *Home Loss and disturbance payments* (Legal Services Agency Ltd, Shelter Scottish Housing Law Service with Castlemilk Law Centre, 1996)

Cailean Gallagher, Amy Westwell and Rory Scothorne, *Roch Winds: A Treacherous Guide to the State of Scotland* (Luath, 2016)

Tom Gallagher, *The Illusion of Freedom: Scotland Under Nationalism* (C. Hurst & Co, 2009)

George Galloway, 'Just Say Naw . . .' with George Galloway MP: The Official Booklet (Respect, 2014)

Andrew Geddes and Jonathan Tonge (eds.), *Britain Votes 2015* (Oxford University Press, 2015)

Gerry Hassan (ed.), *The Modern SNP: From Protest to Power* (Edinburgh University Press, 2009)

Gerry Hassan and Douglas Fraser, *The Political Guide to Modern Scotland* (Politico's, 2004)

Rob Johns and James Mitchell, *Takeover: Explaining the Extraordinary Ride of the SNP* (Biteback, 2016)

Patrick Kane, *Tinsel Show: Pop, Politics, Scotland* (Polygon, 1992)

Peter Lynch, *SNP: The History of the Scottish National Party* (Welsh Academic Press, 2013)

David McCrone, *Understanding Scotland* (Edinburgh University Press, 1992)

Hamish Macdonell, *Uncharted Territory: The story of Scottish devolution 1999–2009* (Politico's, 2009)

James Mitchell, Lynn Bennie and Rob Johns, *The Scottish National Party: Transition to Power* (Oxford University Press, 2012)

Joe Pike, *Project Fear: How an Unlikely Alliance Left a Kingdom United but a Country Divided* (Biteback, 2016)

Murray Ritchie, *Scotland Reclaimed: The inside story of Scotland's first democratic parliamentary election* (Saltire Society, 2000)

Tim Ross, *Why the Tories Won: The Inside Story of the 2015 Election* (Biteback, 2015)

Alex Salmond, *The Dream Shall Never Die: 100 Days that Changed Scotland Forever* (William Collins, 2015)

Brian Taylor, *Scotland's Parliament: Triumph and Disaster* (Edinburgh University Press, 2002)

David Torrance, *The Battle for Britain: Scotland and the Independence Referendum* (Biteback, 2013)

Gordon Wilson, *Scotland: The Battle for Independence: A History of the Scottish National Party 1990–2014* (Scots Independent, 2014)

Archives
Glasgow University Students' Representative Council papers, University of Glasgow Archives (DC157)

Broadcast
Left, Right and Centre (BBC Scotland), January 1992
Profile: Nicola Sturgeon (BBC Radio 4), 30 November 2013
Alex Salmond – A Rebel's Journey (BBC1 Scotland), 19 November 2014
Scotland 2014 (BBC2 Scotland), 19 November 2014
2014 – The Rory Review (BBC Radio Scotland), 23 December 2014
The Week in Politics (STV), 30 October 2003
Women's Hour (BBC Radio 4), 18 December 2013
Tonight (STV/ITV), 23 April 2015

Bibliography

Panorama: The Most Dangerous Woman in Britain? (BBC1), 1 June 2015

Dream Job (BBC Radio Scotland), 15 October 2015

Desert Island Discs (BBC Radio 4), 15 November 2015

Online

In conversation with Nicola Sturgeon, 2 December 2013 (Five Million Questions)

https://www.youtube.com/watch?v=AWfomb99QKw

All Back to Bowie's, 4 August 2014 (Edinburgh Fringe)

http://www.allbacktobowies.com/podcast/all-back-to-bowies-mon-4-aug-2014-in-the-eye-of-the-storm-nicola-sturgeon-interview/

Speeches

'Bringing the powers home to build a better nation', Strathclyde University, 3 December 2012

http://www.scotland.gov.uk/News/Speeches/better-nation-031212

'The benefits and possibilities of independence', Glasgow, 13 May 2013

http://www.snp.org/blog/post/2013/may/benefits-and-possibilities-independence

'Independence can transform Scotland', St Andrews University, 6 January 2014

https://www.youtube.com/watch?v=_hXSNSd85DE

'Scotland's Future: the case for an independent Scotland', UCL, 13 February 2014

https://www.youtube.com/watch?v=RhVI8LDIpxs

Index

Ahmed-Sheikh, Tasmina 78, 84, 191, 235
Aikman, Gordon 213
Alexander, Douglas 45, 55
Alexander, Wendy 142, 148, 202
Allan, Alasdair 35, 39, 40, 206
Anderson, Yvonne 64
Anwar, Aamer 35
Archer, Gordon 34
Armstrong, Rob 164
Attlee, Clement 140

Bain, Donald 55
Barroso, José Manuel 179–80
Bartholomew, James 232, 236–37
Bateman, Derek 33
Beckham, Victoria 126
Bell, Alex 192, 247
Bell, Fergus 59
Bell, Ian 221, 226
Bell, Ricky 33, 44, 81
Bell & Craig (law firm) 59, 74
Benn, Tony 37
Bevan, Nye 140, 151
Bhatti, Adil 64
Birt, Chris 242
Bismarck, Otto von 1
Black, Cilla 22

Blackburn, Lynsey 228
Blackford, Ian 118
Blair, Tony 57, 71, 72, 142, 176, 192, 202, 227
Blyton, Enid 229
Bonnington, Alistair 51
Borgen 168–69
Bowditch, Gillian 141, 207, 213
Boyd, Colin 107
Boyle, John 34–35, 36, 38
Bradley, Niall 35, 36, 37, 40
Bremner, Rory 21, 212
Brookmyre, Christopher 126
Brooks, Libby 188
Brown, Gordon 102, 127, 144, 148, 202
Brown, Keith 205
Brown, Paul D. 74, 75
Burgess, Margaret 44
Burns, Sir Harry 140, 162, 165, 210
Butt, Faisal 103

Callaghan, James 17
Campbell, Sir Menzies 51
Cameron, David 2, 4, 11, 148, 161, 171, 180, 212, 220, 223, 232

Campbell, Alastair 192
Campbell, Glenn 6
Carlaw, Jackson 162
Carmichael, Alistair 186
Caskie, Kathleen 42
Cathcart, Craig 38, 39
Chalmers, Tom 53, 59
Charlotte Street Partners 209, 238
Chisholm, Malcolm 76–77, 99
Clark, David 235
Clegg, Nick 133
Clinton, Bill 126
Clinton, Hillary 126, 231
Coburn, David 191
Cochrane, Alan 180, 192–93
Collins, Simon 74
Connery, Sir Sean 113, 126, 225
Constance, Angela 35, 39, 40,
    45, 129, 190, 206, 242
Cook, Robin 127
Corbyn, Jeremy 2, 235
Corrie, John 17
Costley, Tom 254–55
Craig, George 59
Craig, Sarah 74
Crawford, Bruce 91, 169, 198
Crawford, Ewan 187
Cunningham, Roseanna 33, 53,
    55, 77, 78, 85–86, 91, 109,
    110, 111, 112, 113, 116,
    117, 118, 121, 206
Currie, Brian 122
Cuthbert, Mark 218
Cyrus, Miley 221

Dailly, Mike 76
Dalai Lama 163
Dalyell, Tam 162
Darling, Alistair 193
Davidson, Lorraine 87
Davidson, Ruth 208–09, 249
Deacon, Susan 99
Deacon Blue 31
Deerin, Chris 223, 225, 254

Dewar, Donald 35, 47, 86, 88,
    208, 229
Dinwoodie, Robbie 78
Docherty 229
Dolan, Noel 76, 140, 152, 187,
    193, 207
Don, Lari 35
Douglas, Dick 53
Drew, Catriona 51
Drumchapel Law Centre 74–76
Dugdale, Kezia 231, 233, 240,
    242
Duncan, Dr Ian 108–09
Dunlop, John Boyd 15

Eagle, Angela 5
Eisenstadt, Naomi 239
Elder, Dorothy-Grace 96
Evans, Leslie 230
Ewing, Fergus 56
Ewing, Margaret 42, 53, 55, 132
Ewing, Winnie 16, 54, 55

Fabiani, Linda 43
Fairbairn, Sir Nicholas 55
Farage, Nigel 220, 222
Farquharson, Kenny 130
Finnie, John 174
Foot, Michael 26
Forsyth, Lord 212
Fraser, Murdo 45
Fraser, Sir William Kerr 40

Galbraith, Sam 89, 91
Gall, Gregor 233
Gallagher, Eamonn 177
Galloway, George 143–44, 190
Gardham, Magnus 176
Garner, John Nance 146
Gibson, Kenny 96
Glasgow University Student
    Nationalist Association
    (GUSNA) 31–32, 35–36,
    38–39, 40

Goldie, Annabel 52
Gordon, Tom 187, 195, 196, 219, 224
Gove, Michael 6
Graham, Paul 103
Grahame, Christine 117, 118
Grant, Professor John 51
Grassic Gibbon, Lewis 21
Gray, Iain 152, 157
Gray, Jim 74–75
Gray, Michael 208
Greig, David 45

Hamilton, Duncan 90
Hanif, Humayun 64
Hannay, Dr Rosemary 98
Harrow, Craig 45, 46
Harte, Stephen 29, 35, 38
Harvie, Patrick 6
Hassan, Gerry 65, 68
Havel, Vaclav 37
Heath, Edward 15
Higgins, Kate 71, 78
Home loss and disturbance payments 74
Horsburgh, Frances 76, 81
Hosie, Stewart 35, 52, 205, 230
Howell, Claire 228
Hue and Cry 31, 37
Hunter, Allison 62
Hussein, Saddam 100
Hutton, Alasdair 17
Hyslop, Fiona 33, 41, 43, 49, 53, 55, 77–78, 92, 93, 94

Iannucci, Armando 219
Irvine Development Corporation 15
Islam, Badar 66
Islam, Faisal 3

Jack, Ian 225
Jackson, Gordon 78, 84, 103, 131–32

Jamieson, Cathy 107
Jenkins, Ian 90
Jofre, Shelley 16, 20, 27
Johns, Rob 146, 224, 255
Johnson, Boris 5, 6
Jones, Liz 212
Jones, Peter 53
Juncker, Jean-Claude 9

Kajagoogoo 27
Kane, Pat 29, 30, 31, 37–38, 39–40, 49
Kay, Jackie 229
Kearny, Peter 91
Kellet, Michael 35, 38, 40
Kelso, Roy 20, 26
Kendall, Liz 231
Kennedy, Charles 56
Kerevan, George 246
Kerr, Andy 134, 138–39, 139–40, 166
Kerr, Professor David 139
Khan, Mohammed Aslam 84
Kinnock, Neil 26
Kipling, Rudyard 7
Knudsen, Sidse Babett 168–69
The Kraken Wakes 229
Kvist, Jon 182

Lambie, David 15, 24
Lamont, Johann 173, 188–89
Lawson, Nigel 137
'Letter from America' (song) 22
Liddell, Helen 71, 73
Limahl 27
Lindsay, Isobel 130
Linklater, Magnus 220
Lloyd, Liz 168, 207
Lochhead, Richard 114
Loudon, Monica 136
Lynch, Peter 70

McAllion, John 50
MacAskill, Kenny 53, 56, 110, 117, 233

McCarthy, Charlie 84
McClure Naismith (law firm) 51–52, 59
McColm, Euan 155, 166, 197, 205, 206
McCombes, Alan 65
McConnell, Jack 15, 99, 102, 104, 117, 120, 121, 127, 128, 142
MacCormick, Iain 38
MacCormick, John 31
MacCormick, Marion 38
MacCormick, Professor Sir Neil 175
McCrone, David 30
McDermid, Val 229
MacDonald, Margo 60, 78, 97
Macdonell, Hamish 121–22
McFadyen, Siobhan 126
Macfarlane, John 64
McGarry, Natalie 251
McGuire, Julie 228
McIlvanney, William 229
Mackay, Colin 119, 121
Mackay, Derek 41, 202
McKenna, Kevin 151
Mackenzie-Stuart, Lord 177
McKinney, Paul 63
MacKinnon, Sandy 38, 39
Macklin, Marie 237
McLeish, Henry 92
MacLennan, Stuart 64
McLeod, Fiona 87
MacMahon, Peter 143
Macmillan, Harold 150
Macwhirter, Iain 56, 109, 234
Mair, Eddie 220, 223
Majeed, Abdul 64
Major, John 52, 229
Mandela, Nelson 30
Mandelson, Peter 58
Marr, Andrew 8
Marshall, David 48
Martin, Campbell 44, 131

Martin, Iain 36
Marwick, Tricia 88
Mason, John 54
Massie, Alex 249
Massie, Allan 128
Maxton, James 64
Maxwell, Jamie 234
May, Theresa 10–11, 231, 232
Mazzucato, Professor Mariana 239
Merkel, Angela 212, 231, 232
Miliband, Ed 220, 222, 228
Mill, Alma 13
Mill, Christian 13
Mill, Joseph (great-grandfather) 12–13
Mill, Robert 13
Millan, Bruce 53
Miller, Calum 71–72
Mirren, Dame Helen 218
Mitchell, Claire 50–51, 76, 194
Mitchell, Holly 228
Mitchell, Professor James 61, 118–19, 146, 224, 255
Monteith, Brian 87
Moore, Michael 54–55, 169, 170–71, 186
More Powers for the Scottish Parliament 202
Morrison, Stuart 81, 87, 127
Mortimer, Norman 48
Mundell, David 169, 203
Munro, Steve 193
Murdoch, Jim 51
Murdoch, Rupert 163, 229–30
Murphy, Jim 45–46
Murray, Craig 247
Murrell, Peter 27, 34, 93, 102, 109, 113, 123, 124, 132, 135, 147, 155–56, 173, 202, 218, 225

Neil, Alex 11, 47, 53, 54, 56, 67, 91, 92, 113, 118, 138, 177

Neil, Andrew 236
Nelson, Fraser 186
Noel, Emile 177
Nyborg, Birgitte 168–69

Oliver, Sheila 39
Orskov, Joan 48
Osborne, George 189, 220,
    239, 240, 248
Owens, Ethan 125, 147
Owens, Harriet 125, 147

Paxman, Jeremy 160
Peterkin, Tom 224
Picken, Mary 55
Poe, Edgar Allan 15
Pollock, Robert 31–32, 34
The Price of Inequality 210
Pringle, Kevin 242, 246–47,
    256
The Proclaimers 22
Puttick, Helen 165

The Queen 9, 86, 123, 255

Radcliffe, Zoe 228
Rankin, Ian 126
Rauf, Abdul 151–55
Reid, George 67, 96
Reid, Harry 73–74
Reilly, Hugh 88
Rennie, Willie 213
Rhodes, Mandy 212, 225, 227
Riddoch, Lesley 2, 234
Rifkind, Hugo 253
Ritchie, Murray 73–74, 78–79
Robertson, Angus 33, 114, 174
Robertson, George 94
Robertson, Ria 228
Robinson, Nick 230
Robison, Shona 33, 35, 45, 61,
    85, 88, 96, 104, 114, 138,
    145, 190, 200, 206, 227,
    244

Roden, Alan 229
Roosevelt, Franklin 146
Roosevelt, Theodore 141
Ross, Peter 21, 28, 164, 212,
    225, 227, 228, 245, 253
Rowling, J.K. 2
Roy, Graeme 242
Rudd, Amber 5
Runrig 31
Russell, Mike 58, 70, 83, 85,
    91, 95, 96, 97, 113, 116,
    117, 118, 138, 198, 242

Sadiq, Haji Mohammed 64
Salmond, Alex 3, 4, 11, 25,
    31, 33, 40, 41, 44, 46, 48,
    55, 56–57, 58, 64–65, 67,
    68, 69, 70, 71, 72, 78, 80,
    82, 83, 85, 86, 87, 90–91,
    94, 96, 101, 110, 115–19,
    123, 127, 130, 136, 137–67
    passim, 164–65, 169–95
    passim, 196–204 *passim*,
    204, 205, 206, 213–14,
    217, 220, 222, 223, 238,
    240, 241, 243, 244, 245,
    247, 252
Salmond, Bob 40
Sarwar, Mohammad 61, 62, 63,
    64, 65, 66, 67, 68
Scanlon, Mary 88
Schulz, Martin 9
Scotland: The Case for Optimism
    25
*Scotland's Future: Your Guide
    to an Independent Scotland*
    185
Scott, Jimmy 103
Sex in the City 125
Sheppard, Tommy 248
Short, Clare 88
Sillars, Jim 7, 16, 25–26, 29, 41,
    48, 60, 61, 62, 78
Sloan, Henry 57

Smith, Calum 31–32
Smith, Elaine 54
Smith, Elaine C. 168, 218
Smith, John 35, 55
Smith, Margaret 87–88, 97
Smith, Nigel 67
Smith Commission 200–01, 202, 205, 215
Soubry, Anna 231
Stark, Edi 126
Steel, Sir David 54–55
Stephen, Nicol 86, 137
Stewart, Bob 65
Stewart, Jon 225
Stewart, Kaukab 78
Stewart, Kevin 57, 114
Stewart, Susan 55
Stiglitz, Joseph 210
Stuart, Gisela 6
Sturgeon, Gillian (sister) 12, 20, 22, 27, 155, 226, 230
Sturgeon, James (great-grandfather) 14
Sturgeon, Joan (mother)12, 20–21, 23, 27, 46, 81–82, 95, 112, 126, 147, 203, 230
Sturgeon, Margaret (née Mill, grandmother) 12–13
Sturgeon, Nicola
  character 20–21, 23, 25, 27–28, 29, 43, 49, 56, 61–62, 68, 70–71, 75, 81, 87–89, 108–09, 115, 125–26, 129, 134–36, 151, 225, 226–28
  family background 12–14
  childhood 13–16, 20–21
  schooldays 16–18, 22, 26–27
  decision to join SNP 18–20, 23
  CND membership/Trident 22–23, 47–48, 160, 174
  1987 general election 23–25
  Glasgow University 27–28, 29–51

  Nationalism of 21, 26, 30, 57, 58, 72, 162–63, 175–77, 183–84, 201, 234–35
  political ideology of 46, 69, 72–73, 105–07, 114, 123, 130–31, 143, 172–73, 209, 234–38
  and the Poll Tax 32–33, 43
  as a media performer 33–34, 45–46, 54–55, 69, 160
  SRC presidential election 38–39
  'Youth for Salmond' campaign 42
  and Young Scottish Nationalists 40–43
  work ethic 28, 36, 44–45, 50, 63, 147, 254
  1992 general election 46–49
  'Scotland United' rally 49–50
  Law degree and legal career 50–52, 59, 74, 74–75, 109
  relationship with Alex Salmond 46, 64–65, 70, 80–81, 83, 91, 115–19, 137–67 *passim*, 171–72, 192–93, 196–204 *passim*, 213–14, 223–24, 237
  views on the European Union 3–5, 53–54, 106, 110, 114, 177–80, 214–15
  candidate in local government elections 54
  election to NEC 55–56
  Vice-Convener for Youth Affairs 57, 61, 63, 78
  1997 general election 59
  and Govan constituency 59, 60–84
  appearance and image 27, 33, 56, 83, 97–98, 123–24, 136, 212, 228, 230

Vice-Convener for Publicity 68, 71–72, 80
as education spokesperson 61–62, 68–69, 71, 72–73, 79–80, 86–87, 89–90
on women in politics 70–71, 77, 89, 124, 127, 135, 189, 190, 230–31
1999 Scottish Parliament election 78–84
republicanism of 85–86, 123
and LGBTI rights 89, 107, 164, 231–32
as health spokesperson 91–93, 95, 98–99, 134
2001 general election 92, 93–94
as a debater 95, 127–28, 147, 186, 219
2003 Scottish Parliament election 94–95, 101–04
and Iraq War 100–01
as justice spokesperson 104, 107–08
and economics 107, 143–45, 209–12, 237–39, 239–41
relationship with Peter Murrell 27, 34, 93, 102, 109, 113, 123, 124, 132, 135, 147, 155–56, 218, 225
2004 SNP leadership contest 111–19
relationship with Roseanna Cunningham 33, 55, 78, 85–86, 91, 111, 112, 113, 117, 121, 206
leadership prospects 56, 70, 82, 110–12, 116, 119, 129
as deputy SNP leader 115–19, 120–36
love of books and reading 20, 21, 125–26, 228–29

2005 general election 128–29
2007 Holyrood election 135–36, 137–38
as Health Secretary 137–67
Abdul Rauf affair 151–55
2010 general election 156
2011 Holyrood election 157–59
and the Independence referendum 161–62, 165–67, 168–95
2014 SNP leadership contest 196–205
election as First Minister 206
2015 general election 216–23
education policy 242–44
use of social media 193–94, 220, 221–22
as First Minister 206–15, 216–56
and a second Independence referendum 245–49, 254
2016 Holyrood election 248–52
response to Brexit 1–11, 252, 256
Sturgeon, Robert (or Robin, father) 12, 14, 18, 82
Sturgeon, Robert (grandfather) 12–13, 14
Summers, Caroline 50–51, 52
Sunset Song 21
Swinney, John 41, 70, 82, 85, 91–92, 93, 94, 96, 101, 106, 108, 109–10, 113, 116, 118, 140, 146, 179–80, 189, 197, 205, 240–41, 243

Taylor, Brian 82–83
Thatcher, Margaret 16, 17, 23, 26, 126, 203, 228, 229
Thomas, William 65
Thomson, Michelle 251

Thomson, Patsy 61
Tickell, Andrew 226
Tomkins, Adam 7
Torrance, Michael 89
Totty Rocks 228
Tranter, Nigel 21
Trump, Donald 231
Tuesday Club 209
Tusk, Donald 9

Ullrich, Kay 23–24, 25, 27, 42, 46, 55, 67, 90, 92, 102, 112, 206
Understanding Scotland 30
Urquhart, Jean 174

Vorderman, Carol 98, 124–25

Wade, Mike 250
Walker, Bill 164
Walker, Professor David 51
Wallace, Jim 86–87
Watson, Mike 61
Webster, Jamie 79
Wheatley, John 142

White, Sandra 96
Whiteford, Eilidh 35, 40
Whitelaw, Tommy 164
Wilcock, Mary Jane 12
Wilcock, William 13
Williams, John 67
Williamson, Cliff 41, 43–44, 45, 56
Wilson, Andrew 58, 61, 70, 90, 93, 96, 209, 238
Wilson, Bill 104–5
Wilson, Brian 68–69, 87
Wilson, Gordon 25, 33, 41
Wilson, Harold 17
Wilson, Lena 237
Woods, Kevin 140
Wyndham, John 229

Young Scottish Nationalists (YSN) 23, 27, 31, 40–43, 85, 92, 174
Younger, George 15, 17, 25, 26, 39–40
Younger, Professor Paul 236
Yousaf, Humza 41, 184